IMPACT ZONE

IMPACT  ZONE

THE BATTLE OF THE DMZ IN VIETNAM, 1967–1968

JIM BROWN

The University of Alabama Press • Tuscaloosa

The University of Alabama Press
Tuscaloosa, Alabama 35487-0380
uapress.ua.edu

Hardcover edition published 2004.
Paperback edition published 2021.
eBook edition published 2013.

Typeface: ACaslon and Frutiger

Designer: Michele Myatt Quinn

Cover image: Jim Brown at Camp Carroll; courtesy of the
author

Paperback ISBN: 978-0-8173-6020-7
E-ISBN: 978-0-8173-8709-9

A previous edition of this book has been cataloged by the
Library of Congress.
ISBN: 978-0-8173-1402-6 (cloth)

CONTENTS

List of Maps   vii

Acknowledgments   ix

1 Why   1

2 The Transition   7

3 Arrival   15

4 The Rockpile   29

5 A Mountaintop Experience   47

6 The Ambushes   60

7 Dong Ha   82

8 Con Thien   97

9 Fix Bayonets   135

10 Camp Carroll   151

11 R&R   166

12 Tet   175

13 Ca Lu   185

14 Khe Sanh 201

15 LZ Torch 217

16 The *Repose* 243

17 The Final Days 247

Afterword 261

Glossary of Military Terms and Acronyms 263

Index 267

Photographs follow page 126.

MAPS

1. South Vietnam   14

2. DMZ Northern I Corps   28

3. C-2 Bridge   96

4. LZ Torch   218

All maps by Katherine Brown

Acknowledgments

When one steps back from a personal endeavor and attempts to sort through the results of whatever success has been achieved, there is often the realization that what has been accomplished came not only from the efforts of the individual but also from others who have in one way or another directly helped or influenced the outcome. Sometimes those forces are minimal, but an honest appraisal usually reveals that other people have more impact than meets the eye. As Tennyson so aptly pointed out in his *Ulysses,* "I am a part of all that I have met." In my own case, I know that to be true, and for that reason I recognize that any attempt of mine to identify all the individuals who have brought me to the point of actually having a book published will be inadequate.

Nevertheless, there are some who had such a distinct influence on me that I must speak of them. I will begin with my mother, Marion Park Brown, who with her English degree from Duke University imparted to me a love of literature that has continued as a profound part of my life. Complementing that, my father, James S. Brown, instilled in me a work ethic emphasizing persistence, a tendency that allowed me to actually complete this book, which was a much bigger undertaking than I ever imagined. Who would have ever dreamed at the time those seeds were being planted that they would ultimately be manifested in a book? For that I am eternally grateful to them.

On the other hand, whatever technical literary abilities I acquired came from the excellence demanded by Frances Smith, my high school

English teacher. She was a taskmaster who made all of her students more focused on the proper use of language, regardless of whether they appreciated it or not. For me and many others, however, she made us see and feel things that inspired us to reach for greater understanding and expression than we likely ever would have otherwise. As I hammered out the pages of this manuscript, Miss Smith was always there in the back of my mind, frequently prompting me to reconsider whether there might be a better way of saying something.

Later, as the idea of this book began to form, other people encouraged me to pursue it, and so I want to give proper credit to them. Certainly, my aunt, Laverne Brown Barr, must be thanked because on hearing me speak of my experiences in Vietnam, she immediately began to encourage me to put the happenings down in writing, and this went on every time we had occasion to be together. An English teacher herself, she perhaps saw even better than I did the potential for a story that might be worth telling. Then there is Katherine Brown, my delightful daughter-in-law and also an English teacher, who proofed my early manuscripts and made invaluable suggestions as to better wording. Her encouragement and enthusiasm as I went through numerous drafts were continual sources of motivation.

Later, Lieutenant Colonel Jody Trimble, my good friend, fraternity brother, and editor of the *Sewanee Purple* from our college days, was particularly helpful. Not only is he a scholar, he is also a highly decorated member of the Special Forces from the Vietnam War. His comments pertaining to military matters were extremely helpful as was his critical literary eye.

Of course, special thanks must go to the staff at The University of Alabama Press for their professionalism and the way that they encourage writers. Without taking away from the essence of what the author is trying to get across, they unobtrusively point the writer in the right direction. Any would-be author can only grow and improve if he or she is fortunate enough to be invited to participate in their publishing program.

I know that many others have contributed in one way or another. Thank you, everyone, and know that I am deeply grateful. Whether it was a word of encouragement or actual suggestions to improve the manuscript, your efforts mean more to me than you can imagine.

Finally, I must thank my wife, Jody McKnight Brown, who has had to put up with way too many evenings when I was glued to the word processor and, more important, who has had to endure the re-creation of the Vietnam experience. In many ways, the actual war was much harder on her than it was on me because she could only helplessly wait out my tour of duty. At the time, I at least had something to do. However, inability to participate combined with the uncertainty of the situation created a genuine stress. To dredge that all up again has not been easy for her this time around, and for that reason I applaud you, Jody, for sticking by me through not only Vietnam but this book as well.

IMPACT ZONE

Why

The airliner banked to the west as it climbed away from the Memphis airport. Smiling stiffly, a stewardess demonstrated how to use an oxygen mask and blandly went about her performance. Just going through the motions was a way of life to much of America in that May of 1967. As the jetliner began to level off, I mulled over how indifferent people seemed to the world around them and realized that the Marine officer's uniform I wore could have been a business suit for the lack of interest it had generated. True, the airports these days were filled with military personnel, making uniforms a common sight, but I thought there should have been at least some sign of acknowledgment for those of us involved in the Vietnam War effort. That conflict had escalated over the last several years, and now great quantities of men and equipment were being shipped overseas at an increasing rate. Not only that, actual incidents of combat had become daily fare for the news media as film footage depicted just how bloody the fighting could be.

Although polls at the time showed a majority of the public in support of the war, Vietnam had evoked little emotion in the early years. Americans more typically staked out positions on one side of an issue or the other and became outspoken about their feelings. Granted, there had been some emotion in the student demonstrations against the war in Berkeley, Manhattan, and Washington, but most people endorsing the campaign had been reticent with their views. That lack of vigorous support had begun to prick my interest, especially because I had just been on thirty days of leave in my hometown. My return there as a service-man had hardly been more than a curiosity to anyone, other than family, and had made me recognize that not everyone was as interested in Viet-nam as I was. Although most people vaguely supported the war, it was an inconvenience that many wished would just somehow go away. Was this disinterest symptomatic of some fundamental change taking place in the American psyche, or was it perhaps an indication that Vietnam was not as necessary as the leadership in Washington had led us to be-lieve? Questions of that nature seemed much more pertinent because this flight to California was the first leg of the journey that would take me to Vietnam.

With those thoughts beginning to form they nevertheless were secon-dary to other considerations and feelings. Instead, I focused on what Vietnam would be like and how I would fit in. Fresh out of Marine training and highly motivated as most new officers were, I enthusiasti-cally looked forward to whatever my new duty might hold as long as it involved me in the active war effort. In my mind, it would have been a real letdown to go to Vietnam and end up in some rear area job. As it turned out, that should have been the least of my worries.

I was scheduled for an afternoon arrival at the Marine staging base in Camp Pendleton. My imagination had been running wild as to what the next year might hold, and my thought process was working overtime. Other than speculate about the war, I could only think back on the past to what seemed like a scripted set of circumstances guiding me toward this moment. What was it that had seemingly put me out of step with America's current mood of indifference and was instead driving me with passion toward an experience that would exceed what I had envisioned? Reclining in a seat by the window, I looked out at towering thunderheads and reminisced on how I happened to be here.

Born in Leland, Mississippi, in 1942, I had come into a world at war. Life in those days had been impacted by World War II, and the Ameri-can people were strongly behind their country's efforts. My earliest memories bring back images of this period and are defined by my father in his Air Corps uniform at a base in Laredo, Texas. The military seemed to be everywhere then, and serving America was the proper thing to do. Although I was too young at the time to comprehend what it all meant, I vividly recall visits to our home by my uncle Charlie in his Army attire and my uncle Harold in his Navy garb. The excitement inspired by their military uniforms was thrilling to a child.

America had been through a major test of character, leaving most citizens proud of their heritage and pleased with the accomplishments of our forces overseas. Of significance, the men and women making those sacrifices were acknowledged as special patriots, and for many years their stories were told and retold. Contributing to that admiration, Hollywood exalted the American soldier with a never-ending sequence of war movies. Watching John Wayne in the *Sands of Iwo Jima*, most of us understandably took it for granted that this was the way "red-blooded Americans" ought to conduct themselves. Young boys in those years could hardly avoid a respect for the military, and in my case I needed only a war to fulfill my imagination.

My childhood was a pleasant one in which I acquired middle-class values in a relatively sophisticated environment. I grew up in the Mississippi Delta, an area dominated by a plantation economy but one that contained pockets of culture in several communities. My hometown of Leland was one of those spots, and our family lived there in a modest white frame home surrounded by picturesque oak trees. The community itself had a scenic creek meandering through it, and the area could easily have been a model for one of Norman Rockwell's paintings depicting small-town America.

Leland was particularly fortunate for several reasons. First, the federal government had established a major farm research center just outside of town, bringing many well-educated individuals from diverse backgrounds into the community. It was unusual for such a small town to have so many people with doctorate and master's degrees. These individuals made positive intellectual contributions to the social structure, and their presence created a broader mind-set than might have been normal. Second, Greenville, the economic center and cultural mecca of the Delta, was only ten miles away, with a population of forty thousand supporting a progressive and upscale lifestyle. Finally, a nearby Air Force base trained pilots and, with its ever-changing cast of students and staff, added to Leland's unique situation in that a much wider perspective was gained through interaction with people from all over America.

By the time I reached junior high school, I had acquired a passion for football and found myself somewhat awed by the "heroes" of the senior high team. It happened that several of them joined the Marine Corps on graduation. One in particular, Y. C. McNease, made a deep impression on me. After going off to Parris Island, the Marine boot camp, he returned the following year in time for spring football practice. The coaches had persuaded him to work with the ninth-grade players, and he really did a job on us. Filled with Marine Corps motivation, Y. C. pumped us up in a way I had never before experienced. Football seemed like combat to me already, and under his influence I began to associate his concept of the fighting marine with what I thought football was all about. The Marine Corps, in my mind, was becoming something to which I could aspire. That awareness was reinforced during my junior and senior years on the arrival of Perry Jones, a Marine sergeant recently returned from Korea. His hard-charging manner as a coach and history teacher influenced the entire student body, and, through passionate history lectures, he became the talk of the school. My own contacts with him, however, came on the football field, where he enthralled us with stories of the Korean War and virtues of the Marines. Consequently, the Marine Corps became even more special, and their high standards reinforced the patriotic inclinations I already had. By the time I graduated from high school, service to country and loyalty to America were regarded by me as some of the highest principles of life.

Attending college at the University of the South at Sewanee, Tennessee, I tended to associate with people who had strong military leanings, and as it worked, out my two closest friends participated in the Platoon Leaders Course summer program for aspiring Marine officers. Their influence contributed to my admiration for the military services in general and the Marine Corps in particular. The likelihood that I might join up lessened, however, when I became a senior. I had been dating Jody McKnight from my hometown of Leland for several years, and she was wonderful. Jody had been named most beautiful and was the homecoming queen at Leland High. At Sewanee she was chosen Sweetheart of Phi Delta Theta, my fraternity. We married shortly after my graduation, and whatever interest I had in the military went on the back burner as the more pressing issue of making a living became my main focus. By the end of 1965, however, Vietnam was capturing the headlines, and I became overwhelmed with the notion that America was at war again and here I was, not making a contribution. In February of 1966, I signed up for Officer Candidate School (OCS) to begin training on March 21.

There a real test of perseverance began because the program was designed to eliminate those not suited to being officers. Everyone in the program felt a tremendous amount of anxiety because we never knew who would be the next person removed from the class. This intentional stress was the Marine Corps' method of finding out who could take pressure, and the program did what it was supposed to do; nearly half of the candidates had washed out by the time our class graduated on May 27, 1966. Even though I finished in the top 20 percent of my unit, I was always wondering in any given week whether I would be the next to get the boot.

Those of us who successfully completed OCS were commissioned as 2d lieutenants, and Basic School immediately followed. That new training period reversed the objectives of the OCS program, and the Corps now began to build us up and provide the basic skills necessary for infantry officers. At the same time, they instilled in us the motivation that Marines are noted for, not a hard thing to do with Vietnam making daily headlines.

Prior to graduation from Basic School, we were given an opportunity to request a military occupational specialty (MOS). We had no guarantee that we would receive what we applied for, but we were at least allowed to rank our top three choices of the service branch we preferred. Mine were artillery, infantry, and armor, in that order. The big guns had always fascinated me, and because most 2d lieutenants started as forward observers with the infantry, it seemed like a sure way to find out what the war was all about. I did receive my first choice, along with orders to report to the Army artillery base at Fort Sill, Oklahoma, for further training. That assignment, however, was delayed for several months so I could remain with Jody, now pregnant and about to deliver. Our daughter, Cathy, finally arrived in December, and two months later, on February 28, 1967, I, along with Jody and Cathy, reported to Fort Sill. The school was a superior learning experience, and on completion I thought I was thoroughly prepared for what I imagined to be ahead. That was a good thing because my next set of orders directed me to duty in Vietnam.

My final days on leave in Leland were quite emotional, and the last good-byes on leaving the Greenville airport were heart wrenching for the entire family as everyone prepared for fourteen months of separation. Parting from loved ones is never easy, but the implications of leaving for war made it even more difficult. Now reclining in the big jet, I raced through the sky toward an uncertain destiny and could feel only apprehension about what lay ahead.

2

The Transition

When I arrived at Camp Pendleton, a distinctly different world came into focus that contrasted sharply with what I had left behind. For the last month, I had been among friends and family, and the actuality of parts unknown had taken no form. Camp Pendleton was another story. Here the very fiber of the air rippled with an energy that comes only from frenzied activity, and everything danced in motion with one end in sight, Vietnam. There were refresher classes tailored for the combat tactics of the Viet Cong, and even the survival courses were adapted to the jungles of Vietnam. Lectures on what to do if taken prisoner were presented in such ways as to give us an idea of what we could expect in Asian prison camps, and that formerly abstract thought began to seem much more of a possibility. We also dealt with the more mundane concerns, such as arrangements for family financial support while we were gone. Not the least of those administrative necessities were preparation of wills and instructions to the Corps on who to notify if we were killed or wounded. Almost needless to say, our attention became riveted on whatever waited for us in the days ahead, and the no-longer vague concept of Vietnam began to form a new shape in our minds.

In addition to the administrative details and class time, each of us was assigned a billet, or job assignment, in one of the staging company units. Organized in that structure, we enthusiastically played four weeks of war games across the California hills. With Vietnam staring us in the face, just about everyone wanted to be as sharp as possible for whatever the coming year would bring, and the reality of it all discouraged just about everybody from slacking off in any way on those tactical problems. This simulated combat took up most of our time, and each successful completion of an assigned mission resulted in genuine satisfaction. This climactic setting stirred up a mixture of emotions that might best be described as an elevated feeling of awareness where everything was felt deeply. An acute sense of the love of living began to impact us and became a counterpoint to the new thought of the possibility of dying.

The training and war games continued for the duration of our stay and went without mishap. During this time I had my first real opportunity to have enlisted troops under me, and I developed a great appreciation for the qualities that the Marines Corps had forged in these men. It was refreshing to see just how sharp these enlisted guys were and how dedicated they already were to fulfilling the legacy of being a "Marine." On the other hand, an incident occurred that brought home to me just how young and sensitive most of these men really were. In spite of the tough-guy image so often associated with the Marine Corps, sometimes another side can be seen. It so happened that one afternoon during a survival training class, two instructors walked out in front of the bleachers, with one holding a live cuddly white rabbit. That particular session was to show us how to catch and prepare food if we became separated from our normal supply sources. It must be remembered that many of these men had only recently come from cities and had never thought of meat as anything other than a processed product from a butcher shop. As a practical matter, it was essential that these guys know what to do if they had to kill and clean an animal in a survival situation. One instructor began by pointing to a chart on an easel that depicted various stages of cleaning a rabbit. The other stood by quietly, stroking the live bunny. Gradually it dawned on the group that they were about to see an actual demonstration of the process. Standing off to one side, I could easily see the facial expressions of the men as the class proceeded. Some were visibly shaken as they contemplated the fate of the hapless rabbit, making me realize that "America's finest" were often nothing more than kids at heart. Several eyes glistened, and everyone's attention locked in on the demonstration. In truth, most of our country's fighting force has always consisted of people who are hardly more than teenagers. The common perception of the American soldier usually projects an image of a hard-bitten fighting machine toughened for the job he has to do. Such may be the case after a man returns from war, but most who go into combat for the first time are hardly more than overgrown youths who have been disciplined to take orders and instilled with pride in their particular branch of service.

Continuing to train in this intense curriculum, all of us gained skills that would soon stand us in good stead, but we also had our times away from Camp Pendleton, too. Knowing we were about to walk into a world that held only God knew what, we took every opportunity to go on weekend leave, or "liberty." I spent most of my free time with Ross Blanchard, a lieutenant I had been with since Basic School, and occasionally we would visit his home in North Hollywood. Ross's tour had been delayed for his daughter's birth just as mine had, and, consequently, we attended artillery school at the same time. Now we were both assigned to the same staging company because our last names happened to start with a *B*. After moving together through all of those same rotations, we had become good friends.

One particularly memorable occasion occurred on a visit to Ross's home. His father was a commissioner for the city of Los Angeles and, of course, was well connected and quite prominent. That weekend, Mr. and Mrs. Blanchard insisted that the two of us come up from Pendleton and join them for dinner at their club, and they asked that we wear our appropriate dress uniforms. In my naiveté, it never occurred to me that this would be anything more than just a nice dinner. Attired in our tan uniforms with coat and tie, we looked pretty sharp with gold lieutenants' bars gleaming on our shoulders. Mr. and Mrs. Blanchard drove us to their country club, where we were ushered into the main dining room. Ross and I immediately stood out like sore thumbs as the only apparent servicemen there. Walking through an array of tables, we became aware that our presence was turning many heads. Finally sitting down, I thought for a moment that the unaccustomed attention might be over, but instead the activity picked up. People began coming over to the table to visit, and, of course, Ross and I stood up each time for introductions. I finally figured out that this was not just any club when Walter Brennan, the movie star, came over to greet us. Shaking our hands and talking in his homespun way, he told us that he "really appreciated what you are doing for our country" and wished us well. Several other celebrities and people with names I recognized came up and spoke during the course of the evening. By the end of dinner, both Ross's head and mine were in the clouds. This could have been a movie scene in and of itself, but the highlight of the evening came after dessert. Mr. Blanchard said he had someone he wanted us to meet and asked us to follow him back to the golfers' locker room. When we walked in, there sitting on a bench by his locker was none other than Bob Hope. Relaxing in his underwear, he greeted us like it was the most normal of circumstances. By this time I was in shock, but tried to maintain some degree of decorum. The evening had become totally surreal as we casually visited with a person who was practically a national institution in his own right. He spoke of his USO show at Christmas and told Ross he would be sure to look him up. It seemed on that night as if all the world was a dream and that I had truly left behind life as I had known it.

On our return the next day to Camp Pendleton, the pace of activity picked up even more because our departure date was rapidly approaching. Making frequent phone calls to Jody and the family, I desperately grasped at my old world while being sucked into the whirlpool of Vietnam. Each day it seemed as if some force was pulling us toward a groping and ominous door.

Our staging company had by now reached a high level of readiness, and for that reason it seemed a pity that we would not continue as a unit after we reached Vietnam. Still, we did learn that our company would at least process and travel together until reaching Da Nang. In the past month, many of the men had formed close personal friendships, and most were experiencing a unit camaraderie emanating from the awareness that we were all about to run the same gauntlet. Identifying with the anxieties and concerns of the others, we formed an almost clannish solidarity, remarkable in that we had actually been together only for a short period of time.

Finally, departure day arrived, and we were bussed to Marine Corps Air Station, El Toro, for our flight overseas. After arriving there at dark, I dealt with a little sick gnawing in the stomach that sometimes comes when one approaches the unknown. That last night was an anxious one for many and was one in which the most important event would be a final phone call home. Long lines of serious-faced Marines stood by the pay phones, and when my turn came to say good-bye to Jody, it was like shutting a door on my previous life. The emotion generated from that conversation and the anticipation of tomorrow's early flight did not allow for much sleep.

Daybreak found us standing by a runway where a commercial airliner waited to take us away. On that June morning it was already warm even at that early hour, but a chill settled over us when we saw two hospital planes taxi in from overseas. In the dawn's early grayness, we could only stare at the giant red crosses on the tail sections of the planes, and we took absolutely no comfort when the big transports rolled up to waiting ambulances. Watching them unload their cargo of casualties, I could only hope this first glimpse of the reality of war was not some apocalyptic omen, coinciding as it did with our own departure.

In short order, we boarded our own plane, and to our surprise stewardesses were waiting to greet us. The activity aboard the plane was as routine as if this was a flight from Atlanta to Los Angeles. It made me wonder whether this was some ruse to shield us from some awful truth, whatever that might be. The trip itself went smoothly, and many hours later we reached Hawaii, where we would have a three-hour stop for fuel and servicing. With such a short stop, we had only enough time to wander around within the confines of the civilian airport, but we did experience an unfamiliar aspect of the new world toward which we were headed. Hawaii is in the tropics, and the heat and humidity that would be with us for the next thirteen months slammed us with a physical presence. Profusely perspiring, we boarded for the final leg of the trip to the island of Okinawa, where we would undergo four days of interim processing. Okinawa had been controlled by the Japanese prior to World War II, but since that time the United States had routinely stationed troops there. Now, however, with the hostilities heating up and the island being conveniently located right on the way to Vietnam, Okinawa had become the staging and processing area for Marine personnel entering and leaving the war zone.

Arrival in Okinawa gave us our first taste of being on foreign soil. We boarded buses at the airport and were driven across the island to a Marine base. On the way I saw a tropical countryside interspersed with huts of concrete blocks and wooden shanties, all of which contributed to the distinctly Asian character of the place. This Americanized Japan fascinated me, and our thirty-minute trip went by in a flash. By contrast, when we passed through the gates into Camp Hansen, we could have been at any stateside base because of its orderly arrangements of buildings and neat military appearance.

The following day brought more processing. It seemed like the paperwork was never ending, and we all became burned out with it. To break the boredom of the administrative work, Ross and I decided to go into the local town for the evening. Heading out well before dark, we spent an hour looking at a very different way of life. The village outside the gates was nothing more than a flimsy collection of structures that had sprung up over the years to latch on to American dollars passing through the hands of Marines. Now, a steadily increasing number of personnel coming and going from Vietnam caused the money to flow even more freely. Those going were having one last fling, and those coming were trying to get out of the war mode as fast as possible. Cheap shops and bars were everywhere, and Okinawan girls were on every corner.

As night fell, Ross and I found our way into one of the bars. It was loaded with Marines listening and dancing to a Japanese band that was making a credible attempt at singing American pop songs. The place looked and smelled like all the cheap and gaudy service bars around the world. Cigarette smoke hung across the room, and a smell of stale drinks that had been spilled from countless glasses wafted up from the floor. Okinawan girls swirled through the crowded room, and those Asian beauties, dressed in American-style miniskirts, hustled Marines to buy them watered-down drinks. Remembering that the female world would soon be left behind, the departing Americans were instinctively making the most of the occasion. As the evening wore on, the Japanese band began to play a recently popular song from the States called "House of the Rising Sun." What followed was a glimpse of a form of nationalistic spirit that I had not been aware of. On hearing the reference to the "Rising Sun," the local Okinawans threw themselves into a frenzy of dancing that was much more than just a fun thing to do. A spirit of defiance flashed in their eyes, and you knew that these people were ready to return entirely to the Japanese fold and leave the "protective arms" of America. Chills ran up and down my neck on experiencing for the first time that my country was not loved by everyone, and I left the club with a numbing sense that the security of America was a thing of the past. The lessons had begun of just how wonderful our homeland really is. Two days later we left for Vietnam, and the lessons continued.

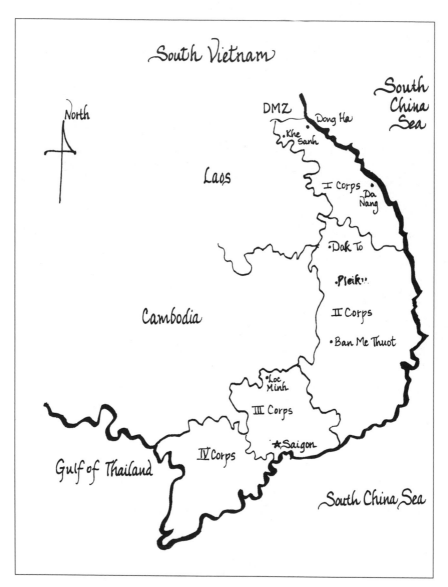

South Vietnam

Arrival

Arrival in Da Nang on June 6, 1967, was chaotic. This was the largest city in the northern part of South Vietnam and the location of the Marine Corps headquarters. Most Marines entered and departed the country from here. Disembarking from the airliner, everyone shot off in fifty directions amid a flurry of hurried good-byes. How everyone seemed to know where to go was beyond me, because I sure did not. Standing there, I wondered how many of these guys I would ever see again. In his typically flamboyant manner, Ross had already conned someone into giving him a ride to his assigned headquarters, which was someplace in the opposite direction from where I was going. Waving to him as he pulled away, I was left standing by myself in the hustle and bustle all about me and no longer could see any of the men with whom I had arrived. In spite of the swirling activity, I felt totally alone and could only try not to appear as uncomfortable as I felt.

Heat and humidity now engulfed me, and my nostrils were attacked by an unpleasant odor that I later found to be common to all Marine base camps. In that busy setting, I made my way over to what seemed to be an information station that had been set up to guide people in the general direction of their new units. My orders were looked over, and a clerk gave directions on how to reach the 3d Marine Division headquarters. By now, darkness was approaching, and another clerk pointed out that it would be useless to report in at this late hour. He did take the trouble, however, to let me know about a makeshift staging area for people caught in my situation. It was near the airstrip, and at least I could be in a tent with a cot for the night. Having managed to miss all the regular chow halls and not having a clue as to where anything was, I decided not to wander around in the dark just yet. Therefore, it was to bed without supper in a strange place without lights. What made matters worse was that the tent was only thirty yards from the airstrip. As soon as I lay down a jet screamed off down the runway, bound for some mission in the night sky. This happened about every thirty minutes for the rest of the evening, and so my first night in Vietnam was not a lot of fun.

The next morning my empty stomach was greeted by that odor from the day before, but now it seemed much stronger. Leaving the tent, I noticed that the smell seemed to be coming from fires burning in fifty-five-gallon oil drums that had been cut off about one foot above the ground. Strolling over to the unpleasant roasting smell, I hoped to find out what was responsible for the obnoxious aroma. To my amazement, I found it to be human waste burning in diesel fuel. This practice, it turned out, was standard procedure for maintaining sanitation in base camps across the country. That smell became a part of the real Vietnam. In self-defense for my empty stomach, I managed to find a chow hall and forced down some breakfast. The food helped, and my spirits improved by the time I headed over to find out about my new assignment.

On reporting in at division headquarters, I learned that I would be meeting with a full colonel in charge of filling billets throughout the division. After I waited a long time, the colonel finally called me into his office, and I made my first mistake in Vietnam. Full of dreams and ideals, I had the misguided fear that I might get stuck in some rear area and never have an opportunity to see war firsthand. Thinking that now might be a time to influence my assignment, I put on my most sincere manner and said to the colonel, "Sir, if there is any way possible, I would really like to be a forward observer in the field with an infantry company." The colonel calmly laid down the papers he was studying, rocked back in his chair, and placed his hands behind his head. He looked me hard in the eyes and seemed to be studying me for an interminably long time. Without any change of expression he finally said, "1/12 supports 3/3, and I think they can use you up there." With that, he stamped 12th Marines on my orders while telling me to catch the next plane to Dong

Ha, which was near the actual demilitarized zone (DMZ). He further instructed me to report to the commanding officer there and repeat my request.

When he said DMZ, I began to comprehend where I was headed. The DMZ was a strip of land dividing North and South Vietnam that had been established by the 1954 Geneva Convention. It was a five-mile-wide buffer strip that was bisected by the Song Ben Hai River to Bo Ho Su and by a straight line from there to the Laotian border. This thirty-five-mile-long buffer zone was off limits to U.S. forces until 1966, when the U.S. 3d Marine Division moved in to reinforce the South Vietnamese 1st Division. Several miles below this "demilitarized zone" ran Route 9 from the China Sea to Laos. Some of the towns and strong points near this once-paved road were Dong Ha, Gio Linh, Cam Lo, Con Thien, Camp Carroll, the Rockpile, Ca Lu, and Khe Sanh. All of these points and anything northward to the actual buffer zone were commonly called the DMZ in the everyday vernacular, although only the buffer zone itself could technically be called the DMZ.

A number of battles in that area had been reported in newspapers back home, so I understood its significance. I also knew that from a geographic standpoint, I would be near large concentrations of NVA (North Vietnamese Army) units. The designations 1/12 and 3/3 represented the 1st Battalion, 12th Marines and 3d Battalion, 3d Marines, respectively, and the colonel had in effect told me I was joining the 1st Battalion of the 12th Marine Artillery Regiment with a good chance of being attached to the 3d Battalion of the 3d Marine Infantry Regiment as a forward observer. I hoped that I had not let my mouth overload my brain. Yes, I wanted to see the war firsthand, but the DMZ might be more than I had bargained for. I also might not have made this request if I had realized that when the Marines assigned you to a unit, for the most part you stayed with that group for your entire tour of thirteen months. The Army supposedly had a system whereby you usually spent the first part of your stay in a more exposed area and then rotated to a less risky location. I had thought that would be a logical thing for the Marines to do as well, but that was not the way it worked.

The afternoon found me on a C-130 cargo plane loaded with medical supplies and half a dozen Marine passengers. This was my first flight over Vietnam, and was it beautiful! I had never envisioned Vietnam as a place of beauty, and it struck me as ironic that we were over here doing our best to wreak havoc in such a scenic place. Tranquil, emerald green jungles and mountains drifted below, while the mystery of what was really down there crept into my thoughts. The chill of the unknown was a feeling I had experienced in the past, but this was different because the unknown might now include someone trying to kill me.

As we neared Dong Ha, the green countryside gave way to an ugly brown scar. Below, I could see a dusty town next to what was obviously the Marine base. The perimeter trenches were clearly visible, and adjacent to the camp an ammunition dump with orderly rows of bunkers and storage bins stood out in contrast to the conglomerate hodgepodge of the rest of the place. Looking down at the runway, I knew Dong Ha would be nowhere near as civilized as Da Nang. The differences were further emphasized when the plane touched down and the crew began madly rushing around, dumping supplies off the plane. They had seen too much enemy incoming fire while landing up here to wait around and find out whether they were going to be a target today. By the time I made it over to what seemed to be the terminal bunker, the big cargo plane was already taxiing down the runway for take off.

Fortunately, I found a truck going to headquarters and was quickly able to catch a ride. That dusty trip took us right through the local village, which, on closer inspection, looked more like a concentration camp, with its squalor and barbed wire, than a town. The shacks and fragile houses were populated by poor-looking Vietnamese who ignored us as we drove through. Later, I learned that Dong Ha and Cam Lo, the other main town near the DMZ, had become hardly more than refugee camps for much of the local population near the buffer zone and now served as places of relative safety from the NVA. At night, all Vietnamese from the Rockpile to Dong Ha were under orders to stay in these camps and, if caught outside, were considered Viet Cong or North Vietnamese sympathizers. Notable exceptions to this were the Montagnards (ancient tribal people) who lived in villages near Ca Lu and Khe Sanh. One big difference in warfare on the DMZ as opposed to that in the southern part of South Vietnam resulted from this refugee camp concept. Down south, our military rarely knew for sure who the enemy was or even who the friendlies were because the villages usually did not have a defense system of their own. Everyone roamed at will wherever and whenever they chose. In contrast, the countryside up here was considered a free fire zone, and unless the Vietnamese were out on a work detail that had been preapproved by the closest American military unit, they could be fired on without any questions asked. Consequently, practically all engagements in the DMZ area were with regular uniformed members of the NVA. Not having to contend with wondering who the enemy was had some real psychological benefits. We also did not have anywhere near the number of booby traps that they did in the south because the NVA frequently moved back and forth across the same terrain that we were traversing. The thought of stepping on a booby trap horrified me, and I was thankful for at least that advantage on the DMZ.

I arrived at the 12th Marine headquarters just before dark and in time for supper. The people in the chow hall cordially welcomed me and told me where I could spend the night before reporting in the next morning. This turned out to be a large tent near the dining area, and because I had not yet been assigned a unit, I would again have to fend for myself another night. Going over to the designated tent, I hoped to at least find someone who could fill me in on the real situation concerning the DMZ. On entering that musty canvas shelter in the fading twilight, I saw the sides were rolled up for ventilation and noticed someone sitting over in the shadows. I spoke and was answered in broken English by a person who turned out to be a Vietnamese army interpreter. After a conversation in which we both struggled to be understood, all I found out was that I could have my pick of cots because he was the tent's only inhabitant. In our further efforts to communicate, it became evident that this small, quiet soldier was not going to be a lot of help in finding out much about anything. Uncomfortable to begin with, I would have preferred to have been alone rather than contend with this mysterious stranger sitting silently in the now-dark tent.

Fatigued from lack of sleep the night before, I dozed off quickly, but around midnight machine-gun fire and explosions awakened me abruptly. Rolling out of bed onto the floor, I could only stare out of the sides of the tent. Eerie shadows stalked across the floor while parachute flares slowly drifted in the night sky. Realizing the firing was some distance away, I went to the door of the tent and saw no activity. The firing apparently had been coming from the other side of the base, and the position of the flares indicated that as well. Going back inside, I turned on my penlight and discovered that the Vietnamese interpreter was nowhere to be found. Now wide awake and with artillery beginning to fire missions at regular intervals, all I could do was lie there in the darkness of a strange new world. I could not even tell whether the booms were incoming or outgoing, and again I hardly slept. Vietnam was beginning to be a pain in the neck. Not until breakfast did I find out what had been going on. Evidently an NVA unit had probed the perimeter; the incident was being nonchalantly discussed over coffee in the mess hall.

Around ten o'clock that morning, I finally got in to see the commanding officer (CO) of the 12th Marines and again requested duty as a forward observer (FO). Colonel William R. Morrison explained that it would be entirely up to the commander of the unit I was being assigned to but that C-1-12 ("C" Battery, 1st Battalion, 12th Marines) needed FOs for 3/3 and he would send me to see the CO of 1/12. He also informed me that he would shortly be flying by chopper to Camp Carroll where they were located and that I could hitch a ride. Within the hour, we were in the air flying parallel to the DMZ, and the scenery was breathtaking. The mountains further inland became rugged, with a lot of bare stone around their peaks, and lower hills and valleys appeared like peaceful meadows from our view high above. In reality, those pastoral fields were covered with elephant grass taller than a man's head and could hide an entire company if the men stayed low. Occasional patches and strips of jungle followed the contour of the land, particularly in the valleys around rivers and streams and on the lower slopes of mountains. Approaching Camp Carroll, which was nine miles west of Dong Ha and one mile south of Route 9, I saw before me one of those gentle meadowlike hills but with a barren brown top for its crown. Its entire crest had been fortified with barbed wire, and trenches traced the perimeter. The ground outside was laid bare, and grass had been cut or burned to a distance of about fifty yards. Camp Carroll looked to be about five city blocks square or a half-mile in diameter and had a road curving around the interior of the perimeter that linked batteries and supply areas. This was the main artillery base for the entire DMZ area and could easily be defended from ground attack, situated as it was on a high plateau with clear fields of fire. For the next thirteen months, this would be the closest thing to a rear area that I would have. Here, adequate supplies, along with showers, dining areas, and tents with wooden floors, made life bearable, but on my arrival at this bleak hill, it would have been hard to convince me that it would become the oasis that it did in the months ahead. In fact, the very hope of returning to Camp Carroll became a positive motivator over the next seven months. During that time I would be in places I never wanted to see again.

I reported to the commanding officer of 1/12 after the regimental commander finished his visit, and on hearing my by now well-rehearsed FO spiel, Lieutenant Colonel W. H. Rice responded by assigning me to C Battery ("Charlie Battery"). My entire stay in Vietnam would be as a member of this entity, and everything affecting me related to it in one way or another.

Charlie Battery consisted of six 105mm howitzer-towed guns that were the work horses of the Marine artillery. Considered light artillery, each gun weighed 4,980 pounds and had a maximum range of eleven hundred meters. It could fire three rounds a minute, and each shell weighed thirty-three pounds. These shells were powered by powder charges, the number used being determined by the distance. Seven bags would be used for the maximum range.

The most common type of round was a high-explosive (HE) shell that normally exploded on impact but that could be set to explode above the target or delayed to explode after penetrating an object such as a bunker. Another type of shell was a plastic anti-tank round that splattered on the hull of a tank before exploding, thereby flaking off pieces of the interior and shredding the occupants. Adding to the versatility of the howitzer were rounds that shot illuminating flares, smoke, and white phosphorus. Rounding out this array was a shell that contained hundreds of flechettes, or little winged darts, that could be discharged from the muzzle of the gun to create a shotgun effect. This high-tech version of the canister that had been used in the Civil War against attacking troops was called "beehive" by us.

These guns were made even more flexible by their ability to shoot high-angle fire like a mortar instead of the typical direct angle of fire of most artillery pieces. Therefore, they could lob rounds into defilades such as those found behind ridgelines or hills. Finally, a gun could be easily towed behind a two-and-one-half-ton truck or slung under the belly of a helicopter for airlift into remote or difficult terrain.

These field pieces could normally get by with a crew of four but in a pinch could be fired by two men if they did not have to shift the gun. Usually there were six or seven men on a crew. In addition to the gun crews, the battery proper had personnel who operated the fire direction center (FDC) where the fire missions were charted. The battery also had administrators and clerks who handled the large volume of paperwork and staff people who supervised various functions of the battery. Other members of the battery included the infantry liaison officer and his staff along with the forward observers and their radio operators, all working in the field to direct fire for the infantry. In Vietnam, where the Marines usually operated below full strength, a 105mm towed battery usually ranged from about 100 to 130 men, depending on the constantly rotating cycle of people moving in and out of country.

Anxious to find out what the new outfit would be like, I immediately went over to report in to the CO and was met by a fierce-looking Marine named Captain Pate. He was lean and trim, with high cheekbones and piercing eyes, yet relaxed and cordial without the military stiffness that I had been accustomed to back in the States. Very poised, he left no doubt that he was quite capable of handling his job, and it quickly became apparent that he was well respected and looked up to by other members of the battery.

During that first meeting, he asked a lot of questions concerning the goings-on back in the States, and his matter-of-fact way made the strange surroundings seem more normal. About that time, however, a seeming explosion rattled the tent and shook the stools and cots. Captain Pate hardly blinked an eye as I crouched in amazement. Seeing my unease, he explained that it was only an Army 175mm battery located right next to us. These guns happened to be some of the largest field artillery pieces in the U.S. arsenal and had a range of twenty miles. Whenever they fired toward the north, the muzzles of their guns almost extended over this tent, and loose objects were constantly being knocked to the floor from the concussion of the rounds being fired. The unexpected blast of those guns became a daily part of life as they routinely shot their fire missions, and I would eventually learn to sleep right through the bedlam when I returned to the battery months later.

My interview ended with Captain Pate telling me, "Yes, you are going to have an opportunity to be an FO." He explained that Charlie Battery supplied FOs to 3/3 and that they had been asking for replacements for some time. That battalion was located at the base of the "Rockpile," a name that had already made headlines back in the States before I left. A lot of fighting had taken place around there during the past year, and it had already achieved a reputation in the Vietnam saga. The Rockpile itself was an imposing rock formation standing alone in the middle of a valley that began near Camp Carroll and ran parallel to the DMZ until it reached that landmark. The valley then turned south until intersecting with another valley that extended to Khe Sanh. Route 9, the principal road across the northern part of South Vietnam, began at Dong Ha near the South China Sea and followed these valleys all the way to Khe Sanh, where it ended on the Laotian border, a distance of about forty miles. That road, deemed essential for operations on the DMZ, was the main supply route along our northern front. The Rockpile, a key strategic location along this route, caused both Americans and North Vietnamese to devote considerable attention to the area. At the time of my arrival, 3/3 had the primary mission of protecting the Rockpile sector from the NVA. They eventually would have their hands full.

Captain Pate suggested that I stay in the battery for several days to get to know the various members and to familiarize myself with operations. Indeed, I was anxious to find out just what was going on and finally to hear from the people who were actually doing the fighting. Besides, I had not even been issued a pistol, and it was time for me to get combat gear and clothes. To this point, I had been in summer khakis and now felt out of place among the field Marines clothed in jungle utilities: lightweight work clothes designed for use in the tropics. I was ready to strap on a shoulder holster for my .45-caliber pistol and blend in with the unit. In no time, I began interacting with the staff and started to feel a part of the battery. One person in particular, Lieutenant Joe McDavid from Alabama, took me under his wing and gave me a clear picture of the situation. Maybe it was our common southern origin that made him so helpful, but he went out of his way to fill me in on what was really happening. He had an easygoing attitude and spoke with an Alabama accent that sounded southern even to me, a native Mississippian. There was no pretentiousness in his manner, and an obvious cynicism came across in his personality, perhaps because he had almost completed his tour and no longer had illusions concerning what Vietnam was about. Filling me in on the history of Charlie Battery, he told me how he perceived the various personalities of its members, and I eventually found his insights to be not only very accurate but also extremely helpful. I was particularly appreciative for his advice on how to stay alive in a combat zone. I have no doubt that I survived in large part because of his no-nonsense guidance on how to avoid needlessly exposing myself or taking unnecessary chances.

During those few days, I had the good fortune to discover that one of my closest friends from Basic School, Lieutenant John Eager, was also at Camp Carroll. He now had a job at the battalion level and was assigned to the FDC. John was another no-nonsense individual, much like Lieutenant McDavid, in that he understood the nature of the war. Outspoken to the point of offending people sometimes, he always said what was on his mind. We had been very close during our earlier association, and I knew him to be a friend on whom I could depend. If you were his buddy, then he stuck by you under all conditions. Over at headquarters, he knew what was happening and later kept me well informed. Because of that friendship, I would know what was going on operationally and also be kept aware of the personal intrigues taking place within the battalion. Not the least of his assistance occurred when he alerted me to unannounced inspections. That type of help would be most useful on my return to the battery many months later. John is one of the really true friends that we so rarely find on this journey through life. On my first visit with him, I learned he had just returned from a hospital stay in Japan where he had been recuperating from encephalitis, also called sleeping sickness. That bit of news reminded me that we had more to worry about over here than the NVA. His dramatic weight loss was evidence of that.

Among John, Lieutenant McDavid, and Captain Pate, I learned a lot about the personality of the unit. Charlie Battery had been involved in numerous actions and had established a certain reputation. The troops were very cocky, or "salty" as we termed it, and bombarded me with war stories while I was getting to know them. One incident that had taken place in early 1967 at Gio Linh seemed to dominate all others. This northernmost outpost, located two thousand meters below the actual DMZ, looked out across a vast, supposed no-man's-land, and it was there that the North Vietnamese launched one of the first major artillery attacks of the war. Because of the demilitarized strip, they were able to position their artillery and rockets very close to our own forces. Our government's policy at that particular time did not normally allow us to cross into the zone, but the North Vietnamese came through at will to attack. They would then, if counterattacked, conveniently fade back into the safety of that area protected by mandate from our government. Knowing we were not going into the DMZ proper, they could set their guns in permanent positions. It was even rumored that they had placed artillery pieces in caves to protect them from air strikes. Almost needless to say, these policies and conditions gave the NVA a greater advantage in this sector of Vietnam than they had in other areas.

An indication of this advantage came from the action at Gio Linh to which many of the men now frequently referred. Charlie Battery had been participating there as part of Operation Prairie III, and a tall wooden tower had been built allowing observation for miles in any direction. From that vantage point, our FOs frequently spotted live targets in the DMZ strip and called in the appropriate type of firepower. The NVA must have felt a need to do something about this because, by cover of darkness, they moved a combination of artillery and rockets to a very close range. Early one night, the North Vietnamese started pounding Gio Linh with an incredible amount of ordnance, and Charlie Battery took hundreds of rounds of incoming fire in the onslaught that followed. This shelling lasted for eight hours, and when day broke, only one of our guns still operated. The casualties were high, and they included Lieutenant Dan Dudley, the forward observer, who had become trapped in the tower when one of its legs and ladder were shot away. He had been a platoon mate of mine at Basic School and was a quiet but likable individual. I never found out the extent of his injuries, but he surely must have spent a night in hell, dangling high in the air with shells screaming in. The North Vietnamese, although they had moved very close, were never counterattacked on the ground because we were not allowed to approach them in the strip.

Before the attack began, one of the troops had been making a tape recording to send home when the first incoming rounds arrived. Diving for cover, he left the recorder on a gun parapet, and it recorded for thirty minutes until the tape ran out. It captured the dramatic sounds of the battle and was now a prized possession of Charlie Battery. The troops took a devilish delight in playing it to newcomers, sending chills up and down the backs of anyone who heard it. Hearing that tape made me wonder how anyone could have survived amid the screaming shells and explosions.

With the telling of such stories, it became obvious that a great deal of pride existed in the unit, and I began to suspect that this was not just an ordinary outfit. This battery had passed the test of Gio Linh and many other trials with verve, creating an esprit de corps that is hard to explain to those not actually involved. Loyalty and feeling went beyond patriotism, creating a bond the likes of which I had experienced only marginally while participating in football. It might better be described as a team pride that comes from mutually shared hardships and endeavors.

The day finally came for me to leave this newfound family and head out to the infantry at the Rockpile. Deploying in a five-vehicle convoy on Route 9, we exited the perimeter at Camp Carroll on the morning of June 19, and a noticeable change came over the troops in the trucks. Everyone pointed their weapons outward and began to watch the sides of the road as the convoy sped along as fast as the potholes would allow. Some sections of road showed evidence of repairs, and I learned later that many of those spots indicated where land mines had exploded. Several miles farther on, it became more mountainous with occasional rock bluffs showing through the tropical vegetation. As we approached a narrow pass between two mountains, a small river came out of the jungle on our right from seemingly nowhere. The sheer bluffs to our left made me feel vulnerable, and I thought how easy it would be for the NVA to spring an ambush.

Leaving the pass behind, we entered a vast valley bordered by tall mountain ridges, and, located right in the middle, an incredible seven-hundred-foot-high mountain of jumbled rock rose up like an ominous monument. Its sheer steepness created a powerful image that dominated the entire panorama; it was the imposing presence so aptly named the "Rockpile." Spread out around its base were what had once been rolling fields and rice paddies, but now the area had a wild, overgrown look. In some past peaceful era, this valley would have been a serene and restful hideaway, but now a pervading sense of unease filled the mountains. Whenever in this area, I always experienced a sinister feeling that unfriendly eyes were looking down from many secret places, and indeed they were. With the wall-like mountains hovering around us, I thought that this is how a gamecock must feel when thrust into the fighting pit. Now, our convoy nervously sped over the dusty bumpy road and anxiously approached the camp at the base of the Rockpile.

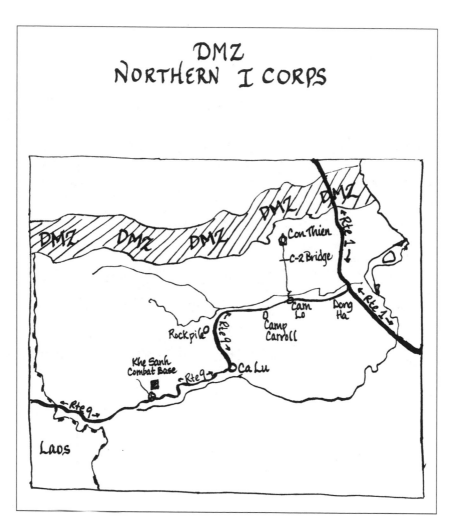

DMZ Northern I Corps

4

The Rockpile

This base differed distinctly from any that I had seen in 'Nam in that it had a wilder, rougher appearance. Here was the ever-present barbed wire, but the location, sitting as it did down in the valley, seemed vulnerable. Adding to this insecure feeling was the fact that the elephant grass grew much closer to the perimeter than it had at Camp Carroll. Inside the barbed wire there were no orderly rows of tents, only low bunkers and trenches that traversed the area with a few random tents scattered about. One of the latter served as the kitchen and another as the mess hall. A third was used for the first-aid station, and all had dirt floors with the canvas sides rolled up. The dining tent had no chairs or tables; instead, long planks were positioned a little over waist high so people could stand and eat. This makeshift chow hall was in a poor location. It was right next to the dusty main road that went through the middle of camp, and whenever a vehicle came by during meal time, clouds of dust would roll across the food. That is just what happened when we arrived during the noon meal. We did not seem a bit appreciated by those eating.

The dust was not something I had anticipated before coming to 'Nam. I had envisioned humid jungles, not the dry heat I was finding. In these hot summer months the base camps up on the DMZ were dry dust bowls, and grit was everywhere. It got in everything you ate and burned your eyes. There was no way to keep clean, and our weapons had to be constantly tended.

After unloading, I inquired as to the location of headquarters and was directed to a sandbagged bunker that had been cut into the ground with a bulldozer. Covered with old tent canvasses, it could hardly be seen for all the elephant grass and vegetation growing around it. The whole area, except for the dining area, was like this and with good reason. It made it harder for the enemy to observe our key operational facilities and more difficult for snipers to get clear shots at us. Inside the bunker, I was introduced to a 1st lieutenant who was the artillery liaison officer for the battalion as well as senior field member from Charlie Battery. His responsibilities included everything relating to the infantry's artillery needs and the supervision of all Charlie Battery personnel. That amounted to five FO teams and the headquarters staff, or about sixteen men in all. He routinely answered to the infantry battalion commander but also received directions from 1/12 back at Camp Carroll. The artillery could override the infantry on some artillery matters, and the position called for diplomacy as well as technical skills. In practice, you actually worked for the infantry commander, and he was the one you had to satisfy. If you did not pass muster with him, he would call the artillery battalion CO and complain or just request a replacement. Whether justified or not, that is just what I understood happened to the present lieutenant and his successor. Sixty days later, I would move into that precarious job. For now, though, I had to contend with entry into a world that I had only imagined and read about. The next year would give a substance to war that was revealed not in words but in sights, smells, fear, discomfort, and elation. Crisis often makes people discover who they really are. This coming period would certainly do that, but it would also change me forever.

The first few days in the field were spent getting acquainted with the artillery personnel and being briefed on how things were done. The lieutenant in charge was a quiet, retiring sort of person who did not seem to belong. Tall and heavyset, he had a polite manner but seemed to have a sense of caution that came across as a form of timidity. His subdued personality was such that I received only minimal orientation from him. Fortunately, though, he had a sergeant on his staff who had a personality exactly opposite the lieutenant's, and he took me in tow. Sergeant Duane Goodridge, a vibrant, outgoing individual, charged around full of energy and ideas. With a boyish, freckled face, he could have been the live-wire kid next door. "Goody," however, was dedicated to his job and relished being a Marine; his salty demeanor merely screened the feelings of a young man who loved life. As the senior noncommissioned officer, or NCO, for artillery personnel out here, he filled a billet that called for an E6 (an enlisted rank) staff sergeant while still only an E5.

We became very good friends, transcending the customary barrier between officer and enlisted. Goody understood the code that had to be observed and never allowed himself or me to be placed in an embarrassing position. Skilled at dealing with the protocol involved, he still managed to communicate on a personal level. I enjoyed him immensely and learned a great deal from him, particularly about how the troops thought. He subtly kept me from making a fool of myself while I was in the learning process and taught me the intricacies of how to get along. Of particular importance was his insight concerning the personalities of the key players out here. It was important to know these people extremely well because they would have to be depended on in critical situations.

I also met Lieutenant Tom Kabler, who became a good friend and whom I would be with for most of my tour. From Washington state, he was a down-to-earth type of guy with whom I could really talk. Tom was serving as an FO out here, the same as I would be, and he made sure I understood the things that really mattered. Later back at Camp Carroll, he became an FDC officer for Charlie Battery while I was executive officer. I never had to worry about where I stood with him because we both respected and related to each other so well.

Another enlisted person with whom I became fast friends was a corporal filling a lieutenant's FO billet. Rayford R. Bebee was from Houston, Texas, and the kind of guy you wanted by your side when the chips were down. Bebee, as he was called, was as brave as they come, yet totally unassuming. He had dark hair and hazel eyes and could have passed for an Indian if not for the eyes. With his Texas drawl, you always felt comfortable around him, but everyone highly respected the way he conducted himself. Bebee, more than any other FO, had seen more combat and performed better in that capacity than anyone in the recent history of Charlie Battery, and the infantry units were always requesting him for touchy operations. He, like Sergeant Goodridge, also knew how to handle the officer-enlisted relationship. In the normal scheme of military matters, officers maintained an arm's-length relationship with enlisted men and were supposed to refrain from forming personal attachments. Under the conditions we found ourselves in, however, it seemed only appropriate to relax the rules a bit. This happened, in part, because the artillery personnel were actually only "attached" to the infantry and not quite part of their fraternity. Even though we lived and functioned as an integral part of their force, those of us in the artillery section developed a particular closeness within our own small group. Also, because of the shortage of lieutenant FOs, we used the more competent NCOs to fill in. Some were really good, and it was hard not to treat those individuals on a more equal basis than military protocol and rank dictated. Consequently, friendships formed that often bridged the officer-enlisted gap, and Bebee and Goody certainly fell into that category. Both of these men later received the Bronze Star and Purple Heart for their performances in combat, and Corporal Bebee distinguished himself even more when he extended for an additional tour in Vietnam. After being wounded for a third time, he would spend several months in a hospital before returning to the field again.

During that first week, I gradually began meeting the infantry. The battalion CO was Lieutenant Colonel Gary Wilder, who had earned the reputation of being a hardnose who sought out action. I think he made people uneasy because his aggressiveness necessarily put people at risk, but as it worked out I was never around him long enough to be able to make my own judgment. I did have time to observe some highly regarded and popular individuals in the battalion, however. One was Captain John W. Ripley, a company commander who had received the Silver Star for his actions in a recent engagement. He was as sharp as could be, and his high decoration, so infrequently awarded in the Marine Corps, had already made him a legend in the lore of the battalion. Obviously, this seasoned combat unit had its own pride and history.

When I arrived at the Rockpile, a lull in enemy activity had existed for some time, and several weeks had passed without incoming fire or perimeter probes. In fact, things had become so routine that the highlights of the days were showers before dark. Real showers were a luxury on the DMZ, and the Rockpile, with its unlimited water supply from the river that ran alongside it, sported hot showers. Not even Camp Carroll had that amenity. Water back there had to be trucked in, and short, cold showers were the only kind available. After a hot, dusty day, nothing could beat a real shower, even if it was in the open air. That first week I did not fully appreciate that amenity, but it would not take long. I also did not yet appreciate the hot meals being dished up in a field kitchen. After later periods of C rations (prepackaged meals of canned goods) for weeks at a time, food prepared in a kitchen would be more than welcome.

That first week passed quickly, and I was assigned to be forward observer for India Company. As a new FO, however, I was not exactly greeted with open arms. These infantrymen had seen a lot of FOs come and go, and until the new man proved his competence, they did not want to get too friendly. There had been less-than-perfect fire missions, and maybe someone had lost a buddy as a result. On the other hand, it could have been simply the realization that the new FO might or might not be cut out for the job. It was one thing to have trained as a forward observer but another to have the personality and skill to get the job done in the field. The infantry wanted to know that you were capable before accepting you as a part of their world. A forward observer was an individual who could save you in a crisis or blow you away on the wrong miscue. Once the FO had proved his ability, he usually was accepted by the company and in some cases even attained a status comparable to that of a good luck charm. Sometimes this happened when an FO did something of a dramatic nature, such as directing artillery fire that saved a unit or consistently performing in spectacular fashion while calling in fire missions. Few achieved deference at that level, but one who had was Corporal Bebee.

Because of the lack of enemy contact, Colonel Wilder decided that we needed to send a company out to look for signs of enemy activity. India Company drew the assignment and received orders to prepare for an extended reconnaissance mission. The selected area was a mountain ridge bordering Route 9 on the way to Ca Lu and separating us from Camp Carroll. A strong enemy presence there could severely affect convoys being run to Ca Lu and Khe Sanh. Ca Lu, only six miles from the

Rockpile, had strategic significance as well because it was at the intersection of two valleys through which Route 9 ran. Khe Sanh could be supplied from either valley, and Ca Lu, consequently, was considered a key location on the DMZ. An old French fort from the French-Indochina war still remained there and indicated that even then Ca Lu had been important enough to justify concrete fortifications. For those reasons the high command decided to keep the Rockpile and Ca Lu as secure as possible.

The mountains on either side of Route 9 provided excellent cover for ambush, and our job would be to patrol miles back on the eastern side. We at times would actually be on the backside of that mountain ridge, away from the Rockpile. Patrols such as this caused considerable anxiety because ground reinforcements would be left far behind and because C rations and water could be supplied only by helicopter. Whenever a chopper resupplied the patrol, every NVA unit in the area was telegraphed our exact location.

Heat was another major problem, and it was almost unbearable as we prepared for the march. With the heat regularly more than one hundred degrees, we knew that heat casualties would be a factor. The artillery staff was most helpful in advising me on how to prepare for such conditions and in particular showed me the proven ways to travel light. They also scrounged up a large supply of canned fruit from the C rations, knowing canned fruit would be one of the few things palatable after miles of heat and sweating. Finally, after demonstrating how to pack the cans in socks tied to my ammo belt, they pointed out other tricks that would make humping the hills a bit more bearable. The socks, incidentally, served two purposes. In addition to being the best way to carry cans, they provided extra changes to give additional relief to the abuse our feet would take.

India Company began the march early in the morning to minimize the heat that was expected to wilt us later in the day. It was an uneasy beginning for me, having been briefed the night before by the company captain who I suspected was nervous about having an untried FO. His very explicit instructions carried the connotation that he had little confidence in a boot lieutenant. This captain impressed me as a man who would do whatever it took to carry out the mission, but he also came across as not being too excited about having the job. Their company had seen a lot of action, and his awareness of the risks might have been showing up in his attitude. At any rate, I knew that I was definitely on trial.

Prior to this patrol, I had developed a cordial relationship with Lieutenant John Anderson, one of the infantry platoon commanders in Mike Company. Tall and lean, with blondish hair, he had an easy, low-key manner. He also had a ready smile and had not minded my endless questions. I learned from him that two or three months earlier an FO had dropped some artillery rounds on India's position while setting in perimeter defensive coordinates. Having heard his account of the incident, I better understood why India's CO might be nervous about new FOs.

As an FO, I had a radio operator who went everywhere with me. The man assigned to me was Private 1st Class Olivari, who would virtually live with me for the next two months. He had dark hair with an olive complexion and looked studious, probably because of the glasses he wore. His father was a major in the Army, and the military had been a way of life to him for many years. "Ollie" did not talk too much, and I never got to know him on a personal basis. However, we would develop a closeness from many tense combat situations and our constant togetherness.

That first day of the march, I found out for myself about those "open meadows" that had looked so tranquil from the air. We literally hacked our way through elephant grass higher than our heads while heat and humidity smothered us. What had looked like a gentle foothill seemed to go up forever in the shimmering heat. I also discovered that the grass had razor-sharp edges that ate up everyone's forearms when pushing it aside, causing me to roll down my own sleeves in spite of the heat. An aftereffect of those cuts was what we called "jungle rot." In this climate, it was very hard for cuts to heal, and those wounds just did not seem to want to scab over. In fact, it sometimes took weeks for them to heal. They were another of Vietnam's torments we learned to live with.

About one o'clock that afternoon, we experienced our first heat stroke. A new trooper, fresh from the States and not yet acclimatized, collapsed near the head of the column. The danger of heat stroke was life threatening, and a helicopter medevac (medical evacuation) was called in to get him out. Much to the CO's dismay, the column had to stop until the chopper could get there. He, of course, felt concern for the trooper but was more worried about the time delay and likelihood that we were broadcasting our location to any NVA troops that happened to be around. Ironically, the casualty, in critical shape when picked up, was envied by many men who could think only of his freedom from the ordeal we were going through.

This reconnaissance mission had only just begun, and it was anybody's guess as to what we would find. That concern, however, became secondary to coping with the incredible heat and humidity. With my head pounding and wringing wet from perspiration, I desperately hoped that I would not be the next to pass out. As the day wore on, I reached a point where all I could do was set my mind on making it to the end of the march without collapsing. In that state of mind I could not have cared less about the NVA. By thinking only of the next twenty steps, I willed myself to make just them. If I had dwelled on how much further we really had to go, I do not know whether I could have handled it. Finally, even thought became impossible, and I simply concentrated on the man's back ahead of me, trying not to show how nauseated I had become. An hour later we topped the hill and took a break while another heat casualty was medevaced.

This was hell, and I found it hard to believe that it was really happening. How had I ended up halfway around the world in this predicament? I had never pictured Vietnam quite like this. Now I better understood why we were put through so much at Officer Candidate School. That program, designed to be a combination of physical harassment and mental stress, taxed would-be officers to the limits of their endurance. At the time, I had found it difficult to understand why we were being forced to take so much abuse, but I now understood that they had been deliberately trying to eliminate those who could not lead when they were emotionally and physically drained. Marine officers are expected to be exceptional individuals under even the most severe war conditions, and that growing awareness gave me incentive to not let myself and all I believed in collapse.

Toward the end of the day, the heat began to subside, and the CO indicated we would set up on a small knoll near the ridge we were climbing. It, too, was covered with elephant grass and had no trees. When we got there, everyone collapsed for about twenty minutes and then tried to regain some semblance of vitality. The heat, I would find out later, had reached 110 degrees each day, sapping our very spirit.

The afternoon continued to cool, canteens were raised to parched lips, and the troops finally began to scurry about. Officers and NCOs had already been moving around to designate where the perimeter should be, and almost immediately the whole company began digging in. A lieutenant then casually came over to me and suggested that I dig my hole near the captain in case I was needed. Watching the others, I saw that the type of holes being dug resembled graves in that they were about the length of a body but were only about twelve or fourteen inches deep. That allowed you to lie prone with no part of your body above the surface of the ground. The reason for these shallow depressions was that it took a minimum amount of digging yet effectively gave protection from mortars unless the round happened to land right on you. Mortars were the enemy's most effective killing tool and a frequently used attack weapon on the DMZ. When one of those rounds came hurtling down from almost directly overhead, the resulting explosion blasted out in a perfect circle. Unless you were below the surface of the ground, the results could ruin your day. Because of this dreaded weapon, everyone prepared at least minimal holes every night that we were on patrol.

When I finished my hole, the CO called me over and assigned me my first fire mission in Vietnam. It was the practice when setting up overnight positions to call in perimeter protective fires. That meant directing artillery rounds to likely avenues of attack and then filing the coordinates with the supporting battery. In the event of an attack, all the CO had to do was call in the code designation for the desired coordinate, and he would have instant firepower without having to waste time adjusting rounds. The few minutes saved often made the difference in repelling an attack or being overrun. A downside to this practice was that when we did this, we also told the enemy exactly where we were for the evening. I was not sure that the procedure served us best for this type of patrol, but the infantry seemed more comfortable with having instant firepower at their fingertips than in being well hidden.

With my heart in my throat, I drew on all my map-reading skills and called in the first coordinates. Waiting for the first round to arrive, I desperately prayed that it would not land on us. The shell impacted relatively near where I wanted it to, and I hoped no one detected my relief. I continued to adjust rounds to the desired point, though they seemed dangerously close to our own position. This first target was a nearby ravine that the CO thought would be a likely approach route if the NVA attacked. One thing for sure, I had never called in a fire mission to such proximity back in the States. Finally, the adjusting round landed in the ravine, and to my relief the captain casually commented, "Good job." After several more protective fire points were set in, my activities were over unless we had visitors later. The thing that had impressed me most during the firing was that the troops paid practically no attention to the nearness of the rounds that were landing so much closer than I was accustomed to. Obviously, they were used to radically different conditions than I had experienced in the highly supervised artillery classes back at Fort Sill.

With that hurdle behind me, I made my way back over to my foxhole and started preparing for the night. The day's exertions had exhausted and dehydrated me, leaving me with no appetite at all. Knowing I needed nourishment to function tomorrow, I forced myself to open a can of fruit cocktail. The liquid soothed my parched throat and helped quench my thirst. We were continually being reminded to conserve water, and the fruit cocktail, with its sugar syrup, was one of the few things available from our C rations that countered the dehydration we were experiencing. The boys back at the Rockpile had guided me well.

That night the Lord truly blessed us. While I was flat on my back and lying exhausted in my foxhole, it began to rain. I did not move a muscle as the drops began to fall and only then opened my mouth to let the rain cool my tongue. Harder and harder the rain came down, filling my foxhole, but all I did was lie there in delight. Stretching out in a mud hole may not seem very pleasant, but that was one of the most refreshing moments I had ever experienced. I did not move until it was my turn to swap with Ollie on radio watch.

Because of my fatigue and inexperience, the night's approach had not particularly bothered me. Vietnam's evenings, however, were particularly dangerous because then, through stealth, the NVA increased their odds of success. Later I learned to respect the danger of the darkness, but for now I was only conscious of having survived an ordeal; nothing else seemed to matter.

When day broke, we started to come alive slowly, but my body seemed like one stiff board as I stretched one limb and then another. The heat, combined with fluid loss and physical exertion, had taken a toll on everyone, as attested by the moans and groans of unlimbering troops. In the early morning coolness, I opened another can of fruit and ate breakfast quickly.

The CO determined that our patrol route for that morning would be guided by likely water sources. If we did not have to be resupplied with water by chopper, it would be more difficult for the NVA to figure out where we were. Using a map, we set out on a route that would take us down the mountain to an apparent stream. Fortunately, the march was downhill and much easier than the day before. Again, we found ourselves trudging through elephant grass with all of its annoyances, but the heat was not nearly the factor it had been. Around nine o'clock in the morning, we reached the stream shown on the map but found it dry, causing the captain to express no small amount of concern. He decided to follow the stream bed on down, hoping we would have better luck at a lower elevation. Two hours later, we came upon a stagnant pool of water, and, without hesitation, everyone began filling canteens and putting in water purification tablets. Normally, the medicinal taste imparted to the water by these chemicals was distasteful, but when real thirst became a factor it did not matter. After a thirty-minute rest we were on our way again and found the going much easier than yesterday. That in part was because we were now moving through trees that had a tropical nature. The accompanying humidity was what you would expect, but the shade from the high and leafy canopy alleviated the sweltering heat.

We moved along smoothly and eventually began climbing back uphill. An hour later, as we scrambled over and around rocks and boulders, the terrain became more mountainlike. Even the trees appeared different than they had earlier in the morning and now and then moved with an occasional breeze. Moving higher up the mountain, I began to experience an uncomfortable feeling, almost like some unseen presence was with us. This ancient land seemed to be warning us that we did not belong.

Vietnam was indeed different in many ways, and I am sure that the tropical vegetation contributed to that strangeness. The differences, however, were in many little things, both good and bad. Of particular significance to me was the fact that there was no poison ivy in 'Nam. With my extreme allergy to it, I had dreaded the thought of catching it over here, but it just did not exist. On the other hand, there were negatives, such as the great variety of poisonous snakes populating the country, some of which we had already observed that morning. Not necessarily a threat, but strange nevertheless, were the different birds and animals we were seeing; the calls and songs of the birds seemed particularly unusual. Those contrasts made for an exotic world and for some reason became more apparent as we moved higher into the mountains.

An uneasiness began to settle over the entire company, and now the normal griping and joking gave way to an ominous silence as the eyes of the troops darted from side to side. Coming to the top of a ridge, we found a well-worn path running along its crest, which made for easier walking, but we also knew that someone else had made it. We confirmed this thirty minutes later when we came on enemy foxholes alongside the trail. Seeing those freshly dug holes was my first exposure to actual evidence of the enemy and chillingly reminded me that the NVA were active and real. It was an uncomfortable feeling knowing that not too long ago somebody had walked this trail who would very much like to put a bullet in me. Being out here, miles from base camp, brought its own set of anxieties, but not knowing what the NVA were up to added to the tenseness. It is one thing to be in a known dilemma, but another not to know who is watching you or what they might be planning. The silence of the column moving along the ridge indicated India Company's unease, and finally the captain called a halt to confer with the platoon leaders. They decided that a major trail such as this could easily lead into an ambush and that we would instead cross over to another ridge, hopefully one less used.

The switch to the next ridge would be one of the most physically exhausting and painful ordeals of my tour in Vietnam. We were going to drop straight down into a valley and climb straight up the other ridge. The CO decided that a direct route to the other side would be the safest bet, and he was not going to waste any time getting there, either. We tumbled and fell down that ridge through a tangle of jungle that I found hard to believe could grow on such steep slopes. Completely forgetting stealth we banged our way down like a herd of wild bulls. On reaching the bottom, we had gashes, bruises, and sprains everywhere, but the captain did not let us rest long. In no time, a three-hour climb began, and we went through hell pulling ourselves up that slope by roots and limbs. Two troopers who had sprained their ankles were particular problems because they had to be dragged and pushed most of the way. The captain passed the word that we must make it to the top of the ridge by dark or we would be in big trouble if we had to spend the night strung out on the slope. Everyone sensed the urgency and went at the climb with a vengeance. There was no talking but plenty of clatter and banging as we scrambled over the rocks. The guys with the sprained ankles did their share of moaning, but they were going through agonizing pain. Actually, hearing them made the rest of us realize how much worse off we could be, and our own pain did not seem quite as bad. Not a stitch of dry clothing remained in the company. The exertion of these men was phenomenal, spurred on as it was by the thought of being caught in such a vulnerable position after dark. Only a few escaped cuts and scrapes, and everyone's body took a battering on the rocks. About a half hour before dark, we made it to the top of the ridge, but by now I was completely nauseated from my exertions, and my head pounded like it never had before. The entire unit collapsed at the top and just lay there for a few minutes.

Finally focusing on my surroundings, I was introduced to my first B-52 bomb crater. A hole had been blasted out of the jungle, and it was large enough in which to fit a small house. The force of the bomb that had done this was hard for me to comprehend. Trees around the crater had been knocked down like matchsticks for a distance of about thirty feet in all directions. It was almost dark now, and we dispersed the company around the crater and set the command post inside. As night fell the captain said we should not worry about perimeter defensive fires because, surrounded by tall trees, we could hardly see any distance at all to adjust fire. The men quietly settled into their positions, knowing we were in enemy territory and realizing that an attack under these conditions could be touchy. A somber feeling of apprehension permeated the mood of the entire company, and a long, restless vigil followed with few having trouble staying awake. Fortunately, we had no enemy contact.

Morning broke with a new problem. The two troopers with sprained ankles were so bad off that now they were going to be a major hindrance moving through this incredibly rough terrain. Therefore, it was decided to medevac them by chopper before we pulled out. Extraction would be extremely difficult because of the thickness of the jungle and would necessitate the helicopter having to descend precisely over the crater. Thirty minutes later a chopper could be heard thump-thumping toward us and without hesitation flew right to the yellow smoke grenade that had been popped to mark our position. This was my first opportunity to see why the helicopter pilots were the real heroes of Vietnam. Those guys seemed to fear nothing and attempted things that only an insane man would do. Much of the time their daredevil performances involved rescue operations where lives were at stake, and their flirtations with disaster created in them a disregard for risk that carried over into even their more routine jobs. They almost had to have that attitude to maintain sanity. This particular pilot flew in and immediately began descending into the crater until the blades of the rotor started pruning the tops of the trees. Men scurried out of the way like ants, and after three attempts it became clear that he was not going to be able to drop to the ground. This left only the option of dangling lines from the chopper and pulling the casualties up one by one. A prolonged extraction such as this really gave the NVA an opportunity to hit us with mortars, and, with the racket all around, we would never have heard the incoming until it was on us. Miraculously, though, no mortars came in, and we were left with a deafening silence as the chopper thumped away. Quickly moving out, we intended to place as much distance as we could between ourselves and the spot that had been so dramatically marked for the enemy.

That day we followed various ridges and in the process found many more signs indicating that the enemy had recently been there, most notably a campsite where they had even built fires. Some of these ridge trails were well worn and probably part of the jungle highway system that allowed the NVA to move so stealthily throughout the country. The North Vietnamese had proved themselves capable of rapidly moving incredible amounts of men and material for strategic purposes; these well-developed paths were the reason why.

At midday, we unexpectedly were directed to return immediately to base camp at the Rockpile. This was received with mixed emotions because everyone wanted to get out of these mountains, but, on the other hand, we had learned that the reason for our recall was that regimental intelligence had determined that a large number of enemy troops were moving into the Rockpile area. This was relayed to us in code over the radio, carrying further warnings to be extremely cautious and get back as soon as possible. The battalion commander did not want his forces spread out all over the place if the NVA were contemplating an attack. At this point, it was anyone's guess as to what they were doing, and we did not need to be taking any chances. With renewed energy, we headed down a major ridge, knowing we would now have to spend only one more night in the boonies. After a hot, uneventful afternoon, we settled in for the evening on a grassy knoll.

Once again, the captain directed me to call in perimeter protective fires, and, with the confidence of having done it before, I routinely set the coordinates for the evening with little attention from anyone. Maybe the infantry was relaxing about me as an FO or else they were just too preoccupied with the new developments.

One of the platoon lieutenants confirmed that when he stopped by to brief me on the change of plans. Our new situation was important, of course, but his final comment was particularly welcome because he let me know that the CO had earlier indicated to the platoon leaders that he thought I was going to be all right as an FO. This came as a relief and eased some of the typical self-doubt that most rookies have until they prove their competence. I finally began to have some confidence that I could function with these guys.

The next day, about noon, we made it out of the mountains to a point on Route 9 about three miles from the base. Transport trucks were sent to pick us up, and within an hour we were back in camp. What a great feeling it was when we passed through the barbed-wire perimeter and into the seeming safety of home base. We were given a two-hour break and allowed to hit the showers. They were like heaven after what we had just experienced. Little things count in times like those, and one learns to savor a good moment because one never knows what the next one might bring.

The physical exertion that I had been through finally caught up with me that night. Relieved to be back, and exhausted as I was, I returned to the bunker where the artillery staff had its sleeping quarters. The liaison officer and Sergeant Goodridge had their cots there and were letting me use them because one of the two was always on duty at battalion head-quarters. The bunker, not high enough to stand up in, barely left enough room to put your feet on the ground if you sat on a cot. In addition, the rats were so bad that you always had to tuck your mosquito netting in around the bedding so they would not scamper across you while you slept. The hot, humid stillness and the cramped quarters, combined with my extreme fatigue, overwhelmed me as I slept. I awoke gasping for breath in the confining space of the mosquito netting and thought I was dying. Tearing out of bed, I crawled out into the night, struggling and gasping on the ground. I really thought that I was gone but gradually brought my breathing under control. The only thing I could compare this experience to was having had my breath knocked out of me. The relief when my wind came back was one of the greatest feelings in the world. Not knowing what was the matter with me, I looked for and found the field doctor, a real M.D., who explained that my exhaustion had caused me to hyperventilate and that it was no big deal. He told me to sleep outside for the evening, and I spent the rest of the night fitfully dozing and wondering why I had gotten myself into this Vietnam thing.

The following day brought new reports of increasing enemy activity, and two nights later this was confirmed by a mortar attack. We actually received only eight rounds, but it was my first experience with hostile fire. The rounds fell a good distance away from me, but there was no question about it being enemy incoming. When the rounds landed, I was sitting outside on some sandbags and scrambled into the bunker with a thumping heart. I waited there calmly for whatever might come next, but nothing did that night. I had finally been shot at, and although it was scary there had been no panic. This would be the first of many times that

I was on the receiving end of enemy fire, and the feelings would always be the same. I never got used to someone trying to kill me.

The next week I accompanied other companies on several day patrols, and we combed the terrain close to our perimeter. These excursions would theoretically keep large enemy units from catching us by surprise and were an integral part of the overall defensive plan. We knew they were out there because we were mortared on two more occasions, one being particularly notable because it happened during the day. Most mortar attacks by the NVA were at night, and this daytime action indicated the NVA were becoming more aggressive than usual. They were definitely up to something with their bold attacks and movement of large units around the Rockpile area.

By that time, I had been in country about a month, and enough had occurred in my short stay to provide some discernment for what Vietnam was about. It was clear that a person could die quickly over here and that personal survival was one of the major objectives. Any romantic notions about searching out combat had long since left my head, and I began to look with relish for a speedy return to Charlie Battery and the relative safety of Camp Carroll. The fulfillment of that desire would be a long time in coming, however.

The battalion, in addition to its mission of keeping Route 9 open, had the responsibility of maintaining an outpost on the peak of the Rockpile itself. A twenty-man contingent, composed mostly of Army technicians, was located there, and they had sophisticated detection and communication equipment that was critical to the entire intelligence operation in Vietnam. What they were doing was supposed to be top secret, but I learned enough to know that it had to do with intercepting NVA radio transmissions. It was Division policy to keep a lieutenant FO up there, thereby having an officer in charge as well as someone skilled at directing fire support. The height of this mountain and its location made for superior observation, and the FO was supposed to report anything of an unusual nature. From there, the FO could see from the South China Sea to Laos and had a clear view of the area bordering Route 9 from near Camp Carroll to almost Ca Lu. The outpost itself was high on a peak of sheer rock cliffs that were on one end of the plateaulike top of the mountain. It could easily be defended and was well within the capability of such a small group's ability to repel an attack.

Every thirty days, the officer on this duty was rotated, and it so happened that I received the assignment. This pleased me because it indicated that I had passed muster well enough to be given such a responsible job. I also knew from my artillery associates that it was one of the more pleasant assignments on the DMZ. My stay there would be a reflective period in which I would experience a complete new set of anxieties and concerns. The coming mountaintop experience would be a time of introspection and would slow me down long enough to place life and Vietnam in perspective.

After receiving the news, I spent the rest of my time hearing friendly farewells and a great deal of ribbing about the soft duty I had drawn. The Rockpile, because of its fortresslike pinnacle, was considered about as safe as any place on the DMZ. Sergeant Goodridge, with his constant good humor and friendliness, loaded me up with helpful information and instructions. Chattering away while I gathered up my things, he said to me, "Lieutenant Brown, your most important gear will be your sunglasses and your swimsuit and be sure and carry plenty of suntan lotion." Goody then briefed me well on how the duties should be handled, and it did seem like the assignment might be a pleasant one. One notable farewell came from my recently made friend, Lieutenant Anderson with Mike Company, who, when I mentioned that I had lost my second lieutenant's bars, gave me one of his sets. He was scheduled for promotion soon to first lieutenant and would not be needing them much longer. Those gold bars would later carry special significance for me because he would be killed while I was on the Rockpile.

5

A Mountaintop Experience

Early the next day the resupply chopper for the Rockpile dropped into our position to pick me up, and away I went to a world that had its own unique place in Vietnam. It would be days of relief from military formality while perched above the war below. Up there, we were removed from actually being part of the action in the valley and yet were involved in an abstract sort of way. The chopper climbed to the peak, and the beauty of the valley and mountains again profoundly impacted me. Vietnam was spectacular from the air. Nearing the top, I saw a plateau of about a hundred acres covered with jungle. I found out later that this little spot was like a land unto itself with its own ecological system. On the edge of the plateau nearest Dong Ha and the South China Sea stood a mass of rocks and boulders rising like some fortress in a fairy tale. It had cliffs that were fifty feet high in the form of a sheer wall on the side next to the plateau, whereas on the opposite side there was just one step to the edge and then hundreds of feet straight down. On top of this rock structure, a massive helicopter pad had been built from heavy timbers; it must have been a major engineering feat at the time of its construction.

As we approached the pad, I noticed that the chopper had a great deal of difficulty settling down. At the pinnacle the frequent updrafts on one side and downdrafts on the other made for treacherous landings. A significant crosswind would make it even more difficult. Again the chopper pilots demonstrated that they either had nerves of steel or were crazy.

They fought the wind like riding a bucking bull and forced the chopper down on the pad.

When we finally landed on the platform, a flurry of activity erupted around the edges. Mail bags, boxes, and water cans were quickly dragged off as a bunch of guys in swimsuits swarmed around the helicopter. Ollie and I jumped out but were able only to wave to the lieutenant and radio operator whom we were replacing because, in the swarm of activity and with the roar of the engine, that was all we could do. The backdraft from the blades was incredibly strong because the rotors were kept at liftoff speed in case a heavy wind gust came along. We then clambered onto some rocks by the platform, and in a flash the chopper was gone. Immediately, the troops bombarded us with multiple questions concerning what was happening below, most of the inquiries being about who was doing what. Someone then guided us over to the artillery quarters, and we came on a tent-looking affair perched on boulders located well away from the pad where most of the troops lived. The hooch, which is what we called our sleeping quarters, was a plank platform about nine feet wide and ten feet long. Poncho rain gear had been stretched over a wooden framework covering two cots with a three-foot walkway in between. This cover was about five feet high and ended just past the cots. Beyond this, the floor extended another four feet, and if you took one more step you would fall forever. The view looking out the back of our hooch was fantastic and gave us a panorama of Mutter's Ridge. This mountain ridge, whose Vietnam name was Nui Cay Tre, had been renamed after the radio call sign of the 3d Battalion, 4th Marines, which had been in a significant engagement at that location in early October of 1966. Of note, it was also there in that fight that Captain J. J. Carroll had been killed, the Marine for whom Camp Carroll was named.

To the east from our little porch, ships were visible twenty miles away in the South China Sea, and with binoculars you could even see the giant red cross on the side of the hospital ship, the *Sanctuary.* That in itself was not too exciting because no one liked to think of why it was there. To the west, the mountains extended into Laos with the skyline dominated by "Ghost Mountain," so named by the Marines because its peak was usually shrouded in the mystery of the clouds. On the rare occasions that its towering top could be seen, it triggered discussions tinged with a certain amount of awe.

Our view down into the valley created an impression of looking at a toy world. People appeared no bigger than ants, and the scene was minuscule in detail. A river crept through the valley and gently curled like a painted ribbon, varying in color whenever it passed through the shade of the mountains or glimmered in the sun. The feelings experienced were those of height and a sense of removal, giving an unreal quality to the activities below.

After stowing our gear, we immediately settled into our duty, which consisted of scanning the mountains and searching for NVA activity. Ollie was certainly capable of doing this as well as I was, and we stood six-hour watches around the clock. If he saw anything, he would wake me to assess it. That first afternoon, we identified all the key terrain features on the map and generally oriented ourselves to the peculiarities of the position. Days and nights of binocular use followed with us combing the nooks and crannies of the DMZ.

In addition to the technicians up here, we had six Marines from 3/3 whose jobs were strictly for security purposes. I met with them, discussing at length the position and its defenses. It seemed that our main protection was the height of the sheer cliff that we were on, and at key points around the top, dozens of hand grenades had been placed in wooden boxes. If we were attacked, simply dropping the grenades over the edge of the cliff would be devastating and probably more effective than anything else we could do. Of course, we all had automatic weapons and with the advantage of our height could spray anything below. Down at the base of the cliff on the plateau side, a ring of claymore mines covered every approach. These devices were attached by electrical wires to detonators in our position and could easily be set off if necessary. The effect of the claymore was like shooting a shotgun at an approaching enemy, and they were highly regarded as a defensive tool. Finally, a wide band of barbed wire had been strung, and attached to that were tin cans containing pebbles with trip flares generously interspersed. Nothing could make it through without rattling a can or setting off a trip flare. It was quite a setup, and it impressed me with its apparent thoroughness.

The only thing left to concern me was the possibility of NVA activity on the plateau. The last time a patrol had gone out had been more than two weeks ago, and I decided to investigate the area myself.

The following day an unbelievable screeching woke me up, and, jumping from my cot, I ran up to the helicopter pad where the commotion was occurring. On arrival, I witnessed one of the most hilarious scenes I had ever seen. A colony of rock apes occupied the plateau with us, and the troops, over the months, had developed an ongoing rivalry with these large monkeys that stood about two-thirds the height of a man. Whenever the rock apes came in range, the men threw stones at them, and these wild and bawdy animals had learned to throw back. On occasions, small-scale rock wars ensued. The screeching came from the apes, and they, in turn, were cursed as only the grinning Marines could do. This lasted for only a couple of minutes until the monkeys faded back into the jungle, but these encounters delighted the men, and they spent many hours trying to entice them close enough to start a battle.

After this intrusion, I gathered the security troops together, and the seven of us headed out on patrol. We followed a tedious trail through the maze of trip flares and then moved into the shade of tropical vegetation. Because of this vegetation we lost the sense of being on a mountain and could have been in a jungle anywhere. This was my first experience at leading a true combat patrol, although I had led many in officer training and during staging at Camp Pendleton. Doing it for real, however, provided an adrenaline rush. It felt quite natural, but knowing we could possibly run into the NVA caused me to take all the precautionary measures I could. An amusing side note to me was that the real interest of the troops centered on the possibility of encountering a tiger. On numerous occasions, a tigress with two half-grown cubs had been seen on the plateau but always from a distance. Before leaving that morning, there had been a lot of boastful talk about tiger skin rugs and such, but I suspected the real concern might have to do with the possibility of an aggressive tiger and our ability to stop it before it attacked us first.

Tiger talk continued on our first break, and we heard a tale from one of the men about what had happened to an ambush patrol some months earlier down in the valley. It seems that before I joined 3/3, a squad had been sent out for a night ambush along a well-used trail. The procedure was to place the men parallel to the path and spaced out evenly; every other man would take a turn sleeping during the long night. The squad leader was on the extreme right of the ambush formation, and during his time to sleep a tiger came walking down the path. Moving silently, the big cat came up to the patrol undetected but evidently smelled the grubby Marines. Expecting an easy meal, the tiger crept up to the sleeping sergeant and grabbed him by the biceps of his arm. You can imagine the sergeant's amazement when he awoke in pain and saw a bizarre face crushing his arm. His first move was one of instinctive reaction and consisted of smashing the tiger in the nose with the clenched fist of his free arm while screaming at the top of his lungs. The startled tiger, confronted with that and the resulting fire from the squad's reaction to what they thought was a triggered ambush, jerked away and ran off. Unfortunately, the cat carried off much of the sergeant's biceps, leaving a mangled arm but also a permanent trip back to the States for compensation. Almost needless to say, the telling of this story in tiger country stimulated a high state of alertness. We continued the patrol until afternoon but found no signs of enemy activity and saw no tiger.

The next week was a carefree one in which nothing eventful occurred and a time during which the essence of Vietnam began to seep into my soul. The wind at these heights constantly blew and never seemed to stop its wailing song among the rocks. Panoramic beauty burned into my mind and remains there forever with the mystic quality of the surreal surroundings. Breezes kept us cool during the days, and it was cold at night. In the evenings it seemed as if we were actually sitting among the very stars, and the closeness of the sky was like nothing I had ever experienced. Freed from the squalor and activity of the war below, one could stop and contemplate the beauty of this strange land. With war raging across Vietnam, it was unusual to have time for this type of introspection except under unique circumstances such as these.

The big events of the days were mealtimes, and for the entire time that I was on the Rockpile, we ate no meals other than C rations cooked over heating tablets. These tablets, which looked like oversized Alka-Seltzers, would burn for five to ten minutes when lit with a match. In spite of that, we came up with some pretty good concoctions by mixing in seasonings from packets sent from home. At night, we amused ourselves by catching rats. On arriving at the base camp a month earlier, I had asked my dad to send some traps when I had realized what a nuisance the rodents were. The traps arrived while I was on the Rockpile and could not have been better timed. The rats we had seen were enormous, and we prepared for that first evening with enthusiasm. Because of the rats' size, communications wire was tied to a trap and fastened securely. After dark, we baited it with peanut butter from C rations and in fifteen minutes had our first rat. His body was approximately a foot long, and with his tail he stretched nearly two feet. The troops on the platform heard all the commotion, and we had to show him off for the next thirty minutes. We then got down to business and caught twenty-one during the course of the night, using just one trap. The troopers up by the pad begged us to let them borrow a trap, and for several nights rat catching dominated our activities until the population began to trim down. Unknown to us, other creatures had as much interest in these rodents as we did. Lieutenant Eager, who had taken a turn up here, killed a bamboo viper chasing a rat from out of the rocks right next to our hooch. When I later found out about the snake, I could only wonder whether there had been others when we were poking around in those holes retrieving rats.

Time moved along in a casual and relaxed way until the war reminded us that it was not really that far off. Regiment had alerted us that there was going to be an early morning air strike on a nearby ridge called the Razorback. This medium-sized mountain rose abruptly from the valley floor and was unconnected to the surrounding ridges in much the same way as the Rockpile. Elongated with a jagged ridge for its crest, it resembled a razorback hog as shown in cartoon caricatures of that famous Arkansas native. It had caves with catacombs that were supposedly frequented by the NVA. Gossip among the troops held that the Japanese had used those caves during World War II because old crates with Japanese markings had been found there on an earlier patrol.

We were eating canned ham and eggs for breakfast and sitting on the helicopter pad, expecting to have a good view of the target area, when the first strike came in. Instead of a distant "show," we were greeted by a wayward bomb that came streaking in right over our heads, narrowly missing us. The bomb, obviously out of pattern with the others, screamed by like a jet plane, and it was not until it exploded a moment later that we realized what had happened. It had been a close call and scared the hell out of everybody. For an instant, I had wondered why the stupid pilot was making such a close pass. Everyone scrambled into the rocks for cover, hoping another was not on the way, while I began trying to raise air control. Several more bombs were dropped, but none came close, and when I finally did reach the air controller, the strike was over. We had just been through something that few Americans in Vietnam would ever experience; we had been on the receiving end of an air strike. For me this happened on one other occasion but not with such a happy ending.

I was calling in fire missions more frequently now, and enemy activity had begun to pick up. One morning a unit on patrol over on Mutter's Ridge started taking mortars, and because we could easily locate the enemy movement, we were directed to call in artillery until the patrol could pull out. I spent most of the day firing away, and was that satisfying! Bringing the adjusting rounds in on target and firing for effect when you knew the enemy was there created a real high. All this was happening while sitting abstractly on top of the world and controlling things down below. I could imagine how Zeus must have felt on Mount Olympus when he hurled his thunderbolts at the mortals beneath him. It also did not hurt our feelings a bit that we were not receiving any incoming ourselves. This was the way to fight a war.

One situation that had turned into a problem was that the liaison officer who had been down at the base camp before I left had been replaced. Evidently, he had not gotten along with the battalion commander. The new man, whom I had never met in person, was the lieutenant preceding me on the Rockpile. I had only a glimpse of him in the brief moment when we had arrived by helicopter. He seemed cocky and unreasonable in his radio communication, and from reading between the lines, I could tell he was not too popular with Sergeant Goodridge or with the other artillery personnel. At any rate, during the day of covering the unit on Mutter's Ridge, I wound up wondering what was going on in the guy's head. With us having the obvious height advantage, recommendations for more effective coverage had been made several times, and each time he countered with something off the wall and completely illogical to the scheme of withdrawal. The only conclusion I could draw was that he must know something that could not be discussed over the radio. Nevertheless, I was not comfortable with the way he handled things and planned to have him explain some of his peculiar decisions when I got back to the base camp.

Not long after this incident, an engagement took place between the Rockpile and Ca Lu when a platoon came in contact with NVA troops. The battalion responded by sending relief troops to reinforce them, and we played a part in that effort as well. Calling in mission after mission on enemy soldiers who were frequently visible from many vantage points, we on the Rockpile and other observers began to have an impact on the action through the combined use of air, artillery, and 81mm mortars. The highlight of the day for me was when I noticed a large unit of NVA troops moving down a draw toward the ambush site. This movement was soon confirmed by Sergeant Goodridge, who had gone out with the reinforcements. From previous radio traffic, I knew jets were on the way for a general air strike, so I relayed in the enemy coordinates to Regiment, hoping they could get word to the air. They must have because in minutes planes screamed in for a look. It was a lucky moment because the NVA were caught totally exposed and hemmed up between two ridge fingers. The jets, carrying napalm, turned the draw into a fiery furnace with flames rolling and boiling down the mountainside. After the smoke cleared fifteen or twenty minutes later, a spotter plane cruised over the area, and I later heard that they had reported a body count of approximately two hundred, a very high number for a single air strike. Eventually, the platoon was extracted but only after a long day of countermeasures. The NVA paid dearly for their morning attack, however.

Everyone now knew the North Vietnamese were back in force in the valley and full of fight. Happy to be sitting high up on the Rockpile, I looked down on the dangerous activity unfolding around us and would have been pleased to spend my entire tour up here. The war was so much closer than I wanted it to be. When the thirty-day assignment was almost over, however, I received the surprise word that my tour on the Rockpile was being extended indefinitely. With only three days to go before the scheduled rotation, I could not believe the stroke of good luck.

Several days later, on July 21, Mike Company was dispatched to the west of Ca Lu to be sure that Route 9 was clear for a convoy taking several of the big 175mm guns to Khe Sanh. Extra precautions were being taken because of the stepped-up enemy activity. One of Mike Company's point men turned a bend in the road and, on seeing an NVA soldier urinating in the road, took a shot at him. That, in turn, triggered return fire from other NVA troops who had evidently been set up to ambush the convoy. Therefore, the fortuitous call of nature foiled what would later be determined to have been an elaborate ambush attempt and one that likely would have resulted in heavy casualties to either Mike Company or the convoy. As it was, Mike Company spent the day in pitched battle while we on the Rockpile, who were not able to see the action, could only sit and imagine what it was like. Listening on the radio network while the drama unfolded, we heard their calls for reinforcements and could sense the stress of the moment as they determinedly dealt with the situation. Requests for medevacs grew, and we knew they had their hands full. Eventually, with the help of Army "twin forties" (double-barreled 40mm guns on a tracked vehicle) they were able to disengage. The 175mm guns never made it to Khe Sanh, however, even though the rest of the convoy managed to get through a couple of days later when it was determined that the enemy had been flushed out. After an investigation of the ambush site, it was evident that the NVA were very serious about stopping traffic to Khe Sanh, and by early August all convoys beyond Ca Lu had been discontinued because of the difficulty anticipated in keeping the highly exposed route secure. Route 9 from Ca Lu to Khe Sanh would remain closed to surface vehicle traffic until Operation Pegasus reopened the road in the early part of April 1968 after the "siege" of Khe Sanh.

Of personal consequence to me in that engagement was the death of Lieutenant Anderson, who had befriended me during my time at the base camp. He was wounded in the stomach, but as he was carried from the field he remained as cool as ever, smiling and cracking dry jokes. By the time his medevac chopper reached Dong Ha, he was dead. It depressed me deeply when I heard what had happened. There would be other occasions when I had friends killed in the same combat action that I was actually involved in, but it was never like this. Hearing about a buddy's death when I was not there always impacted me harder. I guess in the heat of combat, your mind does not have time to comprehend the tragedy. On receiving the news about Lieutenant Anderson, I thought about just how fragile life is and began to accept each new day as a precious gift.

There was plenty of time to consider the follies of man while we sat atop the Rockpile and looked down on the world. At night in particular, I stared out into the vastness of space and found it difficult to understand where we fit in God's great scheme of things. During the long, lonely watches, there was little else to do but think about what it all meant. Halfway around the world, America acted as if nothing was going on; over here the cream of America's youth was being asked to walk through the valley of death. Many of them were not making it out. It made you wonder why these kids, as well as the seasoned professionals, so willingly did their jobs. The spirit of the men up here on the DMZ was incredibly positive. What caused these people to tick? I concluded that there were two major motivating forces.

First, it seemed that for many, it was simply a matter of honor. Most of these men genuinely believed in upholding the highest traditions of America and in standing behind the legacy of those who had sacrificed before them. So what that many back home hardly understood what was going on or even cared about what was happening over here? For the most part, the men in the Marines were volunteers and had, in many cases, actually requested to be a part of America's efforts in Vietnam. Consequently, they felt bound by their commitments to carry on regardless of attitudes back home. The Marine Corps built on those basic sentiments and fostered a profound respect for its own proud history, resulting in a loyalty that demanded action.

The other factor was that war, through the hardships it imposed on its participants, deeply bonded men together in a struggle for a common cause. Whether it was friendship between individuals or the sense of family that comes from belonging to a group, we all carried a feeling of responsibility that made people think of others rather than themselves. Countless stories told of men who had laid it on the line for their buddies. A verse of scripture summed it up well with these words: "Greater love has no man than that he lay down his life for his friends." Even if no apparent feelings of patriotism existed in an individual, oftentimes that person performed heroic acts simply because others depended on him. Most did not want to let their friends down, and many paid the supreme sacrifice just to keep that from happening.

The DMZ was an area where people quickly questioned the war. This skepticism came from concern about political policies that allowed the North Vietnamese to attack us at will from across the DMZ and Laos and yet did not permit us to counterattack and pursue them into North Vietnam. A feeling existed that we were being asked to fight with our hands tied behind our backs. Even so, the men I knew, although they might have griped a lot about the injustice of the situation, met their responsibilities with an enthusiasm born of deep commitment.

Also causing us to reexamine the Vietnam conflict was the antiwar movement with its activist draft dodgers who were beginning to receive some press. This activity began to trouble the participants on the DMZ even if it was not yet being viewed as a widespread attitude of the public. It was hard for us to discern whether the protests back home came from a generation that had turned inward and was merely expressing itself through a selfish "me" philosophy or whether they truly believed we were doing something morally wrong. Most people, including myself, did not want to believe that we were participating in anything other than a high and noble cause. Too much was at stake, namely, our lives, and we needed to believe in what we were doing. Nevertheless, I heard numerous discussions implying that even if America was not completely right, we still owed allegiance to our country. It was generally believed that people could not selectively decide which wars to participate in and that we must stay the course regardless of a particular war's popularity.

During the first part of my time in Vietnam, I believe most of us thought the antiwar movement was generally the product of self-serving nonpatriots who did not want the inconvenience. On the other hand, though, we thought that our leaders were often self-serving as well, with their own politically motivated initiatives and agendas. In spite of the American right to speak out, the protests made us uncomfortable, and we dealt with them in our own ways. Actions from that growing segment of unrest progressively increased the difficulty of our being able to cope with what we were being asked to do in Vietnam. For that reason, the positive spirit of the Marines on the DMZ was all the more impressive.

Aside from all this soul-searching, the routine on the Rockpile produced a pleasant boredom as days ran together. Our biggest inconvenience was the declining water supply, which could be replenished only by helicopter delivery. Baths were out, and we became quite rank on our mountain perch. One day we noticed a black cloud to the northwest that seemed to be moving our way. Some brilliant trooper on the helipad recognized it for its potential and shouted, "Get out the soap, showers on the way!" Twenty grimy guys clutching bars of soap immediately scrambled over the rocks and soon stood stark naked on the wooden platform. There was much verbal coaxing as the cloud moved closer. It edged nearer, and suddenly rain came blowing across us in sheets. The soap flew, and in an instant twenty foamy white figures danced around in an unbelievably cold downpour. Abruptly as it had begun, the rain stopped, and we could only stand there like snowmen, hoping for one more rinse to remove the soap. The rain moved rapidly away, and we all stood shivering and staring at the departing cloud. What earlier had been gentle coaxing talk now turned into some of the most imaginative language that I had ever heard. What a mess! It took the rest of the day to return to normal, with the dried soap causing no small degree of discomfort. You can bet that the swearing went on as well.

Enemy activity continued to be high, and one evening about dusk, while looking toward Dong Ha Mountain to the northeast, I noticed one of our jets crossing the DMZ. It seemed headed toward some mission in North Vietnam. With the sun now sinking below the horizon, the plane sparkled in the red glow of the sunset. At this peaceful time of day we were preparing our evening C rations, and the glint of the jet serenely traced a steady path across the sky. Suddenly, a flash erupted from behind a hill to the north, and a rocketlike comet streaked toward our plane. I shouted at Ollie to look, and we both watched helplessly while it dawned on us that a surface-to-air missile was streaking skyward. A tremendous ball of fire resulted when the two met, and many seconds later in the silence we heard a dull clap as the distant sound of the explosion punctuated our thoughts. Finally, staring at the empty horizon in stunned silence, I picked up the radio and reported the happening to Regiment. Almost needless to say, another evening of retrospection settled in on us as we contemplated the spirits of those who had vanished in that burst of light.

With my grandstand seat I continued to delight in being a distant spectator. I certainly did not want to descend into the maelstrom below me. With a view of just about everything occurring on the DMZ, the panorama of war overwhelmed me. Our little sanctuary with its somnolent activity was like some island on which we were marooned while a turbulent ocean seethed all around. Those of us tucked away in our rock fortress deeply appreciated being above the strife.

I had been on the Rockpile about forty days when I received a call that I did not want to hear. Battalion was bringing me back down to be the liaison officer. The lieutenant whom I had replaced up here and who subsequently had been made liaison officer was already being removed by the battalion CO. He was the second artillery officer in a row who had incurred the wrath of the commanding officer of 3/3. I would hear later that the lieutenant had gone panicky while out with a relief force and, in the process, had called in fire on a Montagnard village. It was my lot to fill his billet, and now realizing that the job had evolved into a risky undertaking for lieutenants, I could only wonder how I would fare with the new battalion commander. Clearly, he did not have much confidence in artillery officers.

My vacation was over, and from that day on, life became more precarious as the war reached up and pulled me back down with firm tentacles. I had been in the field for two and one-half months, and typically at the end of that interval, lieutenant forward observers could expect to rotate to a safer battery job. Now, however, a sinking feeling began to eat at me; it was the growing realization that if I proved competent, I would likely have an extended tour with the infantry.

6

The Ambushes

The descent back to the valley occurred without mishap, and in no time I was thrust back into the other world. Gone was the constant breeze of the mountain; instead, the tropical heat of the valley enveloped me like a shroud. There were, however, those wonderful showers by the river, and I had my first real bath in forty days. Putting on fresh clothes, I hustled over to the mess tent to enjoy a kitchen-prepared meal after having had nothing but C rations on the Rockpile. What a pleasure these trivial things were that had seemed so matter of fact only a month ago.

After indulging in those luxuries, I went over to the artillery sleeping bunker to find out what was happening before reporting in to the CO. Sergeant Goodridge met me with his cocky grin and steady stream of chatter, all the time giving me a general rundown on what had been happening. More important, he filled me in on the scuttlebutt concerning the lieutenant I was replacing. My apprehension grew when I heard the scoop that had not been transmitted over the radio, and it became clear that the new battalion CO was going to be on me like a hawk. He wanted perfection, and my two predecessors had been relieved in short order when they failed to measure up to his standards. Perhaps they were merely victims of a nervous house cleaning, but the colonel's concerns properly reinforced the fact that the artillery segment of the battalion should be functioning at a high level of competence.

After visiting with Goody, I reported in to Lieutenant Colonel

Robert C. Needham and found a situation that promised to become uncomfortable. He was a tall, lean man who looked older than many others of his rank. He had served in Korea, and I later learned that he had been awarded the Silver Star during that conflict. In the coming months I found him to have a serious personality; he was not inclined to joke around. I also recognized, however, that he had a sense of fairness in dealing with the men. Unlike his two predecessors, he was cautious and not inclined to make snap decisions, a trait that made everyone more comfortable because they realized he would not needlessly put them at risk. He eventually earned the respect of just about everybody. When I reported in that day, however, I knew none of this and found him to be exceptionally reserved and cold. In fact, my new CO seemed downright unfriendly and was obviously distrustful of the artillery personnel. He spelled out just what he expected and made it plain that everything I did had to be cleared through him first. As I walked away from the bunker, the magnitude of the job sunk in and, quite frankly, scared the hell out of me. I had a fire-eating CO to work for, and the prospect of increased combat had grown considerably.

I spent that first afternoon in the battalion operations bunker, where all infantry and fire support functions were coordinated by the colonel's staff. This bunker served as the nerve center for all operations and had been dug in well to protect it from incoming artillery and mortar fire. Its one large room enclosed an area about the size of a one-car garage, and arranged around the walls were military radios that hummed with the lifeblood of communications. This place was the brain directing hundreds of men, yet was attached by its own umbilical cord to a higher command, thereby making the battalion a functioning part of the total war machine. In spite of primitive conditions, the room looked impressive and important. The senior players, besides the CO, were the executive officer, Major Harper, and the operations officer, Major Mike Harrington. Seven or eight other men tended to various responsibilities while those two kept a watchful eye on the entire proceedings.

On entering the bunker, I was introduced to Corporal Patrick Foy, who would be the radio operator when I was on duty. He proved to be a fine, even-tempered individual, confident in his job and not easily rattled when things got wild. He had a pleasant personality and sense of humor, and he seemed wise beyond his years. Both he and Sergeant Goodridge began at once to show me how things were done on this level and familiarized me with the nuances of handling the radio from a battalion perspective. It was a comfortable session, and they soon had me filled in on the different artillery procedures. They were enthusiastic, and they genuinely seemed to want me to succeed; for sure, they did not need someone else bringing down the colonel's wrath on the artillery personnel.

That night at the sleeping bunker I drank two cold beers. Now that does not seem like a big deal, but considering that it had been almost two months since I had enjoyed a cold brew, it was great. The battalion had just received its first beer shipment in some time, and everyone enjoyed the treat. Never mind that it was Carling Black Label, a beer I would never have drunk at home, or that we had bought an expensive chunk of ice no bigger than a grapefruit from a South Vietnamese ice truck for four dollars. Forget that we carefully packed this ice around six beers for three of us and watched and waited for two endless hours as it cooled. To pass the time, we played Hank Williams and Skeeter Davis on a little flashlight-battery-operated record player and, taking turns, helped the record turn with our fingers as the batteries weakened. It was a good night, and I slept like a baby after slowly draining every drop of the cool liquid.

The next morning, August 21, 1967, proved to be a key test for me when a convoy ran into another ambush on the road to Ca Lu. In this attack, which came only a mile from our position, a string of trucks was completely pinned down. The colonel immediately sent out two companies to assist them, and shortly we started taking mortars in our own position. I could not believe it—my second day on the job and all hell was breaking loose.

Earlier I had noticed an Army lieutenant in the convoy who was in charge of the twin forties, that 40mm antiaircraft gun of World War II vintage. The gun fired rounds from two barrels that pumped back and forth alternately, each round being a tracer that visually showed the path of the projectile. The gun itself was mounted on tracks and could rapidly swing on targets, making it exceptionally effective for convoy protection. Now the Army lieutenant came bursting into the bunker. At the rear of the convoy when the ambush began, he had been wounded but managed not to get pinned down with the rest of the column. Colonel Needham, on hearing that he had made it back inside the perimeter, had sent for him so we could find out just what was happening at the ambush. His entrance got everybody's attention because he had taken a piece of shrapnel in the face and a hole now gaped in his swollen cheek. You could actually see his teeth through the wound while he talked. Soaked in blood and excited, he looked like a soul from hell as he rattled on to the colonel. This was the first person I had seen with a serious combat wound since my arrival in Vietnam.

It was not long before things got so chaotic that the colonel finally had to start relying heavily on others in order to meet the demands of the crisis. He came over to me and said, "Lieutenant Brown, there is no way I can check on everything that the artillery is doing. You are going to have to handle fire support, and you better damn well not blow any friendlies away." The adrenaline started to pump with the realization that an infantry battalion was in a major action and that oversight of artillery had just been turned over to me. This could not be happening so soon on the job. I just locked my mind on the problems and threw myself totally into the effort. Sergeant Goodridge had gone out with the relief force, and Corporal Foy sat next to me while we monitored radio frequencies of different units. He was invaluable in helping me sort out what needed to be dealt with first.

Between the compass readings from Sergeant Goodridge and another FO, we obtained reverse triangulation on the NVA's tubes (mortars) and soon were firing the full strength of our own 81mm mortars along with artillery from the batteries at Camp Carroll. Reverse triangulation was an excellent method used to determine the precise location of a target. To be effective the technique needed just two observers who knew their own coordinates (location) and who could take a compass reading to the target. The convergence of those two readings determined extremely well the location of a target. Otherwise, with only one observer, the distance to the target often had to be estimated if there was no significant landmark nearby, and consequently many adjusting rounds might be needed to get on target.

With our pouring in of multiple barrages and then walking mortars up and down the sides of the road, the enemy fire finally slackened. Then as our relief troops began approaching the ambush site, we shifted our own rounds away from the road but still pounded the NVA mortar positions. The rest of the time, we worked over the draws that seemed to be their most likely escape routes.

During all of this activity, I did not even think about the colonel, but just did what I thought would be most effective. Around noon, the colonel came over and said that he was getting reports that the artillery was having a significant impact and to keep up what we were doing. About three hours later, we were finally able to get the ambushed convoy up and soon had them rolling toward Ca Lu. The NVA had faded into the hills, and no sign could be found of them, even with assistance from the FO in the spotter plane that had recently arrived. By nightfall, everything returned to normal, and the convoy was safe in Ca Lu. It was a day in which the artillery had been used extensively, and the effect had been significant. Relief flooded over me when I had time to comprehend that I had not "blown away any friendlies," and satisfaction ensued when I overheard that artillery was being given major credit in the successful relief effort.

That night after supper, the colonel called me over to his hooch and told me that we had done a good job. Furthermore, he said that I could take on more responsibility in directing the artillery support as long as I stayed within the scope of his assigned missions. Boy, was I happy! I had dreaded being under his scrutiny after what had transpired with my two predecessors and had wondered whether I could hack it at this level. Because fate had seen fit to throw me in the fire on my second day on the job, I would not now have to go through a prolonged period of assessment and possible harassment. From that day on, Colonel Needham told me what he needed in general terms and let me take care of the details. The artillery staff welcomed this development as much as I did because he had made life miserable for everyone, watching for even the slightest foul-up.

Also of particular significance that day, Sergeant Goodridge distinguished himself with the relief force when he did an outstanding job of calling in supporting fire. He was in the thick of the firefight when he was wounded in the arm and knocked unconscious by an NVA recoilless rifle. When he regained his senses, he moved to an even more dangerous position where he had a better view of the enemy and continued to call in artillery strikes. He would later receive the Bronze Star for his actions, but for the short term this probably added a great deal to the confidence that Colonel Needham seemed to be developing for the artillery staff.

That ambush and subsequent relief effort left us with six KIAs (killed in action) along with thirty-five wounded. Although I had not personally been in danger, deep as I was in the bunker, I now felt thoroughly involved and a part of this conflict. Vietnam, with the DMZ, was beginning its peak year of activity, as history would later show, and I was right in the middle of it. Growing up, I had fantasized about war and what it all meant. Now, it was happening for real, and the excitement of it all made even the slightest detail important. People pulled together as they subconsciously realized that survival depended on everyone carrying his share of the load. Never before or since has life been as intense, and my subsequent activities have never seemed more meaningful than they did then. It was a heightened period of existence, acutely tuned to the fragility of life. We had objectives that mattered, and even our daily routine seemed to count. Friends were treasured, and bonds were strengthened by the danger around us.

The next morning I was on my way over to the headquarters bunker when, all of a sudden, incoming rocket fire came screaming into our position. I jumped in a trench when the first rounds impacted on the other side of the perimeter, and as I slowly poked my head up, another volley came roaring in. This time one of the rounds landed about ten feet away. Fortunately, I had been low enough that I was not hit, but the explosion made my ears ring, and I smelled the distinct odor of gunpowder drifting around me. It was a helpless feeling and very scary because I could do nothing but hope I would not take a direct hit. When it seemed that the NVA had finished firing, I scurried over to the headquarters bunker and began trying to determine where the rockets had come from. We had difficulty pinpointing them, but the FO on the Rockpile gave us a general bearing, and we called in 105mm artillery fire just to let them know we were still kicking.

One of their rockets had not exploded and so gave me an opportunity to examine in detail just what they had fired at us. It turned out that this rocket was not one of the dangerous 122mm types, which were sophisticated and equipped with super high explosives, but was instead the 140mm kind, which was five or six inches in diameter and four feet long. Its warhead made up about a foot of that length and contained black powder. Fortunately, they did not fragment into tiny pieces of shrapnel like the 122s did. The 140s exploded in big chunks, and the rocket portion of the missile looked like a peeled banana. It appeared wicked enough but was not nearly as devastating as the 122s.

Rockets suited the NVA tactics of stealth and quick strikes. A round could be transported by one man, was easily launched, and could be fired from behind a hill. By the time we figured out their location, the rocketeers could be making a hasty getaway without the weight of a round to carry. In their lightened state, they then often seemed to fade into nowhere. We received several of those attacks, along with mortars, over the next several days, and with the pot beginning to boil, those of us in the fire support section were getting a bird's-eye view of everything happening.

In contrast to the natural tendency for artillery men to view combat from a more removed perspective, the closeness of the war seemed to thrust itself on us and reminded me that we were not involved in some abstract exercise. That awareness was accentuated one night when the NVA were actively probing our perimeter, an action that the troops had responded to with considerable rifle and machine-gun fire. As I ran from my hooch over to the headquarters bunker, my senses were inundated by the eerie light of parachute flares floating above and the rapid crackle of firing only yards away. Usually, I was in the command bunker and did not get to see the dramatic display of firepower in the night. An artillery liaison officer typically functioned on tactical levels somewhat above the fray of personal combat and was often visually shielded from the action. The officer's job, if things were to function properly, required an objective attitude and a dispassionate approach. In that particular dash to the headquarters bunker, however, it became clear to me that, even though it was necessary to focus on the big picture down in operations, we could not forget that we were still in the thick of it all. On entering the bunker, I pushed that realization to the back of my mind and quickly put myself back into the routine of our duties. In spite of the closeness of the fighting, we still had that mission and others to coordinate. It might have been different, however, if the NVA had gotten through our lines.

By this time, I had been in country almost four months and under a normal rotation schedule would have already been back performing staff functions with Charlie Battery. Realizing the dangers of the field and now suspecting that the war was being politically mismanaged, I hoped my return to Camp Carroll would be forthcoming. One morning on entering the headquarters bunker to relieve Sergeant Goodridge, I was met with a furor of excitement from the artillery staff. Lieutenant Colonel W. H. Rice, the CO of 1/12, which was the parent unit of Charlie Battery, would be arriving that morning. This was "big doings" because he did not come out here often, and the thought crossed my mind that maybe he would have a replacement for me. My hopes soared until he arrived. I knew at once that something other than my rotation was in the works because the CO of the 3d Marines from Dong Ha, Colonel James R. Stockman, was with him. Colonel Stockman told Colonel Needham that he wanted a full briefing on the increased enemy activity. The battalion was given an hour to prepare for a formal briefing and told to meet in the headquarters bunker. Talk about a scramble. Everyone began gathering facts and putting thoughts together. Colonel Needham came over and told me to present an overview of enemy fire-power and suspected positions and our master plan for artillery support. Maps and grease-pencil highlights would be necessary for that part of the briefing. A frenzy followed while the artillery staff prepared the appropriate data, and I went over to a corner and hastily began working up a presentation that would make some sense.

Colonel Needham opened the meeting with a tactical overview of the activities, and Major Harrington gave a report on the status of the troops. This was followed by a report from the intelligence officer and then my own briefing. I did not blow it and felt pretty good about the way it went. Colonel Stockman then asked a lot of questions, of which I got my share, and when it was over I felt a rush of relief on realizing just how uptight I had been. In those days, a presentation before an audience was something I dreaded, and being thrust to center stage in front of these senior officers had scared the hell out of me. Enemy incoming had been a snap compared with the last few moments. Sometimes it takes extremes to put things in perspective, and I had learned that, for me personally, the desire to be perceived as competent motivated me more than concern about my own physical safety. Combat with its dangers was tough, but fear of not performing well could be agonizing.

Later, Colonel Rice pulled me aside outside the bunker and let me know that Colonel Needham was pleased with the job I was doing. He also said Colonel Needham had requested that I not be rotated anytime soon because of the recent increase in enemy activity. As he put it, "I don't need Colonel Needham calling every other day letting everybody know what is wrong with the artillery. You are just going to have to stay in the field for a while." He then added that two lieutenants, one of whom was a 1st lieutenant, were on the way out to beef up the artillery contingent and that they clearly understood that, although I was only a 2d lieutenant, I was in charge of all artillery personnel with 3/3. This greatly concerned me because I was uncomfortable having an officer under my control who outranked me. After discussing it with the CO of Charlie Battery, I was told that I would be writing all officer fitness reports for those working under me, including the 1st lieutenant's, who had also been made aware of this. A fitness report was the periodic formal report that evaluated an officer in every aspect of his leadership; it was most unusual for an officer junior to another officer to be grading that person.

The significance of having that authority would be highlighted later when it was made known to me at C-2 Bridge that this 1st lieutenant, who shall go unnamed, had been smoking marijuana with several enlisted men (the only such incident involving drug use that I was ever aware of in Charlie Battery). On learning that, I informed him that I was giving him a bad fitness report and that if he protested or if I found out about him being involved in drugs again, I would charge him under whatever statutes were appropriate for drug use in a combat zone. The bad fitness report gave me the leverage to maintain stringent discipline in the field without ruining his career as an officer; in a way it worked out best for both of us. I never had problems with him again or ever heard of any drug use in the battery after that. He transferred to another unit within a few months after that incident.

The fact that I was given this authority to write a senior officer's fitness report emphasizes how important the two battalion COs considered it to be to have the artillery functioning smoothly with the infantry. After almost two months of severe tension, neither of my bosses wanted anything rocking the boat as far as my ability to control those working under me. As soon as the conversation was over, Colonel Rice and Colonel Stockman hopped in a chopper and disappeared before it could sink in on me what had happened. I could only stand there stunned, realizing I was not headed back to the battery anytime soon. My experience, limited though it was, still was the best available at the moment—and besides, Colonel Needham was not raising hell anymore. No one ever said that life is fair.

The next week brought more incoming and additional evidence that the NVA were operating heavily in our sector. Although we did not know it at the time, they were readying themselves for the siege of Khe Sanh. Located as we were on Route 9, the main supply artery to that remote base, we were getting plenty of NVA attention. Already three major ambushes had taken place between the Rockpile and Khe Sanh. There were also other things to ponder when, on September 3, I saw a towering cloud of black smoke reaching higher than I had ever seen before. At Dong Ha, about nine miles away, an NVA 130mm artillery round, one of forty-one, scored a direct hit on one of the bunkers in the big ammo dump near the main airstrip. This major staging area for all of the ordnance coming to the DMZ had an extensive stockpile of munitions. The original explosion set off a chain reaction, and the results were spectacular. Making a tall black column, the smoke went up and up until it seemed to reach the stratosphere. The inferno roared for at least an hour before it diminished, but the smoke continued in lesser degrees for a few days. That anyone in the dump itself could have survived the blast seemed impossible, but I found out later that no one was killed, although seventy-seven were injured. This proximity to the NVA 130mm guns forced the Marine high command to relocate their logistics base to Quang Tri.

Several days later, on September 7, the morning dawned fresh with a cool dew that would shortly transform into sticky heat. As the sun rose above the surrounding mountains, I savored a cup of instant coffee while enjoying a moment of welcome respite before the heat and intensity of the day's activities closed in around us. At that early hour, there still was time for privacy of thought before the ever-changing saga of events dictated the mood of the day. Later in the headquarters bunker, some pursuit would soon be demanding our concentration, making this quiet time special. That morning seemed like any other until I saw a convoy from Dong Ha roll into our position, and, knowing that often brought trouble, I immediately went over to the headquarters bunker. Anything could happen with all the enemy activity that had recently transpired, and I noted on passing that the waiting trucks had twin forties with them. This indicated that Regiment, with its better intelligence resources, saw a special need for additional protection.

On reaching the bunker, I found Sergeant Goodridge visibly hyped over the convoy, and he made no move to leave even though his shift was almost over. He already knew that the command at Dong Ha had put the battalion on alert for the convoy and that India Company would be riding shotgun for the rest of the trip to Ca Lu. The big room emitted a flurry of activity as instructions were transmitted over the many radios to the units involved. By the time I walked in, uneasiness already prevailed, and many were hanging around from the previous shift to assist in preparations.

About eight o'clock the convoy careened out of our position, evidently wanting to make the trip in a hurry. Within ten minutes, radios began crackling with reports that the lead vehicle had hit a mine. Quickly, a massive firefight developed, and we learned that another mine had disabled a vehicle at the rear of the convoy, effectively trapping them. We found out later that the NVA had dug ten or twelve spider holes (excavations about two feet in diameter and over twice as deep) all along the sides of the road and had placed men inside each one. They had then been covered with grass mats, and dirt was sprinkled on top of that as camouflage. Invisible from the trucks, the enemy merely popped out of the ground and opened fire when the convoy stopped beside them. It was a mess, and soon everyone was pinned down.

After the confusion of the first intense moments, it became only marginally clear as to what was really happening. The artillery FO with India Company became my main source of information as he attempted to call in fire missions. It seemed the attackers were well supported by mortars, and our main objective in the artillery section soon became that of stopping the devastating fire that had our troops hugging the ground. The only trouble was that with the incoming fire so intense, no one at the ambush site could locate the mortars, and we could return fire only in a general direction.

Consternation and frustration dominated headquarters, with only minimal radio information to let us know that the men in the field really did not have a handle on what was going on. For some reason, little information was coming from India's CO, and we could only surmise from other radio traffic what was happening. Finally, Major Harrington, the operations officer, came running over to our table and told me to saddle up because he was taking a command post (CP) group to the field to try to gain control of the situation. The lack of coordination had become extremely dangerous, and the attackers were showing no signs of letting up in their assault. Usually after a strike such as this, there would be at least a partial pulling back by the NVA, but today that was not happening. A chaotic situation of this nature needed stabilizing at once, and Colonel Needham thought the best solution would be for Major Harrington to take over on the scene. Typically, you did not send the CP into the thick of things, but the loss of control demanded a radical solution.

The CP group was to be made up of Major Harrington, Captain Orville C. Hay (the air control officer), me, our radio operators, and several riflemen for security. In all, there were twenty of us, with Major Harrington being the perfect guy to lead the contingent. He was a picture-book Marine. It was my understanding that he had come back on duty through the reserves after several years of civilian life. With his intense gung ho personality, he had volunteered for active duty just to come to Vietnam. It was as if he felt some compulsion to be actively involved in combat. Most officers were content just to do their jobs without taking unnecessary chances, but the major seemed to relish action and did not show any concern for his personal safety. One thing he achieved with his positive attitude was an ability to inspire confidence in those around him. We believed he had a grasp of the situation, and it relieved us to know that we did not have to follow some incompetent into a hot zone.

We quickly piled into our jeeps and went barreling down the road. Relief troops were already moving by foot, and they made way for us as we bounced over the potholes. Elephant grass covered the sides of the road, and the sound of a machine gun could be heard cranking away up front. I do not know how we managed to do it, but somehow we ended up in front of the relief force, which about that time began taking mortars. We abandoned the vehicles, and Major Harrington soon had us all charging down the road. For my part, I could pay little attention to what was happening immediately around me because I had to focus on communicating with the other artillery personnel while trying to get a fix on the enemy mortars. The FO on top of the Rockpile helped us in this regard, and occasionally I had an unobstructed view of the terrain as we hurried down the road. In spite of the preoccupation with my duties, I was conscious of butterflies in the pit of my stomach resulting from the certainty that we were fast approaching a full-fledged firefight. Expecting to see the enemy at any moment, I did not understand why Major Harrington kept barreling ahead like he did, but I just tended to my responsibilities and moved with the group. I had often wondered what it would be like when I finally went into combat; the only comparable experience I could relate all this to was the football I had participated in. Once again I had that same old sick feeling that had overwhelmed me before big games.

We turned a slight bend in the road, and just up ahead, rifle fire intensified near the position of the disabled convoy. I could hear a .50-caliber machine gun working out as well. Not having been aware that the convoy had a .50-caliber machine gun, I wondered whether it belonged to the NVA. Scattered boulders of varying sizes broke up the heavy elephant grass, and it was easier to see greater distances now. A shallow ditch ran along the side of the road, and I noted that it might give at least some protection if needed. Scraggly trees were over to the left, and heavy smoke appeared up ahead where I assumed the convoy to be. The smell of burning oil and gas began to impact our senses, and the sound of weapons fire was ominously close. Something seemed bound to happen, and at that moment explosions started going off in the road around us. My first thought was that we were taking enemy mortars because everyone started scrambling for cover. Corporal Olivari and I dove for one of the big boulders by the ditch. Explosions continued, and some of our group started cranking off rifle shots. Then, twenty yards in front of us and on the other side of the road, our own men seemingly started firing at Ollie and me. One of the bullets struck the big rock that we were crouched behind, and a piece of the copper jacket from the bullet became embedded in my hand. Ollie and I began to yell every Marine Corps expletive that we could think of, telling the guys shooting at us what we thought of them.

Finally, the firing stopped, and I continued my harangue, yelling, "What in the hell is going on?" One of the men in the group that had been shooting at us simply pointed to the other side of the rock, and there in the ditch with us was the answer. Sprawled out less than eight feet away were two dead NVA soldiers. We had jumped in the ditch with them and had been separated only by the big stone boulder. It turned out that what we had thought were incoming mortars was a squad of NVA soldiers throwing satchel charges at us from the elephant grass. After further search, we found one more enemy body back in the grass; Ollie and I had almost joined their group. The CP unit had been hit hard in the skirmish. Of the twenty members, two were killed outright, and thirteen were wounded to varying degrees. Major Harrington had been severely wounded along with three others, but the rest just went on about their duties and shrugged off any minor wounds.

Major Harrington was conscious and coherent, but his leg was shattered. He lay there blasting his luck that he had been hit so soon after joining the battalion, but he also acknowledged that he would have to be medevaced. So much for the "coordination from the field." There was probably even more confusion now with the major out of action. For some reason India Company, the unit riding shotgun, still did not seem on top of things. There was no direction coming from them at all.

About twenty minutes later, Captain Ripley, the CO of Lima Company, arrived with the first of his men. This officer had already proved himself as a competent and courageous Marine, and everyone in the battalion regarded him highly. I was mighty glad to see someone arrive who could take control. Captain Hay and I spoke with him briefly, and he went charging off toward the ambush site. It was clear that his main objective was to find out what was happening. Captain Hay and I then decided that this was as good a place as any to set up what remained of the CP group. We spread the troops out on either side of the road for security and positioned ourselves where we had good visibility of the surrounding hills. As it turned out, this spot became the staging area for medevacs and a coordination point for arriving relief troops. From our vantage, we were able to locate some of the enemy mortar positions and immediately called artillery and air strikes in on them while pounding the draws on either side of the road. For the next several hours all I can remember is the heat of the broiling sun and constantly calling in fire missions on every conceivable target or suspicious location. Right by us on the road was the hub of everyone's coming and going, but we were so absorbed in calling in fire that we had little time to observe what was happening. I could only sense this activity in a removed sort of way while taking care of the artillery responsibilities. With no shade for relief, my head pounded from the heat and from an intense concentration on the fire missions.

About mid-afternoon, an artillery spotting plane arrived on the scene, relieving me from having to call in missions personally. From his vantage point, the spotter could easily see NVA soldiers breaking away from the ambush. They were, in fact, finally leaving. This enemy force (later determined to be the 804th NVA Regiment) had pressed the attack to the limit instead of the usual quick strike followed by a hasty retreat. Their intention today had been much more pugnacious, challenging us and bloodying the battalion with well-disciplined and courageous fighting. Their attack had been conducted in a conventional manner, letting us know we were up against seasoned professionals. This was different from the fighting in the south, which mostly involved Viet Cong units operating stealthily and usually at night. Today, these NVA soldiers had gone toe to toe with us and performed admirably.

With the spotter plane now calling in fire support, I finally began paying attention to what was going on around me. Wounded Marines passed by continuously on the way back to the base camp, and supplies of ammo and medical equipment were being passed out rapidly. The corpsmen (Navy medical personnel) were giving first aid to men with gory wounds, but I heard very little complaining. It was then that I was introduced to the darker side of war. A jeep with a small two-wheeled trailer that was six feet by six feet and that had sides about a foot high had been sent to the ambush site to remove the wounded who could not walk. Now returning, it slowly came rolling by our position in the ditch. What attracted my attention to it was a stream of blood dripping from the trailer that splattered me in passing. I immediately looked up and saw a scene like something from a nightmare. Dead Marines had been placed in the bottom of the trailer, and another layer of severely wounded men had been stacked on top of them. Bags of plasma were suspended on makeshift sticks and protruded at weird angles. Like a ghastly scene from Dante's hell, the jeep and its grisly load slowly rolled on as blood trickled out, drenching the dust of the road. I had often heard ambulances referred to as "meat wagons," and now I understood why. This scene played out to me in an otherworldly sort of way, like I was an observer who was not really there.

Later in the day, I finally had time to think and not just react as I attempted to put perspective on the day's events. As I recalled earlier, the only thing in my background that even remotely related to the day's experience had been playing football. After the kickoff and the first licks had been exchanged, nervousness disappeared, and you just settled down to do your job. The same had been true today when, after the first shots were fired, I became totally absorbed in my own responsibilities. Fear or concern for personal safety had not been a factor, and the dead and wounded simply were a part of the scene. All the incidents of the day were just marginal by-products of the occasion. There had been no time for any special feeling of horror, and even the scene with the trailer full of dead and wounded had affected me only in a detached sort of way. As I began to comprehend what I had just been through, my emotions finally kicked in, and an overwhelming sense of exhilaration came over me with the realization that I was alive and well. I could tell from the attitudes around me that my feelings were not unique. This tremendous high has come only in the aftermath of combat; the emotion of the moment does not allow for depression or sadness. On the other hand, I could experience debilitating sorrow on hearing about friends being killed in other places. I suppose that the mind in its imagination generates images of what it does not directly participate in with a more emotional impact than actual experiences that focus on the events themselves. Concentration on the job at hand makes it less likely that there will be mental distress from the actual trauma of combat.

More dead and wounded came by as the day wore on, and the road became a dusty red. In fact, the casualties that day amounted to five killed and fifty-six wounded. The NVA left ninety-two of their dead behind. Captain Hay and I went on with our duties while 3/3 began to withdraw, and then it became mostly a matter of just firing at likely enemy retreat routes. When the last units moved out, we were finally able to leave ourselves. This had all started eight hours ago, but no one seemed to have a sense of fatigue; the adrenaline had not yet subsided. The vehicles had already returned, which meant we would have to hoof it back, but the return to camp was amazingly easy as the tension of the day faded away behind us. Those of us remaining from the CP group chattered jubilantly as we moved along the road in the lengthening shadows of mountain ridges.

On returning, I reported into the headquarters bunker and was quizzed by Colonel Needham, who let me know that the fire support had played an important part in the rescue operation. The pounding to the hillside had been a significant factor in causing the enemy to break the engagement. Approval from the CO added to my already soaring feelings, and for the moment I was happy to be a part of 3/3 regardless of any reservations about the way our government might be prosecuting the war.

Night came, but adrenaline still pumped through my body, and not until much later would I relax enough to sleep. This had been my first test in close combat and was quite revealing. I had often wondered how well I would cope if faced with extreme personal danger, and the day's events had shown me that I could handle pressure. This new awareness contributed to the elation of the evening. There are key events that mark our journey through this world, and I felt like I had crossed a threshold concerning my own capabilities. I had done nothing heroic, but I now knew I would not likely panic in a crisis. Years later, I could say that I was a better person for this and other experiences of Vietnam but with the full realization that if I had been maimed for life, I might have had a different perspective. As it was, I was spared and in the sparing grew.

The following week it was decided that a Montagnard village near the scene of the ambush could have had something to do with that attack. The Montagnards were mountain tribesmen with their own distinctive culture, and this village was one of only two that I was aware of on the DMZ. The other was at Khe Sanh. Most of the other South Vietnamese up here lived in barbed-wire compounds located in the vicinity of Cam Lo and Dong Ha. This particular village happened to be the one that the liaison officer before me had dropped shells on, an incident that had contributed to his being replaced at the time. Now in a fickle about-face, a higher command determined that the village would have to be burned because that previous sanctuary had become an inconvenience. Villagers were loaded on trucks with their scant belongings and in the blink of an eye were on their way to the refugee camp at Cam Lo. From our point of view, we were simply glad to be rid of any people who might be potential problems regardless of their innocence. The trauma to these people must have been tremendous as they were unceremoniously packed up and hauled away from flaming homes.

I was with the command group at the village site when the evacuation took place. Major Harper, the executive officer, was in charge. With a laid-back style, he directed the activities of the operation amid lazy columns of smoke from burning hooches. A picniclike atmosphere prevailed, and our troops combed the once bloody site, posing for pictures and generally having an enjoyable outing. In the midst of this county fair–like setting occurred one of the more unusual incidents of my Vietnam tour. Two companies of Marines were scouring the area on either side of the road near the village, and men in full combat gear could be seen in all directions. In the midst of this military efficiency, our command group was parked by the road with the communication gear arranged on a couple of jeeps. All of a sudden, I heard a noise coming on the road, but it was screened by smoke from the burning village. It sounded like a motorcycle, of all things, and apparently was getting closer. Abruptly emerging from the smoke, a motorcycle did, in fact, head right into the middle of our full-scale field maneuver, and adding to the absurdity of the scene, we discovered the rider to be a Catholic priest. Everyone stood with mouths open while we flagged down this apparition that had appeared from nowhere, completely out of context to the moment. It turned out that he was a French priest and missionary to the Montagnards living near Khe Sanh. He barely spoke English, and only after a lengthy review of his papers were we comfortable in letting him go. We just did not know what to think at first, and the strangeness of his appearance had caught us off guard. Years later, I would read in Robert Pisor's book *The End of the Line: The Siege of Khe Sanh* (page 236) of a French priest who rode a motorcycle and lived with the Montagnards. His name was Father Poncet, and I understand that he was later killed in the war. I think this may have been the same man and can only admire the dedication that motivated him to carry on a ministry in the midst of such havoc.

After the village was destroyed, the ambushes stopped. Nevertheless, there continued to be evidence that the NVA were still around because we took occasional sniper and mortar fire. The next several weeks were relatively quiet, however, and I had time to digest what was happening and enjoy some of the simpler things of life. Listening to Hank Williams on our scratchy little battery-operated phonograph and receiving care packages full of goodies from home became special events. Little pleasures meant so much now, and friendships seemed even more important. I became fast friends with Sergeant Goodridge and Corporal Foy, good people who enjoyed life. The stories they had to tell and their ideas about everything imaginable could have filled a book. All of this talk helped us retain a sense of the world that we had left behind and made it seem not quite so far away.

One of the major topics of discussion was the presence of rats that lived with us in our small bunker. The rats loved to play on the empty bunks, and if only one of us attempted to sleep, the commotion could be horrendous. Try sleeping when rats start squealing and chasing each other two feet from your head. By carefully tucking our mosquito nets around our cots, we kept them from crawling on us, but nothing could stop their incessant racket. My traps from the Rockpile worked for a couple of nights, but these clever valley rats learned to spring them without getting caught.

On occasion we sat outside our bunker in the evening with our two-beer ration and enjoyed a moment of escape. Sipping a brew, looking at the moon and stars, and playing records, we could almost imagine that we were at home. Of course, the endless deep discussions concerning life and war kept us from losing sight of the fact that this lull was only temporary.

During this fairly calm period, we still had to contend with the re-supply convoys to Ca Lu. Because I knew the ridges and valleys so well from previous ambushes, Colonel Needham thought that it would be particularly helpful for me to be with the convoy in the event of another attack. Therefore, I had the privilege of making most of the runs to Ca Lu, and I detested it. We would load five or six trucks with supplies and troops and madly dash down the road. On arrival we would quickly unload and dash back again. I dreaded hitting a mine and would sit on my flak jacket instead of wearing it.

The troops got a big charge out of watching me because of a habit I had acquired since coming to Vietnam. I smoked cigars incessantly, and when a convoy would leave, I would light up at the beginning of the trip. Instead of the normal thirty or forty minutes that it took to finish one of these delights, I would puff so furiously while running the gauntlet to Ca Lu that only a small stump would be left in the fifteen minutes that it took to get there. The artillery boys thought it hilarious, and many jokes and comments were made about it. Fortunately, we were never hit on any of these trips. This was probably a result of having removed the Montagnard villagers but may have been because two companies swept down each side of the road each morning before we left. There were no more ambushes between the Rockpile and Ca Lu while I was there.

My time with the infantry had now extended considerably longer than the usual tour for artillery officers, and I looked forward to return-ing to the battery at Camp Carroll. Everything being relative, that base would be a big improvement because it had tents with wooden floors, sit-down mess halls, movies, and very little incoming at the time. The new battery commander, 1st Lieutenant Joe Schwerer, had replaced Cap-tain Pate, who had rotated. Joe, who was expecting his promotion papers any day, had been executive officer for some time, and it was a smooth change of command. He had an easygoing personality, and I hoped that I had not upset him earlier when I reminded him of the extended time that I had spent in the field. On a recent visit, I had let him know that I was more than ready to return to the battery, and he had responded by telling me he would take it up with Colonel Charles H. Opfar, the new battalion CO, on his return to Camp Carroll. From the way he talked, I had the feeling that he thought it was time, too. That perceived confirmation raised my hopes and excited me to no end.

The news I actually received was a far cry from what I had wanted to hear. It seemed that Colonel Needham had been up to Camp Carroll and had passed on to Colonel Opfar that 3/3 would soon be replacing a battalion responsible for protecting a key bridge on the road to Con Thien. I immediately became concerned because Con Thien, a strongpoint located approximately three thousand meters below the actual DMZ, had earned a reputation as a place to be avoided. Well within range of the North Vietnamese artillery, it took a continuous pounding, and casualties there were exceptionally high. Its name meant "place of angels," so I was told, and it sat on top of a distinctive hill that arose imposingly in the midst of gently rolling terrain covered with overgrown rice paddies. It may have been a beauty spot before the war, as indicated by its name, but now it was a bald, fortlike mound covered with sandbags, bunkers, and ugly trenches. That location and Gio Linh were the two most forward positions bordering the actual DMZ, and both had panoramic views of the north. Con Thien was about seven miles north of Route 9 and was connected to it by a dirt road. A bridge a mile south of Con Thien crossed a stream not easily forded by vehicles, and for that reason an infantry battalion was kept there to keep the NVA from destroying it. Helicopter resupply had become extremely dangerous because of the proximity of northern artillery, and truck transportation remained the most practical method of logistical support. The battalion assigned to protect the bridge had taken tremendous casualties from ground attacks, mortars, rockets, and artillery. No good news seemed to come from that sector of the DMZ.

Years later, I learned that the action taking place at Con Thien was part of North Vietnam's "General Offensive, General Uprising" plan as expanded on by Otto J. Lehrack in his book, *No Shining Armor: The Marines at War in Vietnam: An Oral History* (pages 182–183). It was a three-part master plan for conducting the war. Phase I started in early September of 1967. Designed to draw U.S. forces away from the major population centers, it would be initiated by NVA attacks on the frontiers of South Vietnam. On the DMZ, much of that effort occurred in an area called Leatherneck Square, which was geographically formed by Con Thien, Gio Linh, Dong Ha, and Cam Lo in roughly the shape of a square. Con Thien was the first target of Phase I, and the action around there was intense and deadly. Another key frontier target was, of course, Khe Sanh. Although Khe Sanh later received the press as a place that took a tremendous amount of incoming, the shelling there was never as persistent as it was at Con Thien in the fall of 1967, at least according to General Westmoreland in his memoir, *A Soldier Reports* (page 447).

Phase II of the master plan called for a general attack on the major cities throughout South Vietnam after the bulk of U.S. forces had been pulled away to the remote borders. That would begin on January 30, 1968, and came to be known as the Tet Offensive. Phase III anticipated that a general uprising against the Americans would occur as the Viet Cong began to prevail amid a frustrated populace growing tired of the destruction.

On hearing we were headed to Con Thien, I immediately got on the radio to Captain Schwerer to find out if my transfer back to the battery was any nearer because I was way overdue for rotation. An hour later, word came back that Colonel Needham had requested that I remain with 3/3 because it would be a real problem having a new liaison officer come on board in the midst of a move to such a critical sector. "Your experience will be needed" was the way it was put to me. This depressed me deeply, but I tried not to let it show. The effort to act like it was no big deal was difficult, but I think I pulled it off. I suppose that I should have considered it an honor to have had the colonel make the request, but by that time I knew how costly honor could be.

Dong Ha

The inevitable day arrived all too soon, and the battalion said its good-byes to the Rockpile. At least one good thing would come out of this move: we would be refurbishing our supplies and worn-out clothing in Dong Ha. Dong Ha was the main base on the DMZ, and we would be able to obtain basic necessities as well as have opportunities for other activities. This created much excitement, and we relished the thought of eating in real mess halls, viewing movies, and drinking cold beer. For three whole days we could act like humans before heading to our new assignment. Although the chance to pause from the intensity of the field filled us with euphoria, thank goodness we could not see the future because the next two months would be hell prolonged. If we had known what those coming days held, there would have been little joy in our short reprieve from war on the DMZ. The weeks ahead would strip our souls down to their very essence, and the things that counted most in our lives would come vividly into focus. Seemingly melodramatic, these words inadequately describe the ordeal that we actually experienced over the next two months.

On our last day at the Rockpile, we loaded onto trucks that had been sent to pick us up, and our thoughts zeroed in on the three days ahead at Dong Ha. Beyond that, no one wanted to even think about the possibilities. It is a truism that emotions can handle just so much, and then reality is blocked out by a subconscious reaction that attempts to maintain stability. No one focused on our coming move to the infamous

Leatherneck Square; we thought only of the creature comforts we expected in Dong Ha.

For the moment, though, we still had to deal with the convoy ride and a possibility of hitting a mine on the way. Off came the flak jackets because most chose to sit on them, fearing wounds from below more than injuries to the upper body. In spite of those concerns, excitement bubbled from the trucks when the convoy finally started moving. A three-day reprieve beckoned, and our experiences at the Rockpile were about to become things of the past. Every man had his own set of memories, and few had escaped personal danger. All had witnessed the pain of war, and many had lost friends forever; it was more than good to be putting this place behind us.

The convoy left just as our replacements arrived, and a chorus of catcalls to the new troops graphically described the worst of outcomes for the newcomers. Our guys took great delight in trying to make it seem as if this place was destined to be Armageddon. I suspect that the outpouring of gloomy predictions was a boisterous way of diverting our own concerns from the dreaded Con Thien.

Moving through the valley, I felt like I was leaving someone I had known for a long time. Every valley, ridge, and gully was burned in my mind from days of constant study as a forward observer. Mysterious and ominous feelings still emanated from the towering mountains, giving the countryside an almost spiritual quality. Now that I was leaving, I felt a satisfaction similar to the smugness one feels at having not been bested by a strong rival. To hell with next week's trials; today I was closing a chapter on events that had made me examine myself like never before.

The pace along Route 9 picked up briskly, and reality zoomed back in as we passed burned-out trucks from earlier ambushes and mines. Occasionally, we glimpsed the tranquil river that snaked along by the side of the road, providing a counterpoint to the destruction of the war. Barreling along swiftly, we would alternately come almost to a standstill and then return to a high speed. This typified long columns where leaders must slow down for whatever reason and then pick up the pace again. Those at the rear either raced to catch up or barely moved. During one of those creeping times, we passed by the site of an old ambush, and I noticed a large mound of earth about as high as a man and as long as a car that had been pushed up by a bulldozer. As I looked closer, I was stunned to see that arms and legs protruded from the raw dirt. A hasty grave had been made to bury NVA soldiers killed in an earlier action, and now a macabre sight awaited passers-by on this forlorn road. To make the scene even more grim, some practical joker had placed the head of one of the NVA on a stake in front of the mound. The head was complete with helmet and goggles, and a cigarette protruded from a toothy death grin. There is no telling how many pictures were snapped as we slowly rolled by. Some cracked jokes, but a certain amount of nervous laughter indicated to me that the joviality was merely an attempt to hide inner feelings. I believe many of the men were experiencing the sobering awareness of just how casual death could be on the DMZ.

After another few miles down the road we came to Cam Lo, the village and refugee camp where many of the South Vietnamese living near the DMZ had been interned. As we passed through, little children lined the sides of the road, hoping to be thrown candy or anything else the Marines might give them. Their ages ranged from around three to ten years old, and with big smiles they were giving us the finger. To me this was shocking until it dawned on me that they were only mimicking the many troops who had come by in previous convoys. They must have thought it was an American greeting because I am sure their intent was merely to entice the Marines into throwing them some favor. Adding irony to the situation, many shouted obscene expletives in English as they happily scampered beside the trucks. Marines, for whatever reasons, had responded to the begging of these children with a callousness probably reflecting their general distrust of the Vietnamese. Sure, there were kids responsible for the deaths of some of our men, but sadness filled me when I saw these children so molded by the perverse environment in which they lived.

Fortunately for me, my tour in Vietnam did not place me in proximity to the South Vietnamese people. Only through brief contacts such as this did I witness the ultimate results of their tragedy. The anguish resulting from the loss of loved ones, homes, and lifestyles could be matched only by the actual brutality of the war they endured. To the historian who studies war in the abstract, there is nothing new or shocking in this, but to those of us who actually confronted those circumstances, the brutalization often changed our perception of the world. Most men exposed to these extreme circumstances began to rely on some value system or defense mechanism to deal with the harshness of life.

For me it was Christianity, and that faith provided me with a solid base of support. Chaos is always with us, and there is much we will never understand, but for me God was always there. On the other hand, I did not allow myself to run emotionally to God for deliverance every time I found myself in difficult situations. For the duration of the time I was in Vietnam, it never seemed right to me that I could amble along in a casual relationship with God in the good times and then, when faced with real danger, have the audacity to scurry to him for protection. Still, I knew that he was there.

We finally made it to Dong Ha without any hitches. That crude military base was greeted with as much enthusiasm as if it had been New York City. Having been in the boondocks for what seemed like a lifetime, we had lost touch with conditions in the rear. People in Dong Ha were much more in tune with the big picture, and the base seemed almost like an extension of stateside. It was late September of 1967, and talk of demonstrations and dissatisfaction in the States was now common at this key DMZ stronghold. Being on the so-called front lines, where we had been more isolated, we had a tendency to dismiss those matters. This especially held true because our main news source had been letters from home, sent by people who thought enough of us to write in the first place. Consequently, they typically did not contain information of a negative nature. Now in the stateside environment of Dong Ha, we were forced to face the thought that some of our fellow citizens might not be supporting us. Reality crystallizes in the admission of a problem, and for the most part up to that point, we had chosen not to accept the few rumblings we had heard as anything more than isolated incidents.

Facing this new awareness, most men among the frontline troops on the DMZ already had an established pride in, or loyalty to, either their individual units or the United States in general. It was not necessarily the war effort in Vietnam that motivated them, but a belief that what they were doing counted. In spite of now having to deal with the validity of our "cause," this growing uncertainty about what we were fighting for created even more allegiance to units and friends, thereby reinforcing that motivation. Also contributing to the esprit of these frontline troops was a lack of troublemakers and losers in our units. The officers had found ways to have unreliable men transferred back to rear area support groups in places such as Hue and Da Nang. Our situation was much too critical in day-to-day combat actions to have to contend with shirkers or misfits. Consequently, the young men on the DMZ were some of the finest members of American society. The reliable Marine who could be counted on to do his job was the rule rather than exception, and genuine comradeship developed as men pulled together toward a common goal. In that environment, who could be blamed for glossing over the unrest in America or elevating the pride in one's outfit?

In the years after Vietnam, a great deal of publicity was given to veterans who were having difficulty readjusting to civilian life. If this was a significant problem, it could have been in part due to so many having chosen to believe that America was behind their efforts only to find, on their return to the States, a shocking indifference and downright contempt for our involvement. Prior to the autumn of 1967, I heard very few conversations giving credibility to the dissent back home as anything more than the rumblings of possible draft dodgers. If anything, there was a disdain for the peaceniks, who we suspected were merely stirring things up so they would not have to serve. After the Tet Offensive, though, a distinct shift began to appear in the attitudes of those arriving and even of those of us who had been here for some time as we began to reevaluate the motives of the protesters. By the time I rotated in the summer of 1968, we were regularly receiving replacements who had been exposed to news reporting that was increasingly critical of the war, and the blind faith of the earlier years was diminishing.

That October of 1967, the troop strength in Vietnam was nearing 500,000 and close to the April 1969 all-time high figure of 543,482 for troops in country. The prior two years had seen dramatic jumps in personnel and was now shocking the sensibilities of the citizens back home as the enormity of the escalation began to sink in. Of particular significance, polls showed that 46 percent of the public thought Vietnam was a "mistake," (Stanley Karnow, *Vietnam: A History,* page 488), making

Lyndon Johnson privately agonize over the war's increasing unpopularity. Moreover, most people had family or friends who had been touched by the war in one way or another, and now television, for the first time in history, was giving living-color news coverage of day-to-day fighting. The cameramen were highly efficient and captured the drama of the war with graphic shots of wounded and dead.

Perhaps creating the most consternation at home was President Johnson's call for increased taxes to fund both the war and his domestic program (Karnow, page 487). The economy could not support both, and when the public's pocketbook began to be affected, attitudes really began to change. To this point, much of the war had been conducted with political concerns in mind rather than with the use of sound military strategy, and the result was a form of micromanagement by Johnson and Robert McNamara, the secretary of defense. Now ordinary citizens were becoming concerned about the rising financial costs and the prospect of contributing even more manpower to America's forces. This seemed to be happening with no apparent winning military strategy in place, and many could not understand the president's seeming timidity in not sending troops into North Vietnam or the Laotian sanctuaries. This troubled those at home but devastated those of us on the DMZ. The men here were acutely aware that something was wrong, and talk of disenchantment back in the States began to reinforce those feelings. Having declared that the United States would stay in Vietnam, the president, it seemed to us, could not summon up the courage to either launch a full-scale invasion of North Vietnam or admit that the hold-the-line strategy being imposed on our troops was nothing more than a war of attrition that we could hardly hope to win. Of course, we did not know what was really going on in the diplomatic circles of the world and could not fairly assess the Vietnam strategy from the field.

Understand that at the time, men in Vietnam had little awareness of what was motivating the decisions being made at home but trusted that some logical strategy was directing the madness going on around them. In retrospect I can see that when I arrived in June of 1967, Johnson already was trying to extricate himself from a politically deteriorating situation. The follies that McNamara and Johnson pursued then can now be recognized as window dressing designed to create an illusion of effectiveness in a war that could not be won as they were attempting to fight it. In military circles, there was a premise that a position, territory, or country must physically be occupied by troops in order to establish an effective and lasting advantage. During Vietnam, however, this traditional military maxim was not being followed, and that concerned many who thought we should be conducting the war in a traditional manner. Action in Kosovo may later have disproved that theory somewhat but under circumstances that, although similar, were not exactly the same.

One interesting concept pushed by McNamara added to the growing concern about the war's conduct. The idea probably sounded great on paper to the "intellectuals" in Washington, but it did not initially receive much support from the military. He pursued the idea anyway, and it began to make headlines as a panacea to the developing quagmire that we seemed to be in. It was dubbed "McNamara's Wall" by the men in I Corps and consisted of an elaborate system of strongpoints across the DMZ that were linked by minefields and sophisticated detection devices. The theory was that the enemy would not be able to move into our territory without our knowledge and that there would be minimum loss of American life in the process.

In the book *U.S. Marines in Vietnam: Fighting the North Vietnamese, 1967,* by Gary Telfer, Lane Rogers, and Keith Fleming, the authors point out (pages 86–87) that in March of 1966 Secretary McNamara brought the idea to the Joint Chiefs of Staff, where it had been under discussion for months. Admiral Sharp, commander of CINCPAC (commander-in-chief of all American forces in the Pacific region) in charge of the overall Vietnam operation, thought the concept had numerous problems and discouraged it. The authors state, "While military leaders showed little enthusiasm for the barriers scheme, Secretary of Defense McNamara believed the ideas had merit" (page 87). After McNamara appointed a task force to develop the idea further, General Westmoreland then suggested modifications, and when McNamara approved the changes, "Westmoreland ordered his staff and all subordinate commands to develop the plan" (page 87). The book clearly demonstrates that the idea was McNamara's baby and one that was wet-nursed by Westmoreland. The idea received significant press coverage in the States, but the troops in the field immediately believed it to be a farce because not only were the detection devices too easily set off by animals but also the NVA were everywhere to begin with. Few of us at the time ever found anything positive resulting from the scheme other than that some really good bunkers were built at the strongpoints. They would later serve as protection for some of the command centers of various units operating in the area.

In Dong Ha, where we were exposed to these new concerns, we chose instead to focus on the available creature comforts and did not dwell on the rumors of failing support. We wanted to enjoy this place that resembled our old world. Why, some of the regulars in Dong Ha even wore starched utilities (work clothes), and enlisted men saluted officers just like back in the States! Where we had been, that would have provided a quick target for the ever-present snipers. Here the luxury of hot indoor showers and meals served at tables with chairs were the types of thing that garnered our attention because they brought us a little closer to civilization. Even officer and enlisted clubs existed where you could get a mixed drink. That first day and night were like heaven as we walked through orderly troop areas. In spite of all the griping about the military spit and polish, we secretly welcomed this environment because it signified that we were that much further removed from the bush and the dangers that went with it. Dong Ha felt like a step closer to the real world even if it was a short one.

That first night I joined the battalion staff at the officer's club and promptly managed to get tipsy on two drinks. Having been away from hard liquor for four months, my system could not handle it. Several of us decided that we ought to obtain a few bottles while we had the chance and after a few queries learned that the source was the Seabees. Since World War II, that organization had been a source for scarce items of every kind, and that held true for Vietnam. We finally found the right man and, after much negotiation resulting in a price that was way too high, bought several bottles of bourbon and scotch. What seemed like a good thing at the time would turn out to be a mixed bag in the coming days.

On our second day in Dong Ha, I was called over to regimental headquarters along with Colonel Needham and other staff members. We were given a briefing on our new mission, which was simple enough: all we had to do was occupy the bridge known as C-2 on the road to Con Thien and patrol the surrounding area. If the NVA blew up the bridge, it would be very difficult to supply Con Thien by land.

Con Thien proper, which was occupied by another battalion, maintained an elaborate bunker system on that scarred hill, and it protected them well. They took countless artillery barrages and were mortared frequently, yet casualties remained lower for them than for those whose mission it was to protect them. We would find on our arrival at C-2 Bridge that practically no bunkers and very few defense works even existed. It seemed that 2d Battalion, 4th Marines, or 2/4, had been at the site for some time, and the constant skirmishing was taking a toll. In fact, they had already taken significant casualties during a month of sustained combat. With a distinguished earlier record, they had acquired the nickname of "The Magnificent Bastards," but now they were really beat up. Accumulating casualties on a regular basis, they needed a break from one of the war's more prolonged and intense periods of enemy contact.

After the briefing, Colonel Needham obtained permission for key staff members to make a jeep run up to the bridge to check out the situation before taking the whole battalion in. The group would consist of Colonel Needham, Major Harper, Captain Hay, and me. Each of us would coordinate with our counterparts in 2/4 in order to make the switch as smooth as possible.

That night we spent another wonderful evening at the officer's club, and I saw my first movie since California. It was no less than the *Sands of Iwo Jima* with John Wayne. What could be more appropriate! Interestingly enough, we laughed a great deal as we observed the awful military methods being used by the actors for the sake of making a good film. We were now so acutely aware of the danger of bunching up in groups that we were more concerned about that than the story line. Other things that in our civilian lives would never have even been noticed now seemed ludicrous. No matter, though; it was a movie and quite a change of pace. Besides, this movie was about us, and deep down we were probably experiencing a little bit of an ego trip knowing we were part of the organization that some filmmaker had seen fit to romanticize. When "The Marine Hymn" played, everyone watching seemed much more attentive, and the wisecracks stopped while each person dealt with his own private feelings. That night, for the second time in a row, I slept like a baby, safe behind the lines in Dong Ha. It would be a long time before that would happen again.

About ten o'clock the next morning we piled into two jeeps and headed out for the bridge at C-2. Because it was the middle of the day, we did not anticipate any ambushes and figured that with only two vehicles, little attention would be paid to us. After riding west on Route 9 for a number of miles, we turned north on the road to Con Thien. Although it had the official designation of Route 561, it was little more than a ten-foot-wide dirt track that had been bulldozed back by fifty yards on either side to deter ambushes. This area of rolling land, which had once been rice fields, was overshadowed by mountains rising several miles farther to the west, making the terrain seem flatter than it really was. Still, this coastal plain, which had appeared gentle from the air, was really quite rugged with many ridges and draws. As we progressed up the road, it also became apparent that the surrounding countryside was nothing more than a wasteland filled with scrubby little trees and brush. The triple-canopy jungle that we had so frequently seen back in the area of the Rockpile just did not exist here.

After a ride of several miles, we caught our first glimpse of the position that would soon be our home. It was a barren knoll, practically devoid of vegetation and distinguished mainly by a dusty road running along its crest. C-2 Bridge could not be seen but crossed a stream on the other side of the hill. Approaching the perimeter, we saw men scurrying around, and by the time we reached the lines, no one at all could be seen standing up. It was immediately apparent that only minimal defenses existed, consisting of shallow foxholes with no barbed wire. As we pulled to a halt, Colonel Needham looked around and said, "These guys couldn't hold this position if a Boy Scout troop attacked." We got out of the jeeps on top of the hill, and it was as if the Marines lying in the few foxholes did not even know we were there. They all stared intently at the nearby ridges. Finally, a trooper came running up and said he would take us to the command post. As we trotted behind him, he briefly explained that we needed to get away from the jeeps as quickly as possible because vehicles usually drew enemy fire when they came into the position. Immediately, I began noting the terrain around us and, looking out from the height of the hill we were on, saw a nondescript landscape. Along the stream that came through our position, however, there were some good-sized trees with scrub brush and smaller trees following old dikes and hedgerows where rice fields had been years ago. At one time this must have been a pastoral setting interspersed with occasional villages. Now all that remained were the outline of fields that had once been and, to the northwest, an old church tower that arose amid the ruins of a village that was no more.

The bleak overgrown terrain could have hidden untold numbers of the NVA and probably did. Directly to the west, a long ridge stood out because of its length. Behind it, miles away, Dong Ha Mountain dominated the panorama of the entire scene. To the north, deep in North Vietnam, were more mountains that seemed less imposing but that actually contained the real danger of concealed artillery. The long-range guns, hidden in caves, could be rolled out to fire and pulled back in before our counter-air strikes ever got there. We had only a few moments to take all this in before reaching the command post, which was nothing more than a big open bomb crater.

Each of us then sought out our military counterparts on 2/4's staff, and I was told that the liaison officer had a hole over on the west side of the perimeter. Hustling over, I was greeted by "Hey Brownie, what the hell are you doing here?" It was none other than my closest friend from OCS, Lieutenant Biff Mullen. The ensuing reunion was like long-lost brothers finding each other. Before attending to the business at hand, we had to ask each other what seemed like a hundred questions, and then we finally got around to the situation here. Biff kind of sobered up from the euphoric talk binge and quietly began to tell a story of constant NVA attacks and numerous casualties. Recounting their experiences, he seemed somewhat shaken as he described an incredible account of sustained combat. Evidently, they just patrolled around the area, never really establishing a seriously fortified position at the bridge itself. Their strategy might have been to not give the NVA a fixed target and might have explained the lack of fortifications around the bridge. Something did not seem quite right here, and they had an unusually loose form of discipline. I had never seen an outfit so emotionally drained and would not see another like it for the rest of my tour. The next six weeks did, however, give me insight as to how they might have reached their frazzled state, but even in our darkest moments, unit pride manifested itself in a self-discipline that maintained strong morale within our own unit. Leadership was the key, and everyone in 3/3 worked together like an efficient machine. Life would become basic and crude, but our troops stayed busy and focused.

That day on leaving Biff, I experienced genuine delight from the reunion with such a close and dear friend. I had been drawn to him at OCS because he managed to find humor in the most adverse of circumstances, and that had helped maintain our sanity during the trials we shared at the time. Of medium height with a dark complexion, he was a crisp, all-American-looking guy. On weekend liberty the two of us usually made trips to Washington, D.C., to escape the intensity of our military environment. We always took a room at the old Warwick Hotel, which had seen better days but where the rates were reasonable. That was our chance to study, and from the time we got there each Saturday at around three in the afternoon, we prepared for written tests that were given on Mondays. Then at nine in the evening we would go over to a nearby bar to have some drinks and to glimpse the civilian life we had left behind. It helped to know that there was still a world outside of the Marine Corps. I would call Jody from that bar for my weekly visit, and it was there I found out we were going to have a baby. Biff and I stayed up much longer than usual that night, celebrating my news and what it all meant. More than one toast was made, and the prospect of being a dad with all of the accompanying responsibilities made me even more determined to complete OCS successfully.

After our reunion at the bridge, it was to a dear and good friend that I said good-bye. Little did I know that it would be our last farewell and that I would hear two days later that he had been killed that very night.

The trip back was brief and uneventful, but we all concurred that we had our work cut out for us the next day. After we discussed at length the necessary measures needed to defend the bridge, Colonel Needham went immediately to see the regimental CO to request that barbed wire be delivered for our use when we went in. Our recon of the bridge had convinced us that it would be difficult to protect the bridge as the defenses were presently set up. We found out how true that was at about eleven thirty that night.

The command group met late into the evening, coordinating endless details, and was about to wind up the session when one of the staff NCOs came bursting in. He had been over at regimental headquarters, and reports were coming in that C-2 Bridge was under heavy attack. We immediately obtained their radio frequencies and tuned in on the action. Two companies of the battalion were at the bridge position itself, and we listened to their networks and the command group's as well. Drama and tension consumed us as we helplessly listened to their desperate calls for supporting fire and gunships. They were obviously being overrun, and it seemed that they were calling in artillery on their own position in an effort to stem the attackers. This was a massive offensive by the NVA. We sat in stunned disbelief, hearing the panic and finally cries that "Gooks are running through the position!" Then silence settled in as the radio traffic slowed down considerably, and we each dealt with our own private thoughts while contemplating this place that was about to be our new home. Those of us who had been out there earlier in the day were not surprised. Colonel Needham locked his jaw as results of the disaster trickled in, and then eventually he stood up. He looked around the room and said, "Boys, that didn't have to happen, and it won't happen to us like that." I think at that moment it hit the staff that we had a pressing obligation to maintain the right attitude and self-discipline in the coming days.

We found out the next morning that their casualties amounted to twenty-one killed and twenty-three wounded and that the NVA left twenty-one dead behind. The next day I would hear through my radio operator, Pfc. James Stone, who was in communication with 2/4's artillery section on some matter, that my buddy Biff had died in the attack. It upset me deeply. Biff was the first really close friend I had lost, and the irony of having been reunited with him only hours before his death profoundly affected me. Life is strange as it twists and turns in the most unexpected of ways. Nothing should be taken for granted, and every day should be savored as a gift of God. My generation had seldom been confronted with how fragile life really is, but now many were discovering this on the battlefields of Vietnam. Certainly for me and others it was a confrontation with reality. The next forty-five days at C-2 Bridge reduced to the basics every concept I had ever held.

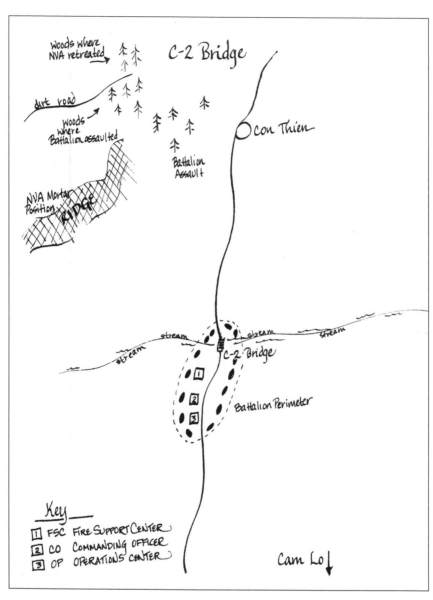

C-2 Bridge

8

Con Thien

After a sleepless night of nervous preparation, we welcomed the day. The whole battalion had heard about the fight going on at our destination, and many wrote thoughtful letters home during the early morning hours. Along with the letter writing, rifles were cleaned to perfection and backpacks rearranged nervously in a subconscious effort of preparation.

Pink light in the east announced the dawn, and the battalion readied itself without the normal vocal admonishments from the senior NCOs. By the time the sun rose, everyone was packed and waiting near the road on what promised to be a beautiful day. The battalion had been given first priority at the chow tent, and we ate knowing this would be our last kitchen-prepared meal for some time. After breakfast we loaded on trucks and were taken on Route 9 to where the road turned north to Con Thien. The plan was to disembark there and walk the final several miles to the bridge. That way we would at least already be spread out if the NVA greeted us with incoming. On reaching the dismount point, Regiment had us wait by the trucks for some unknown reason. It seemed like we were always having to hurry up and wait, and now we spent the morning fidgeting and going over our plans for a quick and efficient occupation. Finally, in the early afternoon, we began the move and fanned out on the right side of the road, both sides having been cleared back for fifty yards. With big intervals between men, the trek began on a bright clear day.

No sooner had we begun than we saw the remnants of 2/4 coming in on the left side of the road. They were about sixty yards away, too far to converse with, and they appeared to be a bedraggled bunch, looking more like a line of walking zombies. It crossed my mind that our earlier delay might have been deliberately timed so we would not come in contact with them. They had been through hell, and there was no sense in exposing our troops to their state of mind.

Our battalion was relaxed, and every person went about his job in a routine but determined way. Attitudes were helped by the sunniness of the afternoon, and the upbeat mood tended to gloss over the disaster from last night. It was hot and humid in this tropical setting, however, and soon we were soaked in sweat as we moved along the road. For some reason Regiment delayed us again about a mile up the road, and the battalion had to come to a dead stop. Colonel Needham now began getting impatient as he realized that we were going to have very little daylight when we reached the new position. If we arrived late we would not have time to orient ourselves or to prepare defenses properly before dark. A half hour later, we finally moved out, much to the relief of the command group.

The day was getting old, and the sky assumed a yellowish tint from clouds that were beginning to build. Moods also changed, and a sense of foreboding crept in with the prospect of darkness looming near. Finally crossing the last hill, we could see our new home on the bleak knoll up ahead, and Colonel Needham passed the word to be ready to take cover at the first hint of incoming. It was gut-check time, and butterflies began to flutter in our stomachs. Every eye took in the panorama; anything could be out there in the brush. About this time, we heard trucks coming from back down the road to pick up the solitary platoon that had been left at the bridge for security. Our troops reached the hill crest just as the trucks arrived, and immediately we heard the distinct boom of artillery in the north. In seconds the scream of the shells were on us, accompanied by the high-pitched crack of exploding rounds. A mad dash ensued to find whatever cover was available, and the unfamiliar knoll became a mass of motion, with people scrambling around on hands and knees. The few foxholes that were found soon brimmed over with many more men than they had been dug for, and bedlam reigned as shells found their mark amid the jumble of men and gear. In short order, everyone had found whatever crevices or hollows were available, and the shelling came to an abrupt stop. Eerie quietness settled on us as we lay motionless in the fading yellow light that now painted the hill a deathly hue. Time seemed to have stopped as everyone silently digested the scene, and then from this still-life picture, the security platoon from 2/4 burst forth like a covey of quail. Rushing toward the waiting trucks, they were gone in an instant, leaving only a cloud of dust and memories of a hill under constant menace.

Now it was ours, and men hurriedly positioned themselves around the perimeter and bridge. Having taken a number of casualties, we sped up our digging efforts because we expected the arrival of the medevac choppers to trigger even more incoming. The troops needed no urging to dig, and shovels churned the earth as soon as each individual had an indication of where his position would be.

The command group found an open trench about thirty feet long on the top of the hill by the road, probably having been put there for protection of off-loading troops. As darkness fell, the troops barely had time to do anything other than scrape depressions in the rocky soil before the medevac choppers arrived. True to our expectations, we began taking mortars when the helicopters came in; the NVA were obviously watching our every move and letting us know we were on their turf. Fortunately, we took no casualties this time. Nevertheless, a general feeling of discomfort prevailed because we still did not know our surroundings well enough to recognize the strongpoints or danger zones. Understanding that the NVA already knew these things, we prepared for a long night.

One positive factor was that the previous battalion had given us their prerecorded coordinates of their perimeter protective fires, so if we did receive a ground attack, we could quickly call in artillery. Colonel Needham and I decided that in the darkness it would be helpful to know where each of those points were, so for about an hour I called in marker rounds on each coordinate. This allowed us to have an idea about how to react if we were attacked from somewhere out of the blackness. As I began calling in the rounds, we were amazed to find out how close they had been placed. Each shell would scream in over our heads at what sounded like tree-top level and crack only a short distance in front of our lines. The first few times we had the battery check their data to be sure they had not made an error. After that we just went ahead and called in the rounds and mentally adjusted to their nerve-racking whine. We knew full well that if someone back in the firing battery made even the slightest error in data being placed on the guns, then the rounds could easily drop in our own position. Later, after a week had passed, we would fully understand why those protective fires had been placed so near. The NVA could approach very close in the heavy brush without detection, and instantaneous artillery support was essential. Adding to our discomfort was the fact that the enemy was located primarily to our northwest along with their main approach routes, whereas our batteries were mostly in the opposite direction to the southeast. That meant our supporting fire had to come directly over our heads whenever we shot a fire mission. I had never seen friendly artillery fired this close to my own position, and the shells came in so low that it seemed that if you stood up they would take your head off. Back home on the artillery ranges, if we had shot this close to our own troops, there would have been no end to inquiries and investigations for safety violations. Here, we quickly found that the proximity of the NVA changed all the rules, and the next several days made this perfectly clear. During our first three days at the bridge, Corporal Bebee and I estimated that the battalion had taken 167 casualties, and, of that number, 81 were from our own weapons. It was impossible to fight in these incredible circumstances without hitting our own people. If we had not fired the close missions or had been overly concerned about hitting our own troops, the casualty rate could have been even higher. The NVA were all around us and close. On the first night in our new surroundings, we were mortared two more times before midnight.

Sergeant Goodridge had rotated just before we left the Rockpile, and now Corporal Bebee was my right-hand man. He and I settled into one end of our thirty-foot trench while Colonel Needham and other staff members took up the other end. It then became a matter of figuring out which were our best defensive moves if we received a ground attack. We were also concerned because reports of sounds in the underbrush had been trickling in from the western side of the perimeter, which could be an indication of enemy movement. After the second mortar attack, Colonel Needham decided he wanted random fire on the protective coordinates to discourage any NVA buildup. Until we learned the nuances of the terrain for ourselves, this seemed to be about the only positive thing we could do. I also had our own mortar platoon work the area over outside the lines to within 150 meters of the perimeter.

Corporal Bebee and I were focusing on this activity when all of a sudden we heard what sounded like a jet roaring in over the position. We both hit the bottom of the trench as something screeched right over us to the other side of the road. In that split second I recognized it as a bomb, having already had a close call with another one on the Rockpile. A deafening crack and flash of light engulfed us when the bomb landed only twenty yards away. Two Marines died instantly, and another six were seriously wounded. The first casualties from our own supporting fire had been taken. The bomb, it turned out, was a scheduled target drop of what was known as an H&I, or harassing and interdiction mission. These missions were designed to disrupt possible enemy troop movement, and targets were picked at random. Through some error along the line, a human or technical mistake had been made. The risk of hitting our own men was inescapable, and many more casualties were taken from "friendly" fire over the coming days and weeks. Still, the NVA were everywhere, moving like unseen ghosts.

We were mortared again at three in the morning. Already we were adapting our survival instincts by attuning our hearing to the distant thump, thump, thump of mortars being fired at our position. That distinctive sound would eventually be discernible even in our dreams. We could be sleeping on the ground near foxholes or bunkers, hear the mortars fire, and be under cover before the rounds impacted in our position. This necessary and constant vigilance eventually caused a numb awareness that permeated our entire beings. Like trapped animals we would be ready to react or fight on at instant's notice.

Day finally broke with a cloudy gray overcast. Cold rations had already been eaten for a predawn breakfast because Colonel Needham wanted everyone up and working as soon as we could see. Several rolls of barbed wire had been thrown out yesterday when the trucks had picked up 2/4's platoon, and in addition to digging, we would be stringing barbed wire. Most important, we would send out patrols to recon the situation beyond our lines.

About an hour after daylight, artillery from across the DMZ started firing at us. We figured out later that they did not fire the big guns too much at night because the flash of their muzzles was seen too easily. Daytime artillery attacks became a way of life for us in the coming days, and because of that and frequent mortar attacks the single most important word to us became the cry "Incoming!" This was the signal to anyone within hearing that the NVA had fired a round or that a shell had actually landed in or near our position. This shout attempted to identify the noise of the enemy fire as distinct from our own artillery or mortars. A person's ability to react in the split seconds at the beginning of an attack could be a matter of life and death. The dreaded word, "Incoming!" fired adrenaline into us in such doses that long after the rounds had stopped we moved around like hopped-up drug addicts.

On this first artillery attack of the day, the NVA found their mark, and another set of casualties was scattered over the hill. What had we gotten ourselves into? Sure, we had been in combat off and on for several months, but this was different. Here the NVA had their own artillery and roamed the area at will. At the Rockpile, we at least seemed to run these guys off whenever they showed themselves. They seemed to be on their own body-count rampage, supposedly an American method of keeping score. If that was the case, then they were making the bell ring. Around one in the afternoon, one of our platoons ran into an NVA unit. Corporal Bebee and I had been setting in protective fire coordinates but quickly dropped that and concentrated totally on the dilemma of the engaged unit. A full-fledged firefight developed, with the NVA positioned between the platoon and our own battalion perimeter, making it impossible to support them with artillery in that overly congested area. Our rounds would have had to come over our own position and then hit precisely between the platoon and us. It was decided that the best bet would be to use our own mortars. By starting to the left and right of the enemy unit and walking the rounds in from the sides, we were able to adjust the rounds onto the NVA without hitting the patrol or our own position. Colonel Needham also sent out relief to hit the enemy from the battalion side. The total strategy put quite a squeeze on the NVA unit.

They left a large number of dead behind, but unfortunately our platoon took casualties as well, most of them having come in the initial contact.

About three thirty we were placed on routine alert because four supply trucks radioed in that they would soon arrive. Everyone found cover, and right on cue the incoming rained down when the vehicles rolled into the perimeter. Troops waited in trenches beside the road, and when the onslaught tapered off, those men jumped up and unloaded as quickly as possible. When the distant booms of guns were again heard, they dove back in the trench. With NVA artillery we did not have as much time to take cover as when we took mortars. The shells arrived in split seconds, and the troops literally had to hurl their bodies toward cover on hearing the far-off guns. Even if we were lucky enough not to have anyone actually hit, there was no end to the bloody noses, sprains, and serious injuries from these truck unloadings. This particular day was not a good one because the unloading party was beaten up badly, and, in addition, one of the rounds landed on the rim of a perimeter foxhole down by the bridge, killing one man and wounding two others. I never heard whether the two survivors made it, but I doubt whether they did from the seriousness of their wounds. Other casualties had been mostly caused by shrapnel flying through the air. Although a direct hit could demolish things as big as a truck or blow a person apart, there was much more danger from the shrapnel. Dead was dead, and a small sliver of steel through the brain killed just as effectively as a devastating explosion; a tiny piece of metal in the abdomen disabled as much as a gaping wound.

The knoll we were on did not provide us with anywhere near the type of protection we needed. It was too low to dominate the surrounding brushy hills, yet we had no choice but to stay because of the bridge. I met with Colonel Needham and Major Harper to discuss defensive strategy, and it was decided that the best solution under the circumstances would be to develop a sophisticated system of covered foxholes and well-placed bunkers for command centers. Rather than put the entire command group in one bunker, we would split it into three separate bunkers located some distance apart. This would, we hoped, insure that someone could still coordinate things if one bunker took a direct hit. We had seen the effects of the NVA's time-delayed fuses, and a direct hit by one of those could be disastrous. One bunker would be for Colonel Needham, the second would be for Major Harper and other operations personnel, and the third would be for the fire direction staff. The CO's bunker and fire direction bunker were small; they were eight-foot-by-eight-foot holes chiseled out of the rocky hill with pickaxes and shovels. The bunker for operations was somewhat bigger but equally as hard to dig. Steel airstrip matting had been obtained from Dong Ha, and these mats with four layers of sandbags were placed on top of the holes, making them essentially mortar proof. Although very secure, they were still vulnerable to a direct hit by artillery or 122mm rockets. Sandbags were added to the sides of the trenches, which allowed us to observe the terrain and attack approaches with even more protection. Airfield matting was also used to cover the perimeter foxholes, making the men less vulnerable to spent shrapnel. That type of construction also gave Colonel Needham another option in the event that we were overrun. In a desperate situation like that, we could call artillery directly in on our own position with the rounds set to explode as airbursts thirty or forty feet high. Theoretically, that would devastate the enemy running through our position while we would be protected by the overhead cover. Although crude, these defenses proved to be very effective in the coming days.

Aside from these defensive measures, Colonel Needham instructed me to pound the surrounding hills and ravines with as much firepower as I could prevail on the support bases to give. As another precaution, he directed our own 81mm mortars to fire regularly just outside the perimeter, convinced that a major part of our defensive strategy had to be disruption of enemy movement. If we hit likely approach points frequently, then the NVA might have a hard time forming for attack. During the day, surveillance patrols would attempt to find out what the NVA had been doing during the night, and we might even be fortunate enough to make contact with some of their units. The more we knew about what they were up to, the better chance we had of countering their ploys. Night ambushes also were set up to try to keep them from getting too close. Finally, listening posts (LPs; typically a team of two men set up in front of the lines to detect enemy movement in the dark) encircled the perimeter for early detection of coming attacks.

Colonel Needham reminded me that when an attack came, I would probably have to be making most of the decisions for fire placement. With that in mind, he discussed at length his notions of how he thought the artillery should be used. It was my job to know where everyone was at any given time and to be aware of likely approach routes. During an attack I was to use my best judgment in directing support, and if I needed to know something, he would get word to me. Corporal Bebee and I rigged up an elaborate map display in our bunker, actually much more complete than the one in the command bunker, and Colonel Needham frequently came over to review it when planning patrols.

We stayed busy with our daily routines, and the perimeter's development continued as an ongoing task. Eventually, we completed an elaborate system of barbed wire with strategically placed claymore mines that would be extremely effective against ground assaults. For the first week, though, we relied heavily on walking artillery and mortar fire in close to the lines to discourage enemy probes. That strategy must have had some merit because the NVA never hit us on the ground during that first week.

The battalion consisted of four infantry companies and a headquarters company. Each infantry company was assigned an FO team, usually made up of the forward observer, who was supposed to be a lieutenant, and his radio operator. In actuality the FO position was often held by an enlisted man. At this time, only two lieutenants were with companies. The third and fourth FO spots were being filled by corporals who were very skilled at the job. Although each team lived with its assigned company, it was still responsible to me for the missions it fired. We were in constant radio contact with each of them, and we approved every mission they shot. The teams not only called in artillery but also directed our battalion mortars, becoming quite adept at walking the rounds in close to the lines as a means of keeping the NVA away.

The artillery bunker was never dull because something was always happening, and the activity kept Corporal Bebee and me totally occupied when we were awake. Both of us slept in the bunker, alternately standing watch and monitoring all supporting fire. We knew the locations of every unit, regardless of size. A unit could be no larger than an LP or as big as a company, but we knew in detail where everyone was. Our radio operators slept in nearby foxholes and came to the bunker when on duty or if we were dealing with something hot. For the first few days of our stay at the bridge, we slept only in snatches during the mornings when enemy activity was minimal. By the end of the first week, a raw numbness had come over us. That actually probably helped us survive the tremendous stress under which we operated. Just being at the bridge and taking incoming around the clock rubbed our nerves, but the additional stress of dealing with fire missions shot at close quarters and having to keep up with all the comings and goings of our troops strained every sense. Our resulting desensitization probably prevented us from blowing a fuse.

After we had been at the bridge for a week, enemy mortar and rocket attacks began to pick up in intensity. We theorized that this was because our perimeter defenses were now improving and that the NVA, recognizing that fact, believed they must do something in lieu of an outright ground attack. On the seventh night of our stay at the bridge, we took six large mortar attacks and two rocket attacks of four rounds each. The mortars did their usual damage, but only two rockets fell inside the perimeter. They were the sophisticated 122mm type, however, and caused plenty of casualties. This first week had been like some World War II combat movie with an incredible amount of incoming. The scream of shells was always with us; sometimes the rounds were theirs, and sometimes they were our own close artillery support. This constant cacophony of sounds, coupled with the tension, left everyone in a state bordering on mild shock and made us focus on the essence of survival. That translated into doing your own job to the best of your ability. Our chances of making it through all this grew in proportion to our ability to function like a smoothly running machine. Fortunately, 3/3 was well run and disciplined, having the esprit that embodied what the Marine Corps stood for. Even though we became callused to the daily carnage, the focus for the vast majority of men was simply on getting the job done without letting their buddies down. It would have been counterproductive to dwell on the ramifications of what was happening around us.

Nature now began to remind us that she could always play a role. One day the rain set in and just drizzled for a period of days. We continued to dig into our piece of real estate but contended with mud and slop. After the first night of deluge and staying constantly wet, the skin on my hands began to shrivel as if I had been in a swimming pool for a prolonged period of time. It took two days before my fingers returned to normal, and trying to use shovels and picks was hell on our hands. The skin peeled right off when handling tools.

Not only was nature uncooperative and the incoming miserable, but also sniper fire became a problem. NVA snipers would creep up to some vantage point, fire one round, and be gone before we could locate them. The really bad part was that they usually hit someone. This dilemma touched us on a personal level and caused much bitterness among the troops. Potential for sudden death or a bad wound from out of nowhere made you hate going anywhere in the position. Digging bunkers was particularly precarious because you had to work in one spot, thereby providing the NVA an easy target. We finally put two FO teams on alert just for snipers and had two mortar crews standing by for an instant response. If any hint of movement could be detected in the direction of a rifle shot, we fired mortar patterns over the sniper's suspected position until the area was saturated. Eventually, this seemed to pay off because the sniper incidents decreased significantly.

We continued receiving artillery volleys during the day and mortars at night. Patterns to their firing eventually became evident, and as we began to recognize them, our odds for survival increased. Artillery could be expected about an hour after daybreak and whenever vehicles came into the position. Mortars started firing a few hours after dark. Our reflexes to these attacks continued to develop, and we could be on the ground or in a hole in a split second on hearing the first sound of incoming. That saved many a Marine's life.

The monsoonlike weather had turned our world into a drizzling, wet, gray affair, and most of the foxholes we had worked so hard to prepare were half full of water. It was in this setting one morning on the way back from a meeting with Colonel Needham when I heard the NVA guns boom from across the DMZ. My reflexes went into action, and I instantly dove for the nearest vacant foxhole. Landing in about one and one-half feet of water was not too bad in itself, but four other Marines happened to be walking by at the same time. Their instincts were as quick as mine, and no sooner did I hit the water than all four men landed right on top of me. I nearly drowned struggling in the bottom of the pit, covered by squirming men. The sensation of drowning created a super-human strength in me that caused me to struggle to a corner where I could finally get my face up. When the incoming subsided, I pulled myself out of the hole, gasping and gulping for what seemed like an eternity. My chest burned in a way I had never experienced and did so for the rest of the day. It hit me that it would have been a hell of a note to have come to Vietnam and drowned in a puddle of water. With amusement, I imagined the headlines in the *Leland Progress*, my hometown newspaper: LIEUTENANT BROWN, DROWNED IN ACION. With all the other ways to die over here, I had almost managed to buy the farm in a mud hole. Such is the irony of life.

As the day wore on, the temperature dropped, and I was downright cold and bedraggled. Somewhat in a state of shock, I found myself losing touch with our surroundings. My chest hurt with every breath from the water I had taken into my lungs, and my hands were wrinkled up like prunes from the constant wetness. I could find no way to get dry. I suppose Corporal Bebee and "Stoney," my radio operator, must have realized what was happening because they came up with a solution for my dilemma. These ingenious guys managed to scrounge up seven or eight of the heating tablets that came with our C rations and after putting a poncho over me lit the tabs one at a time. With only my head sticking out of the rain gear, my body warmed up like toast, and my hands finally dried out. Thirty minutes later, I returned to the land of the living and, after changing into dry clothes under the poncho, found myself semidry for the first time in two days. Although wet again by midnight, I had revived enough to begin functioning as before. Only the chest pain remained to remind me of what had transpired earlier.

At C-2 Bridge, because of the constant incoming, no sanitary burning of waste was allowed for fear the smoke would provide an aiming point for the enemy. Instead, open latrines had been dug that were a real adventure to use. This was highlighted one day when two Marines stopped by to use the facilities, which sat right out in the open on the bare hill. About the time they were taking care of business, artillery from across the DMZ fired off some rounds. In the few seconds they had to react, they found the only cover available, the open latrine. Survival instincts being what they are, these guys dove without hesitation into the waste.

With the rounds landing nearby, they were glad to be there for the moment. When the barrage lifted, however, it was another story. Sheepishly crawling out of their refuge, they were met with a whooping chorus of catcalls and were promptly barred from approaching anyone. They had to throw away their clothes outside the perimeter and wash off in the river before anyone would let them near. The humor of the moment was a welcome relief to the seriousness of our situation and did much to lift the tension under which we constantly lived.

By the second week, it felt like we had been there for a month, with everything now starting to run together. Time was marked by events rather than by hours or days. Such happenings as trucks arriving and the subsequent incoming or more specific incidents such as a recon patrol's encounter with an enemy unit were the ways we related to time. The concept of hours and minutes meant little in our frantic world, and we rarely realized what day it was anymore.

By some stroke of luck, to this point none of my artillery men had been injured, but that, unfortunately, was about to change. Our most popular FO team was made up of a corporal with several years of college and his very intelligent radioman. They were really good, and all of the infantry companies would have liked to have had them attached to their own unit. In addition to their efficiency and professionalism, they enjoyed a reputation for personal courage and were respected for their ability to bring in close supporting fire without blowing anyone away.

I had assigned them to Mike Company because the CO, Captain Ray Findlay, was a stickler for the rule book. He had been an instructor at the Basic School and was there when I went through. He stood six feet, three inches tall and had two prominent canine teeth, making him look somewhat like a vampire. At Basic School he had even been nicknamed "The Fang" because of this resemblance, and the moniker had followed him to Vietnam. Although he was an excellent Marine, his by-the-book demeanor sometimes created attitude problems with men who had already lived through so much combat. My thinking in assigning the top FO team to him had been that he might recognize the regard and esteem with which they were held and not give them as hard a time as he might others. That strategy had not worked, as evidenced by the corporal's now-bald head. Out in the field it had been my policy not to make too big of a deal about keeping hair at regulation length. Although I did not allow anything outlandish, I could not see making life petty under the circumstances we had to live with. At any rate, the corporal's hair length had become a point of contention with Captain Findlay, and he now looked like Yul Brynner, with his shaved head. He and his very tall radioman, who were good friends and went everywhere together, made quite a sight: a bald-headed white guy and a black giant.

One evening, an LP was located out in front of Mike Company's sector. When the men reported hearing movement, they were called back to the perimeter. Colonel Needham, after assessing that information, decided that the area out in front of Mike's sector needed some interdictory rounds, and Mike Company's FO team got the job. The two men started firing single mortars up and down the perimeter. Nobody ever knew for sure what happened, but the corporal FO's last words were "Drop five zero and fire for effect." Up to that point they had been shooting adjustment rounds, and the "fire for effect" was a call for the entire mortar platoon to fire all of its tubes. One of the mortars landed right by the pair's position on the forward edge of the perimeter, and both were killed outright. When the rounds initially hit, everyone thought it was enemy fire, and the usual scrambling and shouts of "Incoming" rang out. When we could not raise the FO team on the radio, I suspected something was wrong, and my anxiety increased when we heard over the Mike Company frequency that they had two casualties. My fears were confirmed shortly afterward over the landline when I was informed that the FOs had been hit. I immediately went over to the first-aid station to check on their condition.

When I came up, I saw them lying on the ground looking like they were just peacefully sleeping. Because no one was tending to them, I realized they were dead. On closer inspection, I could see many tiny cuts on their faces where tiny pieces of shrapnel had hit. Maybe someone had wiped off their faces because there was no blood at all to indicate the trauma of their death. I stood there looking and, in a removed sort of way, thought, "What are the corporal's parents going to think when they see his shaved head?" In the emptiness of the moment, the specter of death had not been what impressed me; instead, it was the notion of how inappropriate it was for one of America's finest to be going home looking like he had been scalped. Out here, death no longer seemed exceptional; it was the unaccustomed that caught our attention. Subconsciously our minds were adapting to a way of life in which dwelling on the obvious could have driven us crazy.

The next day, Colonel Needham's staff conducted an internal investigation, but there was never any clear-cut evidence to indicate whether the mortar platoon had miscalculated the firing data or whether the FO team had simply misjudged how far they were from the previous round. In any event, they were officially reported as killed in action, and nothing, to my knowledge, was ever reported back to Regiment to the contrary. In my opinion, that was the way it should have been. We had to fight in close quarters, and it would have been demoralizing to try to point fingers at people who were struggling for daily survival where margins of error were tiny. The men out here were the elite of America's forces and, by and large, dedicated to doing their jobs without letting their buddies down. It was also better for the families because their loved ones were returned home with full honors for their sacrifices instead of with lingering doubts that their deaths might have been unnecessary. In fact, they did die in combat, as anyone who lived through that time can attest. That it was an inadvertent bullet, shell, or bomb of our own was irrelevant to the realization that it was impossible to have fought under these conditions without hitting friendlies.

Cold, rainy days, mixed with an occasional sunny one, became standard fare as the monsoon season approached. On the morning after our FO team was killed, the sun broke through about ten o'clock, just as a chopper came in to pick up their bodies. Nature could have been paying a tribute to the two warriors as the gray day turned on a dazzling display of golden rays shooting through a scattering of clouds. It was one of the few times that we did not take incoming when a chopper came in, and many heads silently turned to see the aircraft wing away with the two who were held in such high regard.

The longer I was at Con Thien, the harder I found it to understand why the Marine Corps did not put more battalions in the area. With all the thousands of support troops scattered throughout the big South Vietnamese cities, it seemed like they could have put together a few more combat units. There was a suspicion in my mind that egos at the highest levels probably influenced a lot of those decisions. The Marine and Army high commands always wanted to appear in control of their sectors. On the other hand, the Marine Corps was a relatively small branch of the armed services and, in fact, did not really have any more personnel available to commit to the area. Our units always seemed to be below the designated number prescribed, but I do not think they wanted to call on the Army for more manpower. That might have made it seem that they could not handle the situation.

President Johnson's political problems, coupled with loss of public support for the war, were also keeping him from sending more troops than absolutely necessary. Whatever the reason, our men on the DMZ paid a price by having to operate in an area with significantly higher ratios of enemy troops than in other parts of Vietnam. The NVA were everywhere, and we had the job of holding a little bridge in their midst. Another battalion would have surely helped.

Toward the end of the second week, our bunkers and foxholes were nearing completion, and it seemed that we would be better able to handle the incoming. Trenches now connected key points such as the three command bunkers, and shrapnel would also have a harder time getting in the foxholes because these pits had good overhead cover. Circling the entire perimeter was an elaborate labyrinth of barbed wire that could not easily be breached, and it contributed to a feeling that we might be on a more equal footing with the NVA. Daily activities evolved into routines, and those established patterns tended to make us feel even more secure. The men had learned not to expose themselves needlessly around the area, and the daily casualty rate was dropping significantly.

Colonel Needham attributed the absence of any serious ground attacks to our daily patrols and nightly pounding of the hills with artillery and mortars. Still, one high ridge to the east, about three-quarters of a mile away, troubled us a great deal. We suspected that it held most of the enemy mortar emplacements because, from the sound of their firing, that area seemed to be the origin of most attacks. We rarely saw muzzle flashes, however, and attributed that to their tubes being set behind the tall ridge. Consequently, Colonel Needham decided to send two companies over to check things out. The ridge was far enough away that we could not send a smaller unit because there was no telling what they would run into behind that ridge. If they encountered a large force, a small group could easily be wiped out before relief troops could be dispatched. The two companies would compose a substantial unit and would, we hoped, be adequate to handle anything the enemy could spring on us. In addition, we would pound the ridge with artillery before the unit reached the objective, and we would call in an air strike as well. The trick for the unit was getting there and returning before dark.

Two days later, everything was set, and the unit prepared to leave shortly after sunrise. In the early light I went over to both companies to speak with the attached FO teams. On arriving at Lima Company, I saw an amazing sight. Their CO, Captain Roger Zensen, who stood about six foot six, was walking around pumping up his troops. This red-headed ex-football player had joined the battalion only recently but already had a reputation as a hard charger. In typical combat situations, the norm was to camouflage yourself as much as possible, but not Captain Zensen. He had found a great big white and fluffy stalk of pampas grass and stuck it straight up on the front of his helmet, creating the effect of a Roman general running around encouraging his legions. I walked over to him and said, "Captain Zensen, are you crazy?" He grinned an impish smile and replied, "Brownie, there is going to be a lot of action out there today, and I just want the troops to know where I am." Almost needless to say, his men were fired up and chomping at the bit. Leadership takes many forms, and that day he set a mood that would have made any Marine proud. The troops loved his style and would have followed him anywhere. Fortunately, his flair for the dramatic did not get him killed or wounded in the ensuing encounter.

Several hours later, after the companies departed, air strikes spread napalm across the ridge objective. When the strike was over, our troops began moving into the area, and all hell broke loose. How the NVA were able to rally for a fight after that air assault was an amazing thing. Those of us sitting back at the bridge and monitoring radio transmissions could only watch the fireworks. Helicopter gunships were called in for support of what was turning into a serious firefight. It was quite a show watching the choppers dive in with machine guns blazing and rocket pods firing. This display impressed us in a positive way until the NVA, with some kind of rocket device of their own, managed to shoot down one of the helicopters. After careening away from the action for some distance, the helicopter crashed into the brush and burned briskly for a brief moment. It sickened me knowing that Americans had died in that smoking wreck. Out here at the bridge, we were used to seeing people die or suffer wounds in the normal course of a day, but seeing our most sophisticated war machines go down in flames made us feel vulnerable. I suppose that prior to this, we had a type of mental security thinking that our superior technology would ultimately bail us out, but when we saw how that technology could fail, it tended to unravel our security blanket.

The two companies spent the rest of the day extracting themselves from the engagement, and we found out there were a lot more Vietnamese out there than we wanted to deal with. Numerous medevac choppers were brought in as the troops slowly pulled back, bringing out all of their dead and wounded with the exception of the helicopter crew that had gone down. They were nowhere near our troops at the time, and a special detail would have to be sent out for them in the coming days.

Colonel Needham conferred with me concerning fire support, and we discussed the continuing strength of the NVA even after our aggressive effort at suppressing them. That area had been pounded for days with artillery, and even today's air strike had seemed to have little effect on the area. They must have been dug in extremely well. Colonel Needham's final solution was to request a B-52 strike to be delivered as soon as possible.

Division gave unusually quick approval, and a raid was scheduled for the next night. These bombing attacks, code-named Arc Light, were one of the most powerful and devastating forms of destruction that U.S. forces had at their disposal, short of nuclear strikes. When the giant bombs (each containing 750 pounds of TNT) exploded, the blast was incredible. Craters were formed that were large enough to contain small houses. Normally, these strikes were not made within two thousand meters of friendly troops because the combined power of the multiple bombs was devastating. The concussion alone could burst eardrums and knock men into shock if closer than one thousand meters. In our case, the bombs were to be dropped about fifteen hundred meters away, so special precautions would have to be made. If one of the bombs spun out of the normal pattern and landed too close, the results could be quite bad. The time of the drop had to be precise, and everyone would have to be in foxholes or bunkers when the bombs landed.

The next day, all the talk was of the "Arc Light," which was scheduled for eight o'clock that evening. We had seen B-52 raids before at greater distances and felt their concussion from miles away, but this would be different. Anticipation and excitement ran high, much like the feeling before a prime sporting event. Everyone buzzed around discussing the anticipated happening, and I heard more wild tales about B-52s than ever before. Some were true and some purely the figment of active imaginations.

No patrols would go out, and everyone was being kept inside the perimeter for safety's sake. As dusk settled in, each man found a spot where he would not be overly exposed but where he could still have a view of the strike zone. After all the tales that had been bandied about, considerable nervousness now ran through the battalion. The appointed time approached, and things became exceedingly quiet. One of the rumors of the day had been that because of the nearness of the drop to friendlies, the B-52s would be flying at minimum altitude to cut down on the margin of error. Most people therefore assumed that we would be able to hear the jets when they approached. I do not know whether what we did hear were the B-52s or just the bombs themselves coming in, but a distinctive hum could be heard before the ridge lit up in a rapid succession of bright lightning-like flashes. Shortly thereafter, the ground itself shook, and a terrifying rumble, sounding like a giant jackhammer, deafened us. We felt the concussion on our faces, and our eardrums vibrated unpleasantly. This seemed to last for about twenty seconds, and then total silence followed. Finally, somewhere on the other side of the perimeter, someone cheered. At once, the whole battalion came out of their holes, jumping around and yelling like fans at a ball game. It had been an awe-inspiring moment and surely would curtail the NVA from operating behind that ridge. Evidently, the bombs did have an effect because we did not take a mortar attack for the next four days. That would be the longest interval to date that we had gone without mortars. If anyone had been on that ridge when the bombs arrived, his survival would have been truly incredible. Having seen the giant B-52 craters firsthand, I believed anything on the ridge during the bombing had to be dead.

We had now been at the bridge for around three weeks. To this point, the earlier activities of digging in and preparing the position had not allowed time for thinking, and we had become creatures of instinct and reaction. In the artillery bunker, we continually worked on projects that required constant monitoring of the different radio frequencies, and I had not even had time to write a letter home. In fact, I would write only one during the whole time I was at the bridge. This was not only because of the extraordinary activity but also because I did not want the folks back home knowing how bad it really was. It would have been difficult not to convey the gravity of our situation, knowing by then how high the odds were of becoming a casualty. Later in the States at some briefing, I heard a statistic that Marines spending a full tour on the DMZ during the peak of the war had a 50 percent chance of becoming a casualty. Our casualty rate was already approaching that percentage in just three weeks of being at the bridge. At the time, of course, we were not figuring the odds but knew we were losing a lot of men. If you took into account the casualties that the battalion before us had taken on the night before we relieved them, then the casualty rate at this bridge had to be an incredible statistic for a monthlong period at one location. We were often reminded of our losses. We would see choppers come in to pick up the wounded, and whenever we passed near the landing zone (LZ), we would see the plastic shrouds, or body bags, containing dead Marines, lying there starkly. It seemed that all too often one or two KIAs were waiting for the next chopper. Because it was too late to help them, they had a lower flight priority than the wounded and sometimes stayed at the LZ for a while. The lifeless lumps, all bundled up like black bags of laundry, were very impersonal.

Periodically, memorial services for our KIAs were held on the side of our ridge, but they were not particularly well attended because the troops did not like to be reminded of the finality of death. Each Marine who had been killed since the last memorial service would be represented at the ceremony by a helmet sitting on top of a rifle stuck in the ground on its attached bayonet. Gazing at that while the chaplain offered prayers sobered us and made death quite official. Having people killed around you in combat was not depressing. These services were. Here you had to deal with the memories of friends and teammates, and the moments of reflection hurt. In action, we fought, reacted, and exhilarated in being alive.

At this point the things mattering most in our lives were getting very basic not only in mental aspects but also in every phase of existence. Excess mental and physical baggage was discarded while we attempted to focus on the essentials. A physical example of this was our clothing. We had packed very little gear to begin with, but by now had thrown away all but the essentials. Most of us possessed only one pair of trousers and carried a long-sleeve shirt to ward off mosquitoes or to keep warm on the sometimes chilly nights. For the most part, though, we wore only trousers and the ever-present flak jacket without a shirt. If you got too filthy, you just walked down to the stream and waded in fully clothed, washing yourself and your britches all at once. We did not have to worry about underwear because we did not wear any. The heat and chafing that it caused had led most people long ago to abandon that civilian nicety. Our wash jobs were thus reduced to total simplicity.

We attempted to focus our day-to-day living on the immediate job at hand and avoided extraneous thoughts. When we did this, things were bearable. Sometimes, though, this was impossible, particularly when we slept. Our dreams could not be shut out, and they would screw up our minds. Imagine dreaming about being with someone you cared about back in the States, only to wake up in a hellhole. It was awful! I would dream about events at home and just about go crazy when I woke up in 'Nam. In our foxhole discussions, I found that others often experienced the same thing but had nightmares as well. They were related to the daily events of our world at Con Thien, and I do not know which kind of dream was worse. At least my dreams of home did not cause me to wake up screaming like some of the others did.

Some of my best moments in Vietnam were after standing the last night watch and seeing the first light of morning. Most nights on the DMZ were filled with danger, and the relief felt at the break of day was something special. Darkness hid the evil and unknown as well as the real threats that existed in the night. Mortar incoming, for instance, was particularly dreaded and usually came after dark, and most ground attacks by the enemy were launched under cover of darkness. The words "dawn's early light," memorialized by our national anthem, took on a special meaning over here. A subtle awareness of life renewed itself each morning in spite of the death and insanity surrounding us. Its freshness was tangible and seemed to permeate the very air. Anyone who has experienced a night of siege has no trouble grasping the essence of Francis Scott Key's words, regardless of whether a flag actually flew through the night or not. Even after those evenings when nothing actually happened, the mornings brought renewal.

We tried to make the days as routine as the situation would allow, and one morning Corporal Bebee and I went down to the stream to fill our canteens and take one of those dressed baths. Suddenly we heard shouting upstream from a returning patrol, and we immediately scrambled for our rifles. It soon became evident, however, that the men coming around the bend were relaxed and jovial, putting us back at ease. The patrol, on seeing us at the water's edge, broke into big grins and started pointing at us in a gleeful manner. On reaching us, they took even greater delight as they began describing the six dead NVA they had found around the bend decomposing in the water. Evidently one of our mortars had caught an NVA squad in the open while crossing the stream. The returning patrol thought it high humor that we had been filling our canteens and bathing in the tainted water. So went the battlefield humor of the frontline Marines.

About ten days after the B-52 strike, we again started receiving frequent mortar attacks and soon were getting hit day and night around the clock. Colonel Needham requested more B-52 strikes, but none were forthcoming. Word trickled down that the Marine brass was having serious confrontations with the Air Force in their requests for support. There had always been bickering between the services, but this was ridiculous. It was also rumored that the high command in Saigon did not want to admit that Con Thien and C-2 Bridge were effectively under siege. In effect, if these rumors were true, our hands were being tied by political decisions and petty interservice considerations. Still, we had to sit within range of the enemy's guns in North Vietnam while they pounded us with artillery and sent probes against us. We could respond only with counterfire and by sending out short patrols to be sure they were not digging in too close.

Colonel Needham finally gave up on getting another B-52 strike and decided to make a second trip over to the ridge where the NVA mortars were thought to be. This time I would go with two companies on a longer-range sweep that would take us well past the ridge. Our last sweep had been planned as a day maneuver, but we needed to reach much farther out, and that would require us to stay in the bush overnight. The last operation to the ridge had been awkward because of a breakdown in coordination, and Colonel Needham thought that in the event of another attack it would be extremely helpful to have a contingent of the fire support staff there to make decisions. Consequently, I was to represent the artillery in the operation. I received that news with scant enthusiasm. Who needed to take a trip into a fool's world directed by bickering leaders far from the scene?

Adding to my discomfiture was my growing perception of the increased risk when I should have already rotated back to Charlie Battery. It seemed that any time an extremely risky situation came up it was the men who had been through the most combat who were the first to be called on to deal with it. Actually, this is the norm in war and makes sense when you realize that experience and competence are critical in dangerous situations. At the time, though, my mind was not that rational, and I could think only of the slackers and incompetents who had been relegated to positions back in such places as Da Nang or Saigon where they were now safe and happy, drinking beer. It was hoped that there they would not cause serious problems because, in theory, those large cities were not likely to be intense combat zones where competency and teamwork were essential. America's most responsible soldiers have always been rewarded with added risk. To those who died in the process or were maimed for life, we owe a special debt for the sacrifices they made while upholding what they believed to be America's honor and freedom. That debt can be multiplied in the case of Vietnam because of the senselessness of the conflict in the first place and the lack of support at home. The involvement there, with its questionable premises, had evolved into a war of attrition that should never have been allowed to happen, yet American soldiers courageously carried on. If any lesson is to be learned from Vietnam, it is that we owe it to those fighting the war to give them every advantage and support, never trading lives merely for the sake of a numbers game. To do anything less is a moral travesty and disgrace.

The next morning after the announcement of the upcoming sweep, Charlie Battery's CO, Captain Joe Schwerer, and the new gunnery sergeant, Bernard McLaughlin, arrived for a field visit. Fortunately for them, we were calling in air strikes on the ridge, allowing them to escape the incoming that usually accompanied arriving vehicles. The NVA respected the bombs and napalm that the Marine jets were dispensing and were not taking any chances of disclosing their positions to the flyboys. It was festive that noon as we sat back watching the air show and enjoying numerous strafing runs, bombs, and rolling fireballs of beautiful napalm. It gratified us to think that those guys out there trying to kill us might not even exist when we went on our operation tomorrow.

Joe Schwerer and Gunny Mac (Gunnery Sergeant McLaughlin) had brought us two new FOs and a radio operator. Talk about big eyes! To them it must have looked like Armageddon, and here we were sitting around eating "C rats" like we were at a picnic watching Fourth of July fireworks. Gunny McLaughlin, a jaunty Irishman and veteran of Korea, had been in country only a week and probably could not believe what he had stepped back into. The new replacements from Charlie Battery were as nervous as cats, and we casually sat around acting salty while watching their discomfiture. A natural tendency always existed out in the field with the infantry to make guys from back in the battery feel uncomfortable, especially because we had to eat the dirt day in and out while those back in the battery rear usually had more creature comforts. Actually, we were privately envious of the "good life" we thought they enjoyed in the rear.

I found out how much I envied that life when Captain Schwerer informed me later that morning that I was being brought back to the battery in five days to become the executive officer. It took all of my composure not to jump up and shout for joy. At last! I was finally going to the rear. Ironically, it would turn out that the rear, which I so envisioned as a haven of comfort and safety, would be sharply changed by upcoming events and the modified role that Charlie Battery would assume. For the moment, though, I did not know that and was ecstatic. If I could only make it through the upcoming two-day operation, I would have survived this daily hell in which we had been living.

Captain Schwerer seemed to be getting a charge out of the action going on around us. He was a gung-ho type and seemed to relish the idea of combat. In his positive, calm way, he carefully studied the action going on out there and quickly grasped the nuances of what was happening. To me, the action was so routine that my attitude probably came across as being unconcerned. Furthermore, I am sure he could not understand my poorly concealed jubilation at the prospect of leaving all this. Gunny Mac seemed much more level about the situation and showed himself to be quite personable. A prototypical Irishman from the Bronx, with red hair and a boisterous temperament, he was humorous in his comments about the action, which was refreshing in itself. In the months ahead, I would find that trait to be a real positive in the tense world in which we would live. Of course, on this day I had not been around him long enough to really understand the full impact of his personality, but it was obvious that he was a true character from the "Old Corps." In my coming role as executive officer, I would closely associate with him in directing the activities of the battery.

The prospects of my future job excited me. I had recently been promoted to 1st lieutenant but had been more preoccupied with survival than in placing any significance on the new rank. The role of executive officer in a battery was one of the more coveted positions for artillery 1st lieutenants, however, and that did turn me on. The job was a hands-on billet with the primary responsibilities of directing the guns and day-to-day operations. The commanding officer assumed ultimate responsibility for this, of course, but had much broader duties, including operation of the fire direction center, clerical administration, and supervision of the forward observation teams with the infantry. The new duty intrigued me, but my true excitement came from the prospect of leaving this hell called Con Thien.

That night I broke out the last bottle of bourbon we had bought from the Seabees back at Dong Ha, the other having been doled out sparingly since arriving at C-2 Bridge. No one wanted to be tipsy in combat, and that first bottle had gone a long way. With that in mind, I rationed out one drink each to the fire support staff in celebration of my pending return to Charlie Battery and poured the rest of the bottle into a spare canteen.

That evening I wrote my first letter home since arriving at the bridge. Perceiving the coming two days to be even riskier than before, I rationalized that I had better say some things to Jody just in case I did not make it. Nevertheless, I made sure that the letter significantly understated the seriousness of the situation. As for my own mail, the battalion had received nothing for several weeks, and Colonel Needham had complained adamantly about that to Regiment only the day before.

The following morning we moved out at daybreak; it was my first excursion away from the bridge since arriving. Moving north, we traveled on the main road for a quarter of a mile, and, finally, I saw Con Thien for the first time. From the bridge it had been screened by a ridge. Now, my first glimpse of that forlorn place revealed a battle-scarred hill devoid of vegetation and rising from overgrown rice paddies in an unnatural way. It seemed like a giant ant mound in an unkempt yard of grass, an impression that was enhanced by busy Marines scurrying about from hole to hole. Even then, the men did not stay above ground any longer than necessary. After seeing that place, I was glad we were at C-2 Bridge with its own set of dangers rather than at Con Thien proper. Their high-profile hill looked like a true sitting duck—and plucked at that. It was, in fact, one of the primary targets on North Vietnam's DMZ firing range, and although we too were in that same impact zone at the bridge, they were line-of-sight targets. We also heard rumors that at night they could hear the clank of tank tracks moving about in the DMZ. I was glad to be based a little farther away, even if not by much.

Leaving the road, we found that in spite of many recently cold and rainy days, this patrol was going to be a scorcher. Everyone carried at least two canteens on his belt, and the wiser of us carried three. We moved quickly and at noon broke to eat with the CP group collapsing in a bomb crater for a short rest. The heat and humidity soaked us in sweat, and I pulled out a canteen to take a big swig. On taking a gulp, I nearly choked; I had inadvertently put the canteen of bourbon on my belt. Furious at myself for the boner I had pulled and appalled at the prospect of being in this heat with a reduced water supply, I thought about pouring it out. I had been through water shortages on an earlier patrol at the

Rockpile, and it had been bad. That afternoon I almost swore off liquor for good because of the intense heat and strong exertions of the march. When darkness fell, however, I made the best of a bad situation by trading jiggers of bourbon for jiggers of water until I had filled a canteen with the precious liquid—meaning the water, of course.

Late in the afternoon, the patrol reached the ridge without incident. On inspection we found the reverse slope quite interesting. The NVA had built an elaborate bunker system and created the most sophisticated foxholes imaginable. The latter were superbly dug, with overhead protection and camouflaged to perfection. They made our own diggings look like crude attempts in a sandbox. These guys were pros, and our respect for them increased on seeing their engineering skills. We had been told that we were up against the 308th and 341st North Vietnamese Army Divisions and that the 320th Division was supposed to be over near Dong Ha Mountain, north of the Rockpile. Back stateside, most of the talk had been primarily about the Viet Cong as if they were the main enemy. Actually they were further south and used guerrilla tactics, but the units we faced were crack troops from North Vietnam. Disciplined and dedicated, these soldiers were as capable and well trained as any army in the world. The NVA were formidable opponents, and we respected them for their dedication and bravery, particularly in the face of massive airpower.

Although they did not have as many of the sophisticated weapons as we had, they did have an extensive artillery arsenal that was quite effective. Along the DMZ and Laotian borders, their 130mm and 152mm guns were reputedly housed in caves and completely camouflaged. They rolled those pieces out at will and, after firing them, rapidly pulled them back in before air strikes or counter-battery fire could be initiated. Also to our north along the DMZ were the 4th Battalion of the Van An Rocket Artillery Regiment and the Vinh Linh Rocket Battalion. These units were equipped with the deadly 122mm rockets that could be fired with uncanny accuracy. I hated the 122s more than their artillery. Their destructiveness on impact was incredible.

On the DMZ we were in contact with an enemy force having significant numbers and artillery similar to our own. General Giap, their minister of defense, was spoken of often and with respect. His generalship at the Battle of Dien Bien Phu had been well chronicled years before, and even the troops were aware of his legend and how effective he had been. Sitting in the lair of the enemy that afternoon, I was acutely reminded of just how formidable the NVA could be, and now we were out rumbling around in their diggings. We were a half-day's march from friendlies and well within range of their artillery to the north, giving me a very uneasy feeling. I could think of a thousand places I would rather have been.

The concern about the enemy was interrupted just before dark. The good old Marine Corps, in all its wisdom and thoughtfulness, decided to deliver our backlog of mail we had been clamoring for. Here we were on a dangerous operation and traveling as light as we could, and the post office at Da Nang choppered in almost three weeks of mail complete with packages. I received probably twenty pounds of Christmas presents; my aunt Laverne, in particular, had seen to it that I would have loads of Christmas decorations as well as food for the approaching "holiday." After all, this would be my first Christmas not spent at home in Leland with the family. I could have cried when I had to bury the excess baggage during the night. It would have been impossible to haul around all those packages the next day. The food was passed out to the troops to consume that night, and my letters were stuffed into pockets to be read later. Out here we were maintaining strict discipline regarding keeping lights out to avoid giving the NVA any possible target, and reading mail would have to wait. Strangely enough, we did not take a single mortar or have any reports of sounds from the LPs as was usually the case. Instead, it was "all quiet on the western front" for the night.

The following morning we checked out the back of the ridge extensively, and although there were plenty of signs that the NVA had been there, they seemed to have vanished entirely. Not a sighting was made, and the only enemy we dealt with was the heat as we trudged through elephant grass and overgrown rice paddies on the way back to the bridge. Approaching the perimeter we chattered with relief about the lack of enemy contact and had a general feeling of good fortune that nothing had happened. As soon as the last troops filed back into the bridge position, we immediately were hit with a big mortar attack. What did it mean? The NVA were probably telling us that they would pick the time and place that they wanted to fight. In actuality, that was usually the case.

I was jubilant that night because I apparently had been on my last patrol with the infantry. Two days hence, I was scheduled to return to Camp Carroll and Charlie Battery. I would have no more of this mind-bending world where every day we functioned like animals reacting to the crisis of the moment. By now, we all moved from place to place in a semi-crouch, ready to sprawl on the ground instantly at the first sign of danger. After more than a month on this dusty hill, we blended into the ground with our filthy rags for clothes, and the prospect of returning to the battery was like a reprieve from some imminent misfortune awaiting those who became too much a part of this place. The odds were clearly against us at C-2 Bridge. Besides, Camp Carroll had showers, tents with cots, and real mess halls. It had been more than forty days since we had eaten any kind of meal other than C rations, and I was definitely ready to leave.

The next morning I got up bright and early, determined to take no chances on my last full day in the field. When the mid-morning mortar attack came, I had no problem at all because I was safely tucked away in the fire support bunker. Actually, I saw no reason for me to go anywhere. At three in the afternoon I got the word that Colonel Needham wanted me to report over to his bunker. This was probably going to be a good-bye visit. After all, I had spent seven months with 3/3, and a lot had happened. Colonel Needham and I had worked closely, and he probably just wanted to wrap things up and coordinate the passing on of responsibilities. Like a prairie dog, I popped out of my bunker, checking sights and sounds to be sure nothing was happening out of the ordinary and then, after deciding everything was clear, darted on over to the colonel's bunker.

I crawled through his door and found Colonel Needham and Major Harper mulling over his small wall map. He beckoned me over and said, "Brownie, Regiment is getting ready to pull a major sweep around Con Thien involving the battalion." To myself I said, "So what the hell are you telling me for? I'm going back to Charlie Battery tomorrow." Stabbing with his hand toward the map, he continued, "This is going to be one of the most aggressive actions on the DMZ to this point. Two battalions abreast are going to sweep around and to the north of Con Thien, then west and back south to C-2 Bridge." Elaborating on this, he drew their routes on the map with a grease pencil as my stomach sank. Why was he involving me in this? Drawing a big red mark on the map due west of Con Thien, he said, "We are going to be a blocking force for this sweep, and our location will be here. The problem is that intelligence tells us that the position we are to occupy is located in a patch of woods presently held by the NVA. We will have to drive them out and hold the ground until the other battalions can sweep around. In effect we should trap any enemy forces caught between the three battalions." Again I said to myself, "Colonel, you have to be totally out of it by telling me this because I won't be here." Turning to me he went on, "Brownie, I know that you are supposed to go back tomorrow, but it is critical that you stay for this one last operation. We don't need someone inexperienced running the fire support in this kind of situation. I have cleared it with Regiment, but we are leaving it up to you. Can we count on you?" With a numbness of mind, I nodded yes, afraid to speak because I did not trust how my voice might sound. My throat constricted as I stared blindly at the markings on the map. It was several moments before I could regain enough composure to start rationally working out the fire support role for the operation.

I left there as soon as I could and walked back to the bunker in a trance. If we had taken mortars at that moment, I probably would not have flinched, such was my mental condition at the time. After telling Corporal Bebee the general plans, I crawled on my bedroll and immediately went to sleep. There was no other way to escape the nightmare I was living through.

Photo taken the day I arrived at Camp Carroll, the main artillery base along the DMZ.

Helicopter resupply at the outpost on top of the Rock-pile.

Moving out on a patrol on the road from the Rockpile to Ca Lu. The Rockpile and Razorback can be seen in the distant background.

French priest on motorcycle is interrogated. The smoke from burning Montagnard village is in the background.

This tank leading the convoy hit a mine; picture taken as Marines passed by.

Now executive officer, I am giving firing directions to guns during a live fire mission.

Corporal DiCaprio and me on the gun line at the second position in Ca Lu. The corporal was one of those soldiers who used to catch spent shrapnel in his helmet.

A live fire mission. The view overlooks the valley leading to Khe Sanh, about ten miles away.

Jody and me on the veranda of the Ilikai Hotel in Hawaii during R&R.

I use the battery commander's scope at Ca Lu.

In front of the operations bunker at the Rockpile. *From left to right:* Captain Orville C. Hay, me, Sergeant Duane Goodridge, Lieutenant Tom Kabler. Used by permission of Duane E. Goodridge.

Sergeant Duane Goodridge. Used by permission of Duane E. Goodridge.

The Silver Star is presented to me at Camp Lejeune, North Carolina for actions at LZ Torch. The presenter is Major General E. B. Wheeler.

Fix Bayonets

I slept until around ten o'clock that night. Coming back into our world at C-2 Bridge that evening was a sobering experience. Reality flooded into my mind as sleep faded away. The bad dream was not over, and here I was. No question about it, I knew now what combat meant with its wounded and dying. Life is so fragile, and there is no sense in taking chances with it. On awakening, I initially had a sick feeling, but there were considerations other than my frustration and disappointment. Simply put, if the battalion was going into this type of battle situation, then I really was still needed. By now, I knew that this war was stupid and insane, but loyalties count for a lot. Somewhere along the line, unit pride and esprit de corps had become stronger forces than dissatisfaction with the Vietnam War and how it was being fought. People pulling together and supporting each other in a mutual survival effort had evolved into something greater than self.

Beyond this bonding, a sense of the patriotism that had shaped America still pulled at my heart, and a deep and abiding belief in honor still remained a part of my makeup. A new generation was now questioning, even distorting, these values throughout the universities and indeed throughout the land. Patriotism, however, was not a matter of debate for me and most of the people of my era. Many today would say our attitude was extremely naive, and, in fact, many of us did not yet recognize the change of mind-set subtly taking place in America. The bottom line for most of the people with whom I came in daily contact was still the belief that if we were going to be citizens of this country, then we should support her. I happened to disagree with the way we were fighting the war and in my mind believed McNamara and Johnson would have to answer to God for having put American lives at risk in a one-sided conflict. Although there were other points that should have been taken into consideration, such as the potential for drawing China into the war, I just was not thinking like that at the time. In the simplistic way that combatants in the field tended to rationalize, I believed that it was wrong to make us play by a set of rules to which North Vietnam did not adhere but instead exploited at our expense. Yet in spite of those reservations, I still believed that a democratic nation needs the loyalty of its citizens if it is to survive. With that rationalization, even in the face of what I then considered to be immoral leadership, I was able to go about my job without losing my sanity.

In spite of those frustrating sentiments, one very positive aspect about the upcoming operation did appeal to my pride as a member of the Marine Corps. There had been few times in Vietnam where an opportunity presented itself allowing U.S. forces to attack the enemy in a classic offensive thrust. Most engagements were initiated by the Viet Cong or NVA because they rarely allowed themselves to be caught or detected in any kind of mass or static position. They usually materialized and vanished at will. Our battalion's role in this maneuver would be to attack a known NVA position in textbook scenario. To be able to participate in such an operation had to stir the emotional instincts of most Marines. The other two battalions in the sweep might, or might not, get into a scrape as they circled Con Thien, but we alone knew that our objective was to take an occupied strongpoint and that we would have the opportunity to employ the attack principles for which the Marine Corps is so well known.

After the dismay of realizing that I would have to run the gauntlet one more time, I settled down and by the next morning had become quite absorbed in working out the fire support plan. This attack was going to use just about every tactic composing a classical textbook assault. We planned the operation for the following day and scheduled a predawn artillery barrage that would pound the position for half an hour before daybreak. When that concluded, the battalion minus one company left behind to secure the bridge would have moved into position for the final charge. Two forward companies would advance on line across open fields to the woods with one reserve company and the headquarters group following closely behind. When the forward troops neared the objective, I would cut off artillery fire, and the front line would rush into the woods where the NVA were entrenched. On taking that position, the battalion would then spread out but not pursue the enemy. Our role from that point on would be strictly that of a blocking force, with the other two battalions circling widely and, we hoped, pinning any NVA against us and Con Thien, which was only a half mile away. This was all supposed to be accomplished in the course of one day, and we would then return to the bridge before nightfall. For that reason, we were not packing excessive gear or water.

Corporal Bebee and I worked on the details of the artillery barrage and asked for every available gun within range of the objective. We, for the most part, got our wishes, including the 175mm Long Toms of the Army and all of the Marine batteries at Dong Ha and Camp Carroll. The firing would commence at five in the morning and continue until it was light enough for us to see. We wanted their ears and heads ringing when we started to move across the open rice paddies.

This planning caused Corporal Bebee to beam with enthusiasm as the details were worked out. Although I did not know it at the time, this would be the last occasion I would have to work closely with him. He loved the field and later volunteered to stay with the infantry rather than return to the battery. A month later he would be severely wounded and medevaced, eventually returning to Charlie Battery after his recovery. On his return, he again volunteered for the field and remained there until rotating back to the States. Some of the men seemed to thrive on combat to the point that it became an addiction, and I must agree that life did seem to have much more meaning and purpose when we were all striving so desperately to survive. My return to civilian life was a downer in that sense. Nothing I have done since has really seemed as important as those jobs we had to do over there. Pulling together in a life-and-death struggle made what we were doing seem to really matter.

Night finally arrived, and we found everyone checking his weapons to be sure everything was totally clean and functional. This time I would check to see that all my canteens contained water and nothing else. Finally, after cross-checking everything I could think of, I knocked off a couple of hours of sleep following a mortar attack at eleven o'clock. At least where we were going, the NVA would not have surveyed coordinates of our position. I awoke around one thirty in the morning and immediately started poring over details. We were scheduled to form up at four o'clock in order to leave the perimeter by four thirty and would then move in total darkness for a half hour before the artillery began. Actually, by three o'clock the whole battalion seemed astir because the anticipation just was not letting too many people sleep. Everyone maintained strict discipline with regard to not using lights, and it was creepy listening to all the activity in the inky blackness. At four o'clock everyone was ready to go. The troops were placed in their respective groups and made to sit down until their turn to leave. I prayed that we did not take a mortar attack at this particular time because with everyone bunched together in groups, incoming would have been disastrous if it came roaring in. To ward off that possibility, we fired 105s from Camp Carroll at the ridge from which we usually took mortars.

The battalion moved out on schedule in single file, each man holding the belt of the man in front of him. It was a night so black that this was the only way to maintain contact without making a lot of racket that would result from giving commands or turning on lights. This attack was supposed to be a surprise, and stealth was necessary. How the point man ever found his way is beyond me, but a guide team had made a practice run the night before, which probably accounted for the successful effort. What a weird feeling it was, moving with more than four hundred men in the pitch-blackness. Amazingly, only muffled sounds could be heard as we stumbled along like a slinking caterpillar. I am sure everyone knew how critical it was to keep quiet. The humidity and wet elephant grass enfolded us, and soon we were soaked in sweat, with stinging forearms from the razor-sharp grass that cut us incessantly. The perspiration came not only from the exertion but also from the anxiety generated by blindly being pulled along to the morning's destiny. Whose last day was this? Few doubted there would be casualties, but it was convenient to think it would be the other guy. On the other hand, there was also that tugging thought that, on an outside chance, it could be you.

At five o'clock, right on schedule, we heard the first shells from Dong Ha and Camp Carroll whistle overhead to boom in the darkness. For the next half hour, we were comforted by the intensity of the barrage. The hair on my neck stood up, and chill bumps covered my body on hearing the scream of those shells preceding us to our destination. We were now mentally pumped up and anxious for the assault to begin.

The battalion reached the attack point about five fifteen, with the sky in the east beginning to show shades of pink across the fields. Two companies quickly formed on line, spread out abreast, and faced the objective. These troops were staggered two deep and about fifteen feet apart to minimize casualties if we started taking the incoming we expected. The front line consisted of around 250 men stretched as far as we could see in the breaking day. Behind that line, the third company formed a loose column that could be sent forward to reinforce any area having difficulty in the assault. Following them was Headquarters Company, to which I was attached.

At five thirty our artillery bombardment ceased, and the most moving and dramatic moment of my Vietnam experience began. As the sun began to rise in the east, we were finally able to see our surroundings clearly, and then the electrifying command of "Fix bayonets!" was heard all up and down the line. The sharp clicks of hundreds of bayonets being attached was a defining moment in the reality of being a Marine. This was what the Corps was all about, and chills ran up and down my back. Regardless of our thoughts about the war and the way it was being fought, this was why we existed as Marines. Many would comment later about the feelings of the moment and the emotions generated.

The forward companies moved out promptly across the open fields, and soon Headquarters Company was moving as well. The physical movement produced a sense of release from the waiting, and the elation of realizing that we were part of a Marine unit actually advancing toward a known enemy lifted our spirits even more. Shortly after my group moved out, enemy mortars and artillery started landing at random points across the open field. No one stopped unless hit, and the battalion moved at a steady walk through the drifting smoke of impacting shells. As the lead men neared the woods, the entire battalion picked up the pace to a slow trot, and a crackle of rifle fire began to rage back and forth across the front. When the front line hit the woods, a battle cry went up that sounded like the wail of some crazed animal, and from left to right as far as we could see, Marines charged into the woods in true "John Wayne" fashion. Obviously, everyone had thrown himself into the heat of the moment, for no hesitation could be seen anywhere. By now, Headquarters Company almost ran to keep up with the surge to the front. It was as if we were being pulled along by some powerful magnet. Yells and rapid rifle fire were punctuated by mortars landing all over the place, and, like a dream without fear, the thrill of the charge burned in our chests.

When the assault line hit the woods, a brief period of hand-to-hand combat ensued while the fury of the attack quickly carried the men through trees to the other side of our objective. Countless tales would later be told about the exploits and adventures of the engagement. By the time the CP group arrived, the NVA had been pushed out, leaving a number of dead behind. Nevertheless, the bulk of their force retreated no further than to another patch of woods seventy yards away and on the other side of a little dirt road. We did not pursue them because we had strict orders to hold the woods as a blocking point, the idea being for the other battalions to swing around and trap them between us and Con Thien.

We were surprised that the NVA had pulled back only to the next tree line. The logical thing for this smaller unit to do would have been to clear out entirely. Instead, they just set up across the road and began firing their rifles at anything moving in our position. We were up against the hard-core troops of North Vietnam, and they were not to be taken lightly. Full of pride themselves and fiercely loyal to their own cause, these men were not easily intimidated and, being elite troops, were well disciplined, determined, and worthy of our respect.

On arrival, the CP group immediately set up operations in a couple of bomb craters, which gave us some protection from the continuing rifle fire. The sound of bullets zipping over our heads sounded like so many angry bees, and the memory is as vivid now as the bullets were real that day. This went on constantly for the next several hours. Next to the crater that I was in stood an old, scraggly, burned-up tree. It was devoid of vegetation, and its gnarled bare limbs stretched over our position. Fate looked kindly on us that morning when suddenly one of the limbs came cracking down, raising a cloud of dust. When the air cleared, we were stunned to realize what had actually happened. A dud mortar had hit the tree hanging over our crater, and if it had detonated, none of us would have likely survived. An airburst would have been devastating at only ten feet above our heads. We hastily found another crater with no trees hanging over it.

Things were happening because North Vietnam decided to show us their muscle. In came their shells from the north as their guns began pumping in numerous rounds. Fortunately, our air support arrived early, forcing their artillery to back off. Their mortars, however, continued to shoot, and much of my time was spent trying to direct counterfire at that source of harassment. I did this largely by sound and guessing. I would get a line on the direction we heard their tubes popping from and then try to figure out which of our support batteries was most nearly on line with our position and the suspected mortars. I then adjusted the fire up and down that imaginary axis. This was unorthodox, but because we had only sketchy coordinates to operate from, I theorized that because normal deviation of artillery rounds was either high or low and not too much to the sides of the line of fire, we would have a better chance of hitting something other than ourselves along that axis. It seemed to work because eventually the mortar fire eased from those sectors.

Sitting in the bomb crater with bullets zipping by provided a new experience. I had been in the firefight at the ambush site along the road to Ca Lu and later had been exposed regularly to sniper fire, but this morning consisted of three continuous hours of sporadic bullets flying by. We made sure we did not show any more of our bodies than we had to and talked away on the radio, directing fire and keeping in touch with the FO teams.

As we went about our jobs, we eventually formed an idea of our surroundings. The patch of woods we held consisted of about four acres of scraggly trees with enemy bunkers scattered throughout. Again, the engineering ability of the NVA impressed us with their neat, ground-level bunkers that were superbly camouflaged. With all the lead zipping about, the thought crossed our minds that their bunkers might be a safer place than our open-air craters. After crawling over to one of the bunkers and peering into the small dark entrance, though, I could not bring myself to drop down into the blackness. For one thing the smell of the NVA was extremely strong, although I did not really think any had stayed behind. It was more the thought of what else might be down there, including booby traps, that kept me from investigating further. Earlier, I had seen my first punji stakes at the edge of the woods, and that type of booby trap remained a real possibility. Those devices were sharpened bamboo spikes that had been dipped in human excrement. If someone managed to hit the point of these stakes while moving through the short grass, the resulting wound, even if minor, could easily become infected from contamination. The thought that the NVA might have left some of those in the bunkers for a greeting disturbed me. The rats could have the bunkers; I would take the sunshine with its lead poisoning instead.

We took our share of casualties that morning. Medevac choppers came in for the first load about an hour after we secured the woods and would make several more visits that day to take out others. Two choppers arrived in the first flight, the first of which landed without incident near our own crater in a whirlwind of dust and debris. The accompanying chopper, however, attempted to come in about thirty yards away near a makeshift aid station and immediately took NVA fire. The chopper veered into some shattered trees, and its swirling rotors disintegrated in a shower of wood and blades, causing even more casualties. As the dust cleared, the crew piled out unscathed from the undamaged fuselage. My men watched this with fascination, patiently waiting for the completion of the medevac. We had stopped our own counterfire so the choppers could enter the area. Most of our own rounds were coming right over our position and could have easily hit one of the birds. Unfortunately, the confusion allowed the enemy mortars to crank up again. The downed chopper must have gotten the attention of the air command because we soon had all kinds of air support, including strafing runs by fighter jets, a highly unusual method of attack. Strafing was probably being used because, with our proximity to the NVA, using bombs might have gotten us as well as the enemy.

During all this time, the men around me functioned efficiently and with precision. I saw no panic or fear, just abstract awareness of the scene around us. It was a beautiful, sunny day filled with the scream of shells and the constant zip-zip of bullets. Everyone performed his duties routinely, absorbing the unfolding cyclorama. The position was a busy place with wiremen running telephone lines to different command posts while corpsmen attended to wounded. Radio operators chattered away with animation, passing on their messages. The woods had been practically defoliated from last night's artillery barrage and previous bombing raids, so we could easily see much of the activity throughout the battalion. Our crater, with a very high parapet, allowed us to have an exceptionally good view, yet we remained semiprotected. There were plenty of bomb craters, and each of the company CPs had used them to set up shop. In spite of the plans for us to be out by dark, almost everyone was digging in or improving his position. Force of habit and a steady hail of mortars and rifle fire accounted for this. A foxhole could very well save someone from a nearby mortar round.

Most of the day I shot fire missions, but I still had plenty of time to reflect on what was happening. We had been through more than a month of constant incoming from mortars and artillery, and during this time we seldom had the opportunity to shoot back at a "for sure" known enemy position. Now we were involved in a standoff engagement with the NVA and facing the issue head-on under conditions of our own choosing. This was great, and everyone responded exuberantly. The prospect of pinning the NVA between us and the other battalions filled everyone with enthusiasm.

Around one in the afternoon I learned from Colonel Needham that the air command was bringing in one of the big cargo choppers to try to save the downed medevac bird. He told me to keep the artillery support going until the last minute in order to hold off enemy fire. This was worked out with the air boys by having the rescue chopper fly in perpendicular to the line of fire from the guns at Dong Ha, thereby allowing us to keep firing until they were ready to land. Everything had to be coordinated to perfection for this delicate and tight operation.

A half hour later, the rescue chopper came in high to the east from the South China Sea, and I fired artillery until the flight was almost at our position. This rescue ship, called a "Jolly Green Giant," was a huge helicopter that could lift massive loads. Straps had already been rigged on the downed chopper by its crewmen, and they could easily hook to the rescue aircraft when it descended. The giant rotors turned the area into a wild dust storm, but the crew had the downed bird attached in no time. The big chopper then lifted the smaller one like a broken toy and began moving off, at which point the rescue crew made a major mistake. I could not believe it, but instead of flying up and away from the enemy as they should have, they for some unknown reason flew directly over the NVA position. The enemy troops opened up on that chopper like participants at a turkey shoot. Moving slowly, the Jolly Green Giant was raked with fire. Something had to give, and what gave was the chopper underneath. In order to get away from the hail of fire, the crew had only one alternative—to drop its load. Down hurtled the broken chopper right into the center of the NVA position, bursting into flames on impact. The NVA scattered like a covey of flushed quail. All shooting stopped on both sides, and our Marines began jumping and cheering. Who would believe it? It was like someone had called time out in the battle while everyone jubilantly watched the scurrying NVA. I guess even the NVA not directly involved in the crash were caught up in the spectacle because for a good five minutes not a shot was fired by either side. Everyone just stood in the open like fools, watching the folly of war.

After that incident, enemy small-arms fire gradually diminished over the course of the afternoon and by four thirty had completely stopped. Earlier, about the time of the bungled helicopter rescue, the other two battalions had made enemy contact northeast of Con Thien, approximately a mile from our position. I guessed that the NVA we were in contact with had probably learned of the other Marine units in the area and were beginning to clear out.

The plan had been that the other two battalions should reach us by no later than four thirty and pass on down the Con Thien road, allowing us plenty of daylight to reach the road ourselves. The other battalions still had not passed our position by five o'clock, however, making us especially anxious to move out because we were not engaged at the moment. Later we heard that the other battalions had been forced to slow down because they could not determine how many NVA they were up against. Whatever the real cause of the delay, it was creating new problems for 3/3.

We had been rescheduled to leave no later than five thirty, but that time came and went, and still the other two battalions had not made it. Our primary orders still remained to hold our position until they had passed, so we had no alternative but to stay there. Just after dark, we finally received word that the other battalions had reached the road at Con Thien. We had never seen them because they changed course in order to reach there while they still had light, but the net result was that we were left stranded in the now-black night.

With this development, Regiment decided it was now too dangerous for us to leave. They figured that the NVA knew where we were and that if we moved out blind in the dark it could be disastrous if they attacked us on the way. For my part, I preferred to go back rather than be left out here in no-man's-land, but Regiment reasoned that at least in our present position we were already somewhat dug in.

On hearing the news, my inner reaction was, "Is this really happening?" I should be sitting back at the bridge by now getting my few belongings together for the return to Camp Carroll. Sure, it had been an exhilarating day, but I did not relish an evening in true "Indian Country." With our job over, there was nothing left to accomplish. Besides, night protective coordinates had not been established, and our perimeter at present was too disjointed for night defense. Our earlier deployment had been designed with the idea in mind that when the NVA were caught between us and the other battalions, we would charge out toward them. Consequently, no preparations had been made in the present position for a night defensive perimeter. Adding to that problem, we had brought food rations for only one meal, instead carrying extra ammo for the anticipated assault on the NVA. Finally, most of our water had been used up in the heat of the day's activities, and thirst was already making it unpleasant for some.

Whatever the circumstances, I did not have much time to think about it because Colonel Needham directed me to start calling in artillery fire immediately to establish protective coordinates that would encompass the entire position. That kept me busy for almost two hours because I tediously had to march in rounds from initial shots that had been fired far enough away to be sure we did not get hit. Colonel Needham wanted them walked in as close as possible so that in the event of a ground attack they could be used effectively.

By nine o'clock that night the coordinates were set as best we could in the dark, and the battalion had adjusted the perimeter for a somewhat better defensive arrangement. Without any prodding from the NCOs, foxholes had been improved with vigor. For a few hours the predominant sound had been that of dirt being shoveled between explosions of the adjusting rounds. It was an uneasy sort of night, and hardly anyone thought about sleep even after the extreme exertions of the day. Corporal Bebee and I had finished our C rations that morning, but we did have water. The extra canteen really came in handy.

By ten thirty, quiet had settled in across the whole area. No more sounds of digging came from the perimeter, and only the whisper of radio operators keeping in touch could be heard. About midnight we were startled by a yell from the darkness outside our lines. You could hear movement all over our position as troops tensed and strained to hear the unexpected voice better. A moment later, in the dead silence of straining ears, we heard a voice yelling in English, but with a Vietnamese accent, these bone-chilling words: "Marine! Hey, Marine! You die!" Not a sound came from our position as we listened to the shrill and plaintive taunt. We sat there in cold awareness as it sunk in that the NVA had returned to their position across the road and were even so bold that they were verbally harassing us. Had we really heard this? Moments later, no doubts remained as the shouting of "Marine! Marine, you die!" began again, followed by laughter. This time the taunt was drowned out by rifle fire from the troops nearest the NVA heckler. When the shooting stopped, he yelled again and successfully worked on our minds with his mocking words. This went on and off for probably twenty minutes during which we were in total darkness because Colonel Needham did not want us popping hand flares and making our position any more obvious than it already was. Now, though, our guys were yelling back between his taunts, and their responses were expletives as callous as only a Marine could manage. Then we had a new sound to contend with when we heard a "swish, swish" followed seconds later by an explosion in our perimeter. The NVA had rigged Chicom grenades on the end of long bamboos and by swirling them around their head were releasing them at the peak of their swing. They were thus able to throw them much farther than our men could throw their own grenades. Almost needless to say, a number of our guys tried anyway. Colonel Needham then had me bring in the protective fires as close to the position as we dared while we began popping hand flares and firing sporadically all up and down that side of the perimeter. By one in the morning a full-scale firefight was going on, and two probes had been made of our lines. Colonel Needham wanted artillery walking the limits of the perimeter, and this occupied my complete attention. I assigned the calling in of these missions to the FO teams closest to the most significant enemy activity.

At one thirty, we started getting hit by a big and determined NVA effort on the east side of the perimeter toward Con Thien. Colonel Needham directed me to move the artillery rounds in even closer and furthermore told me that if we started getting overrun he wanted the artillery brought in on our own position. It was gut-check time for everyone in the crater as he said this. The FO team on the east side was now bringing artillery rounds right up to the lines in single shots. Colonel Needham came over and said the placement was good, but he wanted the whole battery firing. I told him that it was entirely possible that some of the rounds might hit us, but with the attack in full swing, he said fire anyway. After the proper commands and several moments later, in came six screaming shells. The perimeter exploded in flashes, and the sound of shrapnel whined over our heads. Colonel Needham yelled at me to keep it up, and we did for another ten minutes. The NVA attack stopped abruptly, although our guys continued firing their rifles intermittently.

With the lull in the fighting, the colonel now started talking to his company commanders over the radio in an attempt to assess where we stood. I held the artillery in check while waiting for further instructions and prayed that the attack was over. The prospect of calling artillery in on our own position chilled me to the bone. Enemy fire had definitely decreased, and most of the rifle fire was our own by now. Colonel Needham's company commanders confirmed that the attack had indeed stopped, and things began to feel a little less desperate. On the other hand, we had taken several casualties, one of the worst coming from our own artillery rounds. In the barrage of fire, one of our shells had landed in our position and within three feet of an occupied foxhole. The two occupants had not had their heads above the ground, which saved their lives, but the explosion collapsed the foxhole wall in on them. One of the men suffered a broken back, and every time anybody tried to move him he screamed in agony.

As the next few hours passed, it became apparent that the NVA were not pressing the attack. Occasional rifle fire came into the position for the next hour but steadily decreased. A flare ship also arrived, lighting up the entire area and allowing people to breathe even easier. The wounded Marine with the broken back, however, continued his blood-curdling screams every time anyone tried to help him. His pain was genuine and wrenched our stomachs each time he yelled. There were additional casualties, but the situation was so dangerous that Regiment was not letting medevac choppers in. The previous day's helicopter loss might have had something to do with that. The screams of the wounded Marine went on for an interminable time until finally the corpsmen shot him up with so much morphine that he passed out. Hearing such agony may have been the worst part of the night. Anyone sitting there could imagine himself in the guy's place and empathize with the desperateness of his plight. How could he possibly live under these conditions? Sleep was a stranger that night, and all of us examined our inner selves in the eerie half-light created by flares floating in the darkness of this nether world.

Day finally broke, and the battalion instinctively and individually began the business of getting ready to leave. For my part, I had the mortar platoon walk rounds all around our position, particularly the points where we had previously received fire from the enemy. In the full light of morning, medevac choppers finally came in to get our dead and wounded. Three severely wounded Marines were among the casualties and were, for all practical purposes, comatose. These boys, hooked up to their plasma bags, were symbols of our worst fears and hopes. In their crushed and broken bodies we saw our own vulnerability, yet there was also a realization that survival was possible even against the direst of odds. The plasma bags hanging over them could have been banners announcing that even in the hell of battle there was still hope. One of these three was the Marine who had screamed through the night; amazingly, he still lived. Those who chanced to be near these men wanted to know which one had been yelling during the night, his very survival a testament to the possibility of life even in the dark valley of the shadow of death.

When the choppers finally touched down, great attentiveness and gentleness was given to the casualties as they were gathered up and loaded aboard. It was like some precious and delicate treasure being handled. Though these Marines had, in our minds, risen above this chaotic world to a higher plateau, they had paid a price that we all wished to avoid.

The medevac proceeded smoothly, and as the last chopper flew away we immediately began moving out. No one had slept now for practically two nights, bombarded as we had been with emotional and physical stress. Moving and looking like men from the dead, we fanned out across the scraggly rice fields and retraced our route back to the bridge. Although the NVA scattered a few mortars our way, no one seemed to notice, and as it was, we were lucky in that we did not take any casualties on the return. For my part, the thing that I was most aware of was the freshness of the morning and the beauty of the sun in the east. It was good to be alive.

On arriving at the bridge, I had no feeling of elation at the prospect of leaving. I just grabbed my belongings and quickly made my farewells. Two supply trucks hustled into the position, and after they unloaded I hopped on one as it headed back to Dong Ha. At that point, the uppermost thing in my mind was the concern that we might take rockets as we left. The truckers, however, wasted no time, and soon we were barreling down the road. Sitting in the rear of that truck, I looked out across the barren hills at C-2 Bridge fading away and could feel only emptiness and relief. The last forty-five days had left me drained and exhausted. Constant artillery and mortar duels laced with an occasional firefight had taken their toll, and I could now understand how the battalion we had relieved more than a month ago could have reached its bedraggled state. That awareness reminded me of the cliché to "think twice before making judgments on others until you had actually walked in their shoes." Nevertheless, beneath it all I could look at 3/3 only with a justified pride because they had maintained an incredibly positive mind-set through it all.

I looked as bad as I felt in my pair of ragged trousers and filthy flak jacket. Not able to shave for three days, I resembled some kind of wild man. My first stop was Dong Ha, and I did not wait to clean up before going to the mess hall. I was ravenous and had not eaten a real cooked meal in forty days, besides not having anything to eat since yesterday at noon. If a senior officer did not like it, I could not have cared less at that point. They must have sensed my state of mind because no one said a word as I piled my tray high and wolfed down the food. There happened to be new guys in the mess hall who had just arrived in country, and they stared at me like I was some freak in a carnival show.

After that repast, I caught a convoy to Camp Carroll as fatigue and exhaustion began flooding over me. The trip and my arrival blended into a hazy blur, finally ending in the ecstasy of my first shower in more than a month. After that long, cleansing bath, I stumbled into a tent and crashed on a cot. They said I hardly moved until I awoke twenty-four hours later.

10

Camp Carroll

The return to Camp Carroll was like a reprieve from a death sentence. It has been said that people awaiting execution will often enter a trancelike state of acceptance as the hour of death approaches. We had lived with the real specter of death for so long at Con Thien that I think I must have been experiencing the mental condition of a condemned prisoner. It took several days before I could again function normally. A numbness existed, and only slowly did I begin to appreciate fully the joy of life around me. When my spirits finally did return, it was the little things that meant so much. A shower or hot meal was no longer taken for granted. Just being able to walk around Camp Carroll without having to stoop in a crouch stimulated me. In fact, it did not take much to please me at all, and when the numbness faded, life became a conscious delight. Especially enjoyable was sipping a cold Coke; actually, the coldness was the best part because I had not had access to ice for weeks.

My perceptions had changed so much by now. Sure, Camp Carroll took occasional incoming, but compared to Con Thien it was a cakewalk. Everything in this world is relative, and what might seem a hardship to some is a blessing to others. Vietnam brought this home to me more than anything that I have ever experienced before or since. It was a time when I learned about the very essence of life.

I had come to Vietnam in early June of 1967. Prior to that I had been subjected to the rigors of an intense military indoctrination. Devotion to country had been drummed into my head, and the honor of the Marine Corps had been made a religion unto itself. Even before I joined the Marines, my mind was filled with notions of glory and honor for country. Newspaper reports in the first part of 1967 told of successes in Operations Cedar Falls and Junction City, and my concern then had been that the war might be over before I even really joined it. Now, recent news stories increasingly described student protests at college campuses. This was so alien to my thought process that I began to feel disgust toward those at home who, when they heard America's bugles sounding, could think only of saving themselves. America's leaders might have let us get in the war for the wrong reasons and might have subsequently mishandled its execution, but there distinctly had been a call to arms. It was beyond what I wanted to accept that people would so flagrantly reject what to me was a clear and present duty. Now, after returning to a safer and saner environment where I could think instead of react, I began trying to make sense out of it all. That was a difficult task.

Con Thien had opened my eyes to circumstances that seemed grossly out of kilter. There we had been asked to play a deadly game of attrition with each side playing by a different set of rules. North Vietnam was free to do anything it was strong enough to do, whereas we were saddled with restrictions beyond my comprehension. Americans were told to sit at designated points along the DMZ like ducks in a shooting gallery while the NVA took potshots at will. If you were at a major base such as Dong Ha or Camp Carroll, there was a certain amount of incoming, but these bases had substantial fortifications and large numbers of personnel that reduced the chance of ground attack. Lesser positions, however, such as Gio Linh, Con Thien, and the Rockpile, also had ground attacks with which to contend. Of course, other positions with even smaller contingents were even more vulnerable to any kind of attack. They included such places as Ca Lu, C-2 Bridge, Hill 881, Lang Vei, and many others. The NVA had advantages on the DMZ and Laotian border that they usually did not have in other areas of Vietnam. They could move in by night, attack, and be gone before day and, in many cases, return to Laos or the no-man's-land of the DMZ proper before our troops could even think about pursuing them. Much like Brer Rabbit, once they returned to their briar patch they were home free. We could not cross into these areas because President Johnson had made a political decision to play the war by standards that he believed would project America as a protector of South Vietnam, and he in no way wanted to give an impression that we were aggressors. That policy actually encouraged the NVA to make quick and short ground attacks. It also allowed the enemy to develop substantial artillery positions that were never threatened by our own ground forces. Our only response was by air and artillery, and the NVA positioned their guns in ways to minimize the effectiveness of our attacks with extremely good camouflage, engineered fortifications, and the use of caves.

Another factor making it difficult to understand war on the DMZ may have had to do with the nature of the Marine Corps itself. If you were not at one of the main bases, then fortifications were crude at best. An unwritten tradition in the Marine Corps held that we were not programmed for defensive actions but were, by training, assault troops. This underlying mentality may have been reflected in a somewhat cavalier attitude toward elaborate fortifications. On the other hand, our minimal protection could have been because the Marines lacked the resources that Army units had. Only in high-profile positions such as Khe Sanh or Con Thien were there really well-built bunkers and trench systems. One had only to visit Army locations and then observe Marine defenses to be keenly aware of the difference in the quality of fortifications. Whatever the reasons for our minimal defenses, the Marines appeared more vulnerable than they had to be.

To those of us in the field, it seemed that so much more could have been done in an aggressive manner to pursue the war and protect our troops. In retrospect and with the benefit of much historical debate, it is clear that political considerations often influenced the way the war was fought to a greater degree than did pure military strategy. At the time, it was hard to understand why we did not move troops into Laos and physically disrupt the supplies coming down the Ho Chi Minh Trail. Even better, it seemed, would have been an invasion of North Vietnam all the way to Hanoi. Many of us believed that this was the proper way to proceed in the war and often discussed how we would have volunteered to stay beyond our normal tour if a determined effort had been made to invade the north. Of course, we had a very limited view of the overall ramifications of such measures and typically related to the war from the shortsighted perspective of frontline combatants. Although we really wanted to serve our country in a meaningful way, we began to suspect that it was only a political game being played to influence the press and to posture to an American populace that was becoming increasingly restless. The war, to many of us fighting it, seemed to be nothing more than a body-count affair with operations being designed to produce enemy KIA numbers.

That state of affairs, in retrospect, can be traced in large part to Robert McNamara, the secretary of defense, and resulted from his theories of quantitative analysis. As discussed by Edward F. Murphy in his book *Semper Fi: Vietnam* (page 111), McNamara thought war could be conducted by assessing the numbers, much as he had run Ford Motor Company. General Westmoreland, realizing that numbers were what McNamara understood, had begun quantifying his progress statistically, and that evolved into a sophisticated system of body counts. That methodology in time dovetailed into the idea of keeping score by showing that the NVA were losing more men from attrition than we were, and Westmoreland refined those rules substantially. McNamara alludes to these developments later in his book *In Retrospect: The Tragedy and Lessons of Vietnam* (pages 48 and 211). This exercise might eventually have achieved some kind of statistical victory because of our superior firepower and massive supply system, but only in a superficial sense. It actually accomplished nothing other than killing a lot of Americans and a whole lot more North Vietnamese. The NVA just kept on pouring men into our meat grinder while our forces gained no tactical advantage in the process. North Vietnam, on the other hand, actually benefited as American disenchantment at home increased proportionally to the mounting casualties. America began to lose its resolve to fight because the public would not accept the kind of personnel losses that we were taking without perceptible gains in territory or strategic progress.

To have effectively won the war by simply keeping the NVA out of the south would have taken such a massive deployment of troops followed by economic fallout that it would have been entirely unacceptable to America. Johnson and McNamara finally realized this but had unwittingly become players in a game of attrition. The problem, of course, was that, in war, battles are typically won or lost by tactical or strategic maneuvers, much as in chess, and not necessarily because of the size of the opponent's forces. Furthermore, psychological victories can be achieved by the militarily weaker opponent, as was the case in Vietnam, where we were ultimately forced to withdraw without significant defeats on the battlefield.

The United States finally reached such a state of frustration that, by the time Johnson figured out that the war could not be won through body counts, it was too late to count on support from the citizenry for other types of campaigns. America's patience had run out, and even the strongest patriots were losing trust in their government leaders. At that point, if a new strategy had been suggested, it would likely have been met with skepticism by the majority of people. The faith in our government's leadership had been shaken to the core. That mistrust would reshape American attitudes toward elected officials for years to come.

In my own way, I simply lost the naive faith that our leaders would do the honorable and right thing. Political self-serving may well have always been the underlying factor of government, but that aspect of our republic had never been as clearly revealed as in Vietnam. The press threw aside previous reporting restraints and now told everything in all its ugliness. The news media during World War II and Korea had been cautious in the way they released news and, to a large degree, covered mistakes or miscalculations by our leaders. No more. All their flaws and foibles were shown on the evening news with no holds barred. An era of faithful trust was gone.

Now back in the battery at Camp Carroll, I was again with men who had not yet fully experienced the frustrations of limited war. Those who had not spent time in the field were still gung ho and charged up. True, back here we took incoming occasionally and saw a certain amount of combat, but there was not the sense of angst that comes from having been shot at too many times without an assurance of effective retaliation. I loved America and revered the Marine Corps but did not want to die for what I perceived at the time to be President Johnson's notions on how to fight a "limited" war. After Con Thien, my greatest aspiration was to get out of Vietnam alive but honorably. My attitude at that point left me in an awkward position because in my newest leadership role it was important to maintain a positive approach. I clung to my beliefs of standing tall for the country and to the traditions of the Marine Corps and kept reservations about our leadership to myself.

Vietnam differed from previous wars in many ways, but one item impacting the mind-set of its participants was a phenomenon that had supposedly been implemented to boost morale. Everyone arriving in country was given a date that would end his tour and send him back to the States, the theory being that this would give him something to look forward to. In some ways, this was all right, but it often created attitude problems with short-timers and contributed to a certain amount of disarray as people rotated in and out of units. Nevertheless, a fixed return date was a part of Vietnam. It was known as our "DEROS," or the date eligible to return from overseas. Many Marines kept calendars on which they marked off the days as their DEROS approached. The ingenuity of locating these calendars ran quite a gamut—from Bibles to flak jackets or wherever. The most common location was on helmet covers. I had been in country for more than seven months and finally started one of my own, keeping it in my letter-writing kit with pictures of Jody and Cathy. It was a good feeling each night to mark off another day, now that surviving had become so important.

At Camp Carroll, however, I had other things to think about other than going home. Joe Schwerer, the CO of Charlie Battery, was the man to whom I reported. As with most Marine officers, his dedication to the Marines was enthusiastic and intense. As I had noticed when he came for a field visit to Con Thien, he was very capable and tempered his gung-ho attitude with a lot of common sense. This helped keep things in perspective and made my job as his right-hand man much easier. I was executive officer and second in command, and life was as pleasant as could be under the circumstances. I had seen some COs who were so brainwashed by the military aspects of the Corps that they made life a nightmare for those unfortunate enough to have landed in their units. Joe was easygoing, yet dedicated to detail and excellence. More important, I credit him with having taught me how to motivate subordinates without unduly alienating them. His style was laid back, but he always insisted on getting the job done. I am a much more capable person thanks to the four months I spent with him.

As executive officer, or XO, I was given a free hand to carry out tasks in my own way as long as I got the job done. The official role of an XO was to supervise personnel and direct the firing of the guns. Computation of gunnery data was handled by the FDC, and the administration was handled by the CO and first sergeant. It was a great job for an artillery officer, and as far as any job in war can be fun, this one came close. The leadership training that had been hammered into me in Basic School came into full play here. Because of the actual combat missions that we fired regularly and the occasional incoming that we took, the troops were serious about their jobs. The battery took pride in its work and performed efficiently.

The man ramroding the troops was Gunnery Sergeant McLaughlin, the same Gunny Mac I had first met at Con Thien. In his typically Irish manner he kept things lively and upbeat. He was responsible for pushing the troops and keeping order, and he did just that. Being forty years old, the Gunny's many years of experience kept him one step ahead of the men because he had been there himself and knew all the tricks of the trade. It amused me to no end seeing him making the rounds of the gun positions. Like a large leprechaun in a Marine uniform, he would bounce into a gun pit, making the dust fly and giving orders right and left. The men respected him and understood that he knew how to use the power of his position. For all his bluster, the bottom line was that he had a kindhearted disposition concerning the troops and took good care of them as long as he was not crossed. Not many of the men made that mistake.

The Gunny interacted well with the officers also and knew how to play the role of staff NCO to perfection. Personable and outgoing, he carried on an amusing foolishness and banter that did not strain the officer and enlisted status that had to be maintained. The occasional exceptions to this had been a couple of drinking binges. The bottle had been Gunny Mac's devil for some time. He had enough time in the service to be a sergeant major, the highest rank that an enlisted man can attain, but he had been busted in rank twice for alcohol-related incidents. This time he had made it back to gunnery sergeant. Through a quirk of fate, he would again become my gunnery sergeant when we returned to the States and I became CO of C Battery, 1st Battalion,

10th Marines at Camp Lejuene. Again, the alcohol almost got him when we were on a cruise to Vieques, an island off the coast of Puerto Rico near the Virgin Islands. While on liberty he ended up in the St. Thomas jail at the old dungeon on a drunken brawling charge, and his drunken spree probably would have gotten him busted again if I had not gone to bat for him with the battalion CO. Otherwise, he was a great person and a pleasure to work with.

For about a month after my return to Camp Carroll, things rocked along in routine fashion as Christmas approached. My headquarters was the "Exec Pit," an above-the-ground bunker situated next to the six guns of the battery. This sandbagged affair had an observation encasement on top that allowed me to observe the guns when firing. Whenever a mission came into the Exec Pit, I would go up on the platform inside the bunker and give commands over the headsets to the guns. Numerous fire missions were shot each day in support of nearby troops, primarily at the Rockpile, Ca Lu, and Con Thien. Because I had been in those places, the missions were particularly meaningful to me, and I tried to instill in the battery a sense of their importance.

It was here I found out just how much esprit Charlie Battery really had. Our battery had been at Gio Linh on the night when it took hundreds of rounds of artillery incoming, and many members had been wounded. Five of the six guns were even disabled to the point where they could not return fire. The last one, however, continued firing until almost daylight, when the incoming finally ceased. By the time I had become battery XO, the remaining members from that engagement had managed to be assigned to two guns, One and Six. They considered themselves old hands and were arrogant about their status as such. The saltiest of the crew was Corporal DiCaprio, now gun chief of Gun One. One day we started taking incoming while in the process of firing a mission to support engaged troops. Incoming or not, we always continued firing if the field troops were actually in combat. On climbing up to the observation window, I noticed that Guns One and Six were standing around inside their gun parapets as if they were at a Sunday picnic. The other gun crews were crouched down and scampering around like mice while shells landed randomly throughout Camp Carroll. One and Six were looking at the other gun crews and making disparaging remarks. Knowing the danger they were exposing themselves to, I ordered them down on their knees until it was necessary to service the guns. They were further directed to stay in their bunkers if they were not needed outside. I could tell that they were enjoying the impression they were making on the other crews as they grudgingly complied. About that time I had to drop down into the bunker to confer with Captain Schwerer about some aspect of the mission, and as soon as Guns One and Six saw me drop out of sight they took advantage of my disappearance to continue impressing the new guys. Several minutes later, I popped back up to continue the mission and was flabbergasted at the scene awaiting me. Corporal DiCaprio and his crew had their helmets off and, using them like baskets, were running around their gun catching spent shrapnel from the incoming as it flew through the air. The lengths these guys went to in order to play the gungy role staggered me. I, of course, raised hell and forced them back down while completing the mission. This continued to be an ongoing problem, particularly when the new guys became veterans themselves and wanted to prove their own prowess. Charlie Battery was a special group with a real sense of self-identity. The overwhelming majority of its members were proud to be such, and the battery's record for courage under fire was a tradition constantly on everyone's mind.

At Camp Carroll I again had the good fortune to be with my close friend from Basic School, John Eager. John was fire direction officer at the battalion level and in charge of plotting all the missions for the various batteries at Camp Carroll. For better control and to avoid duplication of missions, individual batteries at Camp Carroll did not supervise their own plotting but assigned FDC personnel for this centralized post. John and I now spent a lot of time together, and I found it very helpful knowing someone privy to the goings-on at the battalion level.

Being in proximity to battalion headquarters, I also got to know the battalion staff much better. The CO, Lieutenant Colonel Opfar, was a wiry, distant sort of person with whom I never really had much personal contact. On the other hand, the operations officer and later battalion exec, Major Capenas, was the mover and shaker. A lean man full of energy, he was always buzzing around watching everything while carrying on a constant chatter. Acutely aware of the moods and feelings of the battalion, he did an excellent job of advising Colonel Opfar. In combat, the commanding officer needs to understand fully the attitudes of his men, and then he can more effectively motivate them when he has to drive them hard. The major, a career Marine, walked a tightwire in order to stay tuned into the heart of the battalion, and he admirably fulfilled that need.

Another responsibility of the various batteries required that each provide security for a portion of the perimeter around Camp Carroll. Charlie Battery's sector was located right next to our guns on the western side toward the Rockpile. Assigned to occupy that sector and build it up defensively, we constructed foxholes, strung concertina wire, and laced the area with claymore mines. Each fighting hole had overhead protection, reducing the effect of mortars, and there were good fields of fire stretching to the front. The outstanding defensive location of Camp Carroll, high on a giant knoll, and its vast size minimized the chance of a significant ground attack, but that brought about another problem: complacency. The men tended to be a lot less alert and often fell asleep on guard duty. Vigilance remained essential, though, and that matter needed dealing with. As executive officer, one of my direct responsibilities was maintaining perimeter security on our sector during the night. After a number of attempts by the staff and myself to keep the men awake, I found a solution at some risk to myself.

One night as I quietly walked down the line, I came upon a foxhole where considerable snoring was going on. Silently, I crept up and stole their rifles, taking them back to my bunker where I could easily retrieve them. Then, picking up a board about the size of a baseball bat, I returned to the foxhole where the snoring continued at full speed. In the deep darkness and without any warning, I started flailing the occupants like I was beating rats. As the two troopers started reacting and yelling, I quickly faded back through the grass and into the battery position. With the commotion coming from the foxhole, others along the line started popping flares, and soon the whole perimeter around Camp Carroll was on full alert. I saw Gunny Mac and others running down to the line, but all they found were two guys cut and bleeding with knots on their heads. When he discovered that their rifles were missing, the Gunny gave the two troopers some real abuse. He had the presence of mind to realize something was up that had nothing to do with an enemy attack, and after dressing them down thoroughly, he sent the wayward Marines back to their tents. Of course everyone in the battery knew immediately that the guys were beat up and missing their rifles. Not only did these two guys have hell to pay, but the Gunny raised hell all up and down our section of the line. He read them the riot act and interrogated other men on the perimeter, thinking one of them might have played a prank. When no one shed any light on the situation, the Gunny became irate, believing that the breech of security reflected on himself. In the meantime, I watched developments until I thought the moment was right and then took the rifles over to the staff NCO tent, which was now empty because of all of the excitement and activity. Tucking the two rifles neatly in the Gunny's bunk, I smoothed his blankets over them and returned to the Exec Pit to see what he would do next. Things eventually returned to the normal quiet of two o'clock in the morning, and Gunny Mac went back to the staff quarters. Almost needless to say, when the Gunny got back to his tent, he again went berserk upon crawling in bed with two rifles. Now thinking that the troops were trying to mess with him, he turned out all the battery enlisted men and gave them continued hell for the rest of the night. I turned in no official report on the matter but through John Eager, as an unofficial intermediary, let Major Capenas know that we were dealing with the sleeping problem in an unorthodox way. The two wayward Marines received all kinds of extra duty and were tormented by the Gunny for two weeks. No more sleep problems occurred on the lines after that.

During this first month back at Camp Carroll, an unusual event occurred. Nature, in its own way, showed us just how much we do not control. One tent had been designated as a club for the battery, and there the troops received their daily ration of two beers, when available. Located in front of the club tent stood the battery sign, which was two feet high by three feet wide and quite colorful. The base coat was fire engine red and had a 105mm howitzer painted on it as the main motif with a slogan reading, "The Best Damn Battery in Vietnam." Little plaques were tacked to the supporting legs of the sign, designating the significant places that Charlie Battery had been.

One morning we found that the bright colors had attracted a swarm of bees. They covered the sign to the point that you could not even see it. That alone would not have been so bad, but we found that anyone who came close to the club tent was being attacked by rowdy bees. Unfortunately, a fire mission came in around noon, and we could not even man the two guns adjacent to the tent because of all the stinging going on. Even the other guns had enough bee marauders that the troops were having a tough time doing their jobs. The bees were accomplishing what incoming and flying shrapnel had not been able to do; they were impairing our performance. Battalion finally had to give the mission to another battery. The bees were not going away, and something had to be resolved. After several failed attempts at ridding ourselves of the unwelcome guests, somebody came up with the idea of dressing four men in two layers of the rubberized rain suits that we rarely used and rigging headgears up with mosquito netting tucked into the neck. A red shirt was then stretched on two sticks in such a way as to create a surface nearly as wide as the sign, and honey was smeared on that. The volunteers then went up to the sign and, by holding the shirt against it, enticed the bees to transfer to the honey-coated device.

This was all observed at a distance by the other troops, now enjoying what had turned into a festive occasion and who were cheering on the progress of the operation. The four volunteers hammed it up and made quite a theatrical scene as they proceeded to take the bees toward the perimeter. Then, somehow, a bee managed to worm its way into the rain suit of one of the men, and a show really began as the Marine bounded away from the procession, tearing at his suit. Attracted by this activity, a large flight of the bees chased him as he ran toward the cheering troops. Their laughter soon turned to howls as the trailing bees found unprotected men. People were flying away from him as he made his exit, providing great comedy to those not in the immediate vicinity. Fortunately, the volunteer managed to squash the invading bee and regained some decorum as he returned to the red shirt, where the main body of bees remained. Finally, the bees were carried well outside of the perimeter and deposited in a ravine along with the shirt.

This happening was talked about with glee for months and became part of the lore of Charlie Battery alongside tales of past actions. After all, this was the only time the battery had ever been immobilized, in combat or otherwise. The comic relief of situations like this helped make life in Vietnam more bearable and was a catharsis to the daily stress. For several hours we had totally forgotten the war and, like a group of kids, had enjoyed something radically different from the business of combat.

As Christmas approached, I found myself missing the spirit of the season that I had enjoyed so much back in the real world. Life was routine and often grim as we methodically shot our fire missions and dodged sporadic incoming. The men attempted to decorate the club, but the days were filled with so many fire missions that no one really had time to get in the Christmas spirit. When Christmas Eve finally arrived, I had to accept that it would not be the same in a war that did not observe holidays. Ironically and perhaps for the first time, I saw Christmas in a much clearer perspective. It happened that I always carried a New Testament Bible that Gideons International had given to those of us who wanted them. Mine was kept in the breast pocket of my flak jacket or in the cargo pocket of my trousers. That Christmas Eve, with night falling, I pulled it out and started reading those familiar stories that told of Jesus's birth. Only in that context, amid the bleakness of the routine of war, did Christmas have meaning. The gaiety of the season, with gift giving and festivities, was not a part of this place. That night the only gift that mattered was the gift of God of himself. In the life we were living, our values had been reduced to their basic essence, and Christ's gift of himself was clearer to me at that moment than I had ever perceived before. Sitting there outside the command bunker watching an occasional flare shining in the night sky, I felt a real sense of God's presence in this ungodly place. Christmas morning dawned with a big fire mission in support of a Marine battalion engaged in heavy combat, and life went on with its constant struggle. Since that time, there have been many more Christmases, but the most meaningful ones have been whenever I purged the typical hoopla and focused on the concept of Christ in the simplicity of what his birth really meant. That night I saw and felt a genuine peace.

During this time, one thing really began to excite me. The powers that ran this war had, in their wisdom, decreed that everyone in the military who served in Vietnam was entitled to one week of rest and relaxation away from the war. Affectionately called R&R, this Shangri-La of escape could be taken in any number of exotic locations. There were places such as Bangkok, Taipei, Australia, Japan, Hawaii, and others. Among the unmarried men, the most popular destinations were Bangkok, with its fabled uninhibited females, and Australia, running a close second, with American-like females who particularly liked Marines. The stories of the girls in Bangkok were wild and grew with the telling. Married guys, however, usually opted for Hawaii if they could afford to have their wives fly over and stay for a week.

My R&R was scheduled for January, and I anxiously made all the arrangements with Jody to ensure that we would both arrive in Hawaii at the same time. The anticipation of again being with her was wonderful. Separation had made me realize just how much I loved her, and my new awareness of how fleeting life could be made the prospect of our being together that much sweeter. In many cases, wives also had their own concept of our fragile existence. Having a husband in a war zone created plenty of anxiety in and of itself, but for the first time in history this war was up close and personal because of media coverage. Most evenings, TV news footage showed the horrors of combat as it had never been shown before, and that combat was shown as quickly as the day following the fighting. Reporters covering the war had practically no restrictions on what they could portray, and the more grisly the scene, the bigger an audience it seemed to attract. It must have been a miserable time for those wives when they saw in living color just how deadly Vietnam was. The reunions of husbands and wives meeting in Hawaii would probably rank as some of the great love stories of all time if they could adequately be described in words. It was certainly like a fairy tale for those of us in Vietnam to be plucked from the nightmare of war and placed in the idyllic setting of Hawaii with the love of your life. Knowing I would soon be with Jody created an immense joy as the new year came into being and I anxiously anticipated the R&R date.

Aside from routine fire missions and occasional incoming, another noteworthy event in the life of the battery occurred before my R&R. It happened on New Year's Eve night and exemplified again how much we welcomed a break from the routine of war. This occasion was marked by an extra beer ration, and the troops really tried to get in the spirit of things. When midnight arrived, much whooping and yelling ensued, and soon hand flares were being popped. Some joker out on the perimeter threw a grenade, and soon others followed. Headquarters, hearing this melee, sounded the "attack" siren, and parachute flares came floating down, setting some tents on fire. It took the next several minutes to determine that we really were not under a ground attack and the next thirty getting fires put out and everyone back under control. These guys were always hungry for anything distracting us from the seriousness of our situation on the DMZ. Of course Battalion held an investigation but seemed to get nowhere in pinning any blame. At the battery level no one, including all the staff, wanted to put a damper on the spontaneous enthusiasm that had erupted, and for some reason no one knew anything about anything.

11

R&R

The day finally arrived for me to leave for R&R, a departure time that was actually two days earlier than the scheduled flight out of Da Nang. This early departure supposedly allowed plenty of time to catch one of the aircraft flying out of Dong Ha to Da Nang. The availability of rides varied according to resupply needs and whatever military movements happened to be taking place on the DMZ. Therefore, extra days were given to those men who were stationed west of Dong Ha, especially if they were going to Hawaii to meet spouses who had made airline reservations. I imagine the brass realized that if a lot of wives ended up in Hawaii with no husband to meet, then many members of Congress might be making inquiries as to why. Consequently, R&R trips to Hawaii were particularly coveted because of the extra days allowed for R&R.

On departure day I caught the first convoy leaving for Dong Ha. I was nervous as a cat all the way. The recollection of previous ambushes and the dread of hitting a mine dominated my thoughts. I was much too close to escaping the insanity of war to have something happen now. There were plenty of tales about guys getting zapped on the way home or when leaving for R&R, but in reality that probably happened very little. Nevertheless, those were the stories that usually hung around. When the truck rolled through the wire at Dong Ha, a rush of relief poured over me on realizing that I had cleared the first hurdle toward my anticipated reunion.

Wasting no time, I hitched a ride over to the airstrip and knew as soon as I walked up to the shack serving as a terminal that I had a potential problem. There were fifty or sixty people already waiting to catch flights, and they were sprawled all over the place as if they had been waiting for some time. Nothing could be done but put my name on the list and hope. I breathed a sigh of relief on finding out that going to Hawaii carried a priority rating; that moved me up to nineteenth on the list. The others ahead of me were either headed to Hawaii or had some other type of high priority. Five or six hours later, at two o'clock, the anxiety returned when not a single aircraft had left for Da Nang. I had thought there would be more traffic than this! To make the wait more bearable, I found a shady spot near a supply shack but still sweated it both figuratively and actually. As the afternoon wore on, I noticed a Marine Sea Knight helicopter approaching from the west that seemed to be headed toward our strip. My hopes soared because I knew it had the capacity to pick up at least twenty people, and I immediately went over to the air control hut. There I learned that indeed it was coming in to pick up passengers for Da Nang, and I was told to get in line by order of priority. When the chopper came to a stop, the terminal crew started calling off several numbers at a time. When that group was on they would then call a few more. I began to pray real hard that the Lord would see fit to let me on that flight, making sure he understood how important it was that I get to Da Nang and soon. When they called number eighteen, I just knew that I had it made, and then they announced there would be no one else allowed on the flight. I talked to the sergeant in charge and did everything I could to try to get on that helicopter, all to no avail. Finally, somebody found an air control officer who outranked me and brought him over to make it clear that I was not getting on that plane.

With a sick feeling, I fumbled my way back over to the supply shack and flopped down. Getting out of here was really important, and now my imagination began to conjure up thoughts about the consequences of having to wait around all day tomorrow and then still not being able to catch a plane. The flights today sure had not gone very fast, and with all my fuming and fretting, it was hard to remember a time when I had coveted something so much. So I felt a great deal of relief a half an hour later when a Caribou transport plane came in and picked fourteen of us up. The next morning at breakfast in Da Nang, my emotions concerning the trip took another swing on hearing about a helicopter that had crashed into a mountain after leaving Dong Ha. From everything I could pick up about the incident, it seemed to be the chopper that I had prayed so hard to board. Later that night at supper, I heard that it was thought to have been hit by some kind of ground-fired rocket and that there had been no survivors. I never had a chance to confirm the details, but the probability that this was the ride I had missed hauntingly reminded me that we mortals sometimes do not know what we really ought to be praying for. Fortunately for me, God does not jump through hoops just because we entreat him passionately.

Da Nang differed so much from where I had been. From the primitive world of the DMZ, I had returned to a city, and the transformation was even more pronounced on reaching the R&R Center. For the first time in seven months, I walked into a real building with concrete block walls, doors, and, miracle of miracles, air conditioning. There were indoor showers with hot water and real flush toilets. The sweetest things, though, were the clean white sheets on beds with innerspring mattresses. That night I showered for thirty minutes, collapsed in bed at eight o'clock, and slept until nine the next morning. It was a deep sleep that leaves you feeling like you just went to bed when you eventually wake up. As I became aware of my surroundings, I was rejuvenated by the knowledge that the next morning I would fly out of here to my lovely wife.

The R&R Center had been created as a little oasis in the war. Much like a giant post exchange, it had as much merchandise as any department store back in the States. Everything imaginable could be found, including cameras, stereos, jewelry, clothes, and you name it, all at very reasonable prices. Best of all, there was a grill serving cheeseburgers, milkshakes, and other "American" fare. I think I decided that day that a cheeseburger with fries and a milkshake was my favorite meal of all time. By three o'clock I had eaten four times, ordering the same thing at each sitting.

In between meals, I carefully shopped for Jody, finally settling on two rings. One was a pearl with little diamonds on each side, and the other was a star sapphire. I was very pleased with the purchases and truly looked on them as gifts of love as my heart soared at the thought of being with Jody again. Finally, after spending the day trying to feel Americanized, I went back to the officers' quarters to nap and crashed. Earlier, I had run into some old friends from Basic School who had invited me to dinner, and I wanted to be fresh for the evening.

They showed up about six thirty and took great delight in waking me from a deep sleep. After quickly showering, I dressed in summer khakis for the first time in over half a year, there having been nothing but unpressed utility uniforms in most places on the DMZ. Everything seemed so unreal, and here I was going out with friends in a world that felt almost like the States. My buddies knew the ropes on getting around, and they soon secured a ride in some kind of R&R shuttle van. Within a few blocks, we were traveling through rundown areas consisting of shanties and dilapidated shops, but as we progressed through the city, the homes got larger until we were in what obviously had been a prosperous neighborhood, with big white houses and tropical gardens. An unreal quality permeated the evening as we sped through a shadowy world that was in total contrast to the Vietnam I had known to this point. Obviously, there had been some wealthy Vietnamese before the war. I could only wonder whether they still were well-to-do.

We continued out of this sector and soon arrived at another military compound. We pulled up to a one-story building that could easily have been in urban California, and I gazed in amazement at the Stone Elephant, a nightclub that had been built by either the Navy or Seabees. Impressed as I was with the outside, I experienced culture shock when I went in. For a guy fresh from a long stint on the DMZ, this was almost an unfathomable transition. We could have been in any classy restaurant stateside. Nothing but the finest materials had been used in its construction, and the style was as American as you could imagine. On entering, we were greeted by a madhouse of activity, complete with live entertainment in a large bar area to the right. Even more amazing was the sight of American women throughout the club. On the DMZ where I had been, we had not seen any American women at all, military or otherwise. All of these women were well attended, and each had her own individual entourage of admiring guys. It staggered me how different this Vietnam was from the one I was accustomed to. Where a dry tent had been a luxury on the DMZ, this fantastic creation by the Seabees seemed almost bizarre. In fact, this abstract scene was almost like an affront to those back on the DMZ, who were just trying to make it from day to day in one piece. After several drinks at the bar, my amazement faded, and I had reunions with other old friends from Basic School and even one from my alma mater at Sewanee. Later, my group made its way into the dining room, and there we found a floor show in progress amid tables covered with white cloths. Not a jungle utility uniform was in sight, only crisp khakis and even some Navy guys in their winter blues. We were then given menus and wine lists for perusal, and in time a superb dinner arrived on china plates. I could think only of how much we take for granted.

We returned to the R&R compound after an evening of total contrast to the world I had been living in. This switch from the insanity of the war on the DMZ, only an hour away by helicopter, to a civilized and sophisticated setting impacted my sensibilities in such a way that I have rarely accepted anything at face value since. I had been plucked from a life-and-death struggle and brought into a manufactured environment radically different from the Vietnam I knew. The ephemeral nature of life and the rapidity with which circumstances change impressed me as never before. In control one instant, wiped out the next, we all live a charade. The most serious of endeavors are often contrived, be it war, business, patriotism, or whatever and can change at the whim of man, fate, or God. It hit me that most things in this world lack endurance and that today is all we really have. Very little seemed rational anymore, and rationality itself was suspect. Having lived with radically changing situations for months, I recognized that they are no more than your current set of circumstances. Nothing is forever, and change is reality, for better or worse. In this new awareness, the only stability I could grasp was my faith in God and the belief that his universe transcended the chaos and fantasy of this world. He alone was always there and the same whenever I chanced to acknowledge him.

The morning to leave for Hawaii finally came, and I joined a sea of eager faces gathering at the air terminal. Everyone was in short-sleeve khakis, looking all spic and span. These guys were going to meet their wives and sweethearts in a matter of hours, and the joy was hardly concealed by even the toughest of Marines. The whole group reminded me of a bunch of college guys waiting to board a bus for a visit to a neighboring school for women. Parked next to the terminal, a Braniff airliner waited while we rapidly checked out through the counter for departure. This civilian aircraft seemed so out of place in our military world. No one could board fast enough as smiling stewardesses greeted us at the top of the stairs. Few of the troops had seen American women in the last six months, and they looked like angels beckoning us aboard. Those stewardesses must have felt like absolutely raving beauties as eighty sets of eyes followed their every move. Like a ship of fools, most of the guys made idiots of themselves, inventing reasons to have conversations with these female apparitions from home. When they passed out drinks, the already loud hum of animated conversation rose to a roar. For now, at least, there was little introspection about what had been left behind. The reality of what we were leaving was best put out of consciousness because the thought of our eventual return could be overwhelming. Today, only the expectation of what awaited us in Hawaii existed. We stopped on the island of Guam for refueling, but no one even wanted to get off because we were so impatient to be on with the journey. The flight to Guam had been ebullient, but on leaving the island, many fell asleep as the booze took its toll. Sensibly, the stewardesses were no longer passing it out. I guess they had made enough trips to know that a planeload of drunken Marines was not the best thing to unload in Hawaii.

About an hour out of Honolulu, everyone started getting fidgety. With several hundred miles left to go, you would have thought by the way we were acting that the runway was in sight. Previously snoozing Marines now began preening and primping like a bunch of high school girls. Uniforms were adjusted, hair was combed, and the aroma of cologne soon filled the cabin. Then for the next thirty minutes, with seats in the upright landing position, there was enough craning to look out the windows that it was a wonder half the passengers did not have neck cramps. I know many of the same thoughts ran through all of our minds. Had our wife or girlfriend made her flight, and would she really be there? Would she look as good as she always had? Would things really be the same? These thoughts went unspoken, but the serious expressions and anxious faces indicated that a great deal of contemplation was going on. Finally, the pilot came on over the intercom and, just like in the States, informed us of the temperature and weather conditions in Honolulu. Smiles began to break out, and soon everyone was talking at once. We were really finally here, and Vietnam with all its dangers had ceased to exist for a while.

The tires hit the runway with a squeal, and all faces were glued to the windows. Not until the door opened did anybody leave the windows; each person was straining to see whether his girl was in the waiting crowd. Talk about a fast unloading; we must have set a record getting off that plane. We were promptly herded by ground personnel to a staging area in the terminal where an officer recited the dos and don'ts for our stay in Hawaii. Literature was also passed out, but no one absorbed any of this because our minds were on the other side of those gates where the women were. Finally, after the ritual recitations to incoming R&R troops, the doors opened, and we poured into a large barnlike area where, jammed behind a low wall, rows of smiling, beautiful female faces peered intently at us as we gawked back at them. Squeals started sounding as the women began recognizing their mates, and soon it was a madhouse of hugs and kisses as the two crowds merged. When I finally zeroed in on Jody, she was wildly waving because she had spotted me first. I rushed to her with an overwhelming surge of emotion, and after the initial embrace, all we could do was hold each other and smile. Words would not do; we just grinned at each other like simpletons.

After boarding a bus, with still only the minimum of talking, we could only look into each other's eyes with pure joy. To be rejoined after seven months of separation with the real threat of never seeing each other again created a high that was indescribable. Life cannot be sweeter than it was at that moment. After several minutes we were finally able to have some sort of comprehensive conversation and began babbling like two kids at recess. Talking at the same time, I asked question after question, and Jody jabbered back so fast that we finally sat back gasping for air. Our main topic concerned our daughter, Cathy, now a year old, and I could not hear enough. After what seemed like the shortest of rides, we arrived at the Ilikai, supposedly the finest hotel in Hawaii. Thus began one of the most bittersweet weeks of my life. For all the joy we found over those next days, nagging reality constantly reminded me that we would soon have to part again. Life was exquisite during this time, and we spent one of the most caring interludes that we have ever experienced. Constant jubilation came from just being near each other, and the Hawaiian paradise we were in was totally eclipsed by the overwhelming strength of love radiating from our togetherness.

The highlights of our days were simply walks on the beach and the mai tais that we sipped around the pool. Companionship counted the most. We did, however, decide to see a little of Hawaii, so one day we rented a baby blue Mustang convertible and drove completely around the island. Gorgeous emerald green mountains rose in riblike fashion to sheer heights of splendor, and we watched the giant waves on North Beach as surfers rode their boards with catlike grace. Mostly, though, we exulted in just being together. As the end of the day neared, we wound through pineapple fields and managed to arrive at Pearl Harbor just in time for the sunset lowering of the flag on the *Arizona* memorial. The sobering awareness of that disaster was too heavy for our emotional state, and we silently hurried back to the gaiety of the Ilikai.

One of our other excursions was to a shopping mall where I had fun picking out clothes for Jody and Cathy. In particular, I thought our selections of matching muumuus were wonderful and visualized the two of them wearing them back home in the States. Other activities included a couple of luaus on the beach at the hotel and dinner at a night spot where Don Ho was entertaining. Still, out greatest enjoyment was in just being secluded together.

I particularly appreciated the creature comforts of civilization and, for a while, found the news on TV to be refreshing after no TV at all. It interested me to see how Vietnam was being portrayed by the media at home. This was well and good until the day before I was to leave when the news started covering a new spate of activity in the province of Quang Tri, where I would soon return. That activity, in fact, proved to be the preliminary moves leading up to the Tet Offensive, which began shortly after I got back. Watching all that, I had the foreboding feeling that things might be even worse on my return than they had been before. Coldness settled into my stomach, and I turned off the TV as our parting rushed toward us.

Back in the States when separation had been necessary, good-byes had never been easy. This was much worse, however. The reality of death and an awareness of the carnage of war had been firmly fixed in my mind, and I knew the very real dangers awaiting me. My time with Jody reminded me of how much I really loved her, and the thought that I might never see her again was unbearable. I did not share those thoughts and tried to shield her from how dangerous it was on the DMZ. I suspected she was frightened enough without any revelations from me. Besides, somewhere along in my journey through life I had decided that thinking about things was not the same as verbalizing them. A thought expressed in words gave credibility to the idea, and I sure did not need any more reality in a world too real already.

Our parting was as miserable as could be expected, and words cannot express the sick and helpless feelings that overwhelmed us. The wrenching agony of that departure left an indelible effect on Jody, and I found out much later that she cried for the next five hours on her flight back to the States. Resentments over our separation in general and Vietnam in particular crystallized in such a way that Jody developed a deep resentment of the Marine Corps and the separations it had caused. For years to come, the pride I felt in having served with the Marines could be discussed only discreetly whenever Jody was around.

Tet

I arrived back in Vietnam with no happiness of homecoming. Tension now filled the air and pervaded the attitudes of everyone with whom I came in contact. Activity was definitely up, and Khe Sanh had become a priority of the high command. Later it would be learned that Westmoreland was gearing up for what he thought would be a major thrust by the NVA on the western end of the DMZ. It took me a few days of hopping rides to make it back to Camp Carroll, and everywhere things buzzed with a sense that something big was about to happen because of massive troop movements that had been detected along the DMZ. North of Route 9, from Dong Ha westward, all kinds of activity had been reported.

On reaching Camp Carroll I found things in a flurry. Because the camp was the main artillery base on the DMZ and because of its support role for all combat units, the personnel there were particularly well informed as to movements of both friendly and enemy forces. Hearing their solid intelligence really spiked my attention, especially on finding out that the 320th Division of NVA regulars was directly to our northwest and within striking distance. It was one thing to have small enemy units operating in the area but altogether different to have one of the NVA's top divisions lurking nearby.

Our preparations for a possible attack consisted of no more than beefing up the perimeter defenses and additional clearing of grassy areas outside the perimeter. Inside the lines, Colonel Opfar, the battalion CO, was even on a tear to make the gun positions as barracks-like as possible. No new trenches or protective areas were being constructed, and the tents and living quarters were being squared away to look like something you would see stateside. After a few discreet inquiries, I found out that we were expecting visits from congressmen who would, of course, be accompanied by the military hierarchy. It irked the dickens out of me that these measures were being taken while we were getting hit with incoming on a fairly regular basis now. It did not make sense to me to be prettying up the area when we were in an authentic combat zone.

During this time we received some news that caused just about everyone to reexamine why we were here. A report came over the troop news broadcast from Saigon that the U.S. ship *Pueblo* had been attacked and captured by the North Koreans. As the news trickled out, it became apparent that the ship's crew had made no effort to resist and had given up without a fight. What a bummer this was to the guys up here who were routinely shelled. It seemed to us that the *Pueblo*'s crew had merely rolled over and surrendered at the first threat. This created a real letdown among our troops, who were sucking it up every day and facing death on a regular basis. The *Pueblo*'s apparent lack of action generated endless discussion, with bitter reactions toward the ship's captain for what most considered cowardice in the face of the enemy. Later information, available after we had returned to the States, would reveal somewhat more mitigating circumstances than we were aware of then, but at the time all we had was what we were hearing from the media. Endless grist for the conversation mill came from that incident, but it also had a positive aspect in that it got our minds off of the defensive posture we found ourselves in at Camp Carroll. Not so positive, though, was the growing realization that not everyone was prepared to make the type of sacrifices we were making daily in Vietnam. We had seen the phenomenon of peace demonstrations back stateside and shrugged it off, but to have a military unit seemingly disgrace America so blatantly really got to us.

Conversations continued in that vein as we approached the Vietnamese lunar new year, otherwise known as Tet. For the Vietnamese this was supposed to be a big deal, much like our Christmas and New Year all rolled into one. We kind of expected that, because of Tet's significance to both North and South Vietnam, military activity would slack off for that holiday period. How wrong we were.

The eve of Tet, which fell on January 30, was like any other of our recent days at Camp Carroll. Various units went about their tasks of sprucing up the position, just like we were preparing for a stateside inspection. Plenty of complaining came from that, and talk continued concerning the surrender of the *Pueblo*. Maybe Colonel Opfar realized that morale might not be up to par in this environment, so, for whatever reason, he sent out the word that everyone could have an extra ration of beer for the evening. This was greeted with enthusiasm, and parties were planned all over Camp Carroll by various units. Of course, there could not be too much of a party because an extra beer ration consisted of only one extra can, bringing the total number of beers to three cans per man. Nevertheless, the concept lifted everyone's spirits and served the purpose for which it was probably intended. Charlie Battery, with much fanfare, organized a "Beer Bust" at the tent that had been dubbed "Club Charlie." Festivities began with the officers joining the men for the initial beer and then leaving the troops to themselves so they could relax and finish the evening. Gunny Mac, who I am sure managed to get more than the allotted number of beers, loosened up and, I later heard, was quite the clown, giving the men a welcome reprieve from his normal harassment.

By ten o'clock that evening every beer was gone, and only those who had drawn duty remained up. I decided to check the lines personally so the others could unwind. Even Division seemed to be doing its part for the occasion because there were no H&I fire missions assigned for the evening. That meant the gun crews could get some uninterrupted sleep unless an infantry unit needed supporting fire. After my first round of checking the lines and finding the men reasonably alert, I started back to the Exec Pit to enjoy a cigar I had received in the day's mail. Peeling the wrapper away, I crossed the road by Gun Four and happened to glance toward the north. It was natural to look in that direction because incoming often came from the DMZ. At that moment the Tet Offensive began for us at Camp Carroll. The match for my cigar was never struck because I saw a series of flashes in the north. My thought was, "Surely, that can't be what I think it is with the Tet holiday and all." Then the telltale glow of rockets could be seen arcing toward us, and I knew incoming was on the way. I immediately yelled, "Incoming," as others did the same, and diving for the nearest trench, I cursed the NVA for mess-ing up what was supposed to be a good night. We probably took about twenty rounds of incoming in that first volley, and "Pistol Pete," a 75mm Pack Howitzer up on Dong Ha Mountain, began cranking out intermittent shots as well. I do not know how many rounds we took that night, but it lasted for about two hours. We turned the batteries to the north and fired at the coordinates of known and suspected artillery positions. The troops just got on the guns in the midst of the incoming and, like any routine fire mission, calmly started pumping out counter-battery fire. Battalion gave us new coordinates as well, and we fired at will from the battery. We kept that up until the incoming eventually stopped. A number of men were killed or wounded around Camp Carroll that night, but Charlie Battery took no direct hits. Three men servicing Gun Two did receive minor shrapnel wounds, however. In spite of our lack of casualties, a strange feeling came over us as we sensed that this heavy incoming was a signal that the war was changing. There was certainly no panic or undue nervousness, but a calm awareness pervaded the thoughts of even the gunners out on the firing line. The following morning, those feelings were confirmed by a steady stream of reports coming in that told of attacks launched all over Vietnam. At Camp Carroll the night's activity initiated a series of increased rocket and artillery attacks, which the NVA would sustain on a daily basis for almost a month. Our Tet was not as fierce as it was in many other places to the south, but it was a period of intense personal stress marked by occasional casualties and plenty of strained nerves.

For the next month, our war could be compared with the trench warfare of World War I. It was around-the-clock incoming with much time spent in the trenches and bunkers. Those who had not been out in the field with infantry units found this to be particularly difficult. Having already been through the intense danger of field combat, I kept things in perspective, as did others who had been in more intense settings. Con Thien, for instance, had been a living hell. Tet at Camp Carroll was no picnic, but again, everything in life is relative.

The artillery and rockets from the north were bad enough, but psychologically Pistol Pete gave us the most grief. It was tedious enough to have only a split second to hurl yourself toward a trench after hearing the guns on the DMZ, but Pistol Pete on Dong Ha Mountain would crank off rounds at the most inconvenient of times. He particularly had a way of sneaking in a shot in the aftermath of the confusion resulting from other incoming. Evidently, he had line-of-sight visibility, allowing him to know right when we were most vulnerable. This resulted in people avoiding the open or even being above ground. We particularly steered away from noisy places such as gun positions because we could not hear the enemy fire and have that necessary moment to dive for cover. The chow tent became equally unpopular because of all the noise associated with feeding large numbers of troops. This attitude concerning the dining tent did not take long to develop; it happened in an instant in the week following Tet.

It chanced that it was Charlie Battery's turn to go through the chow line in the midst of all the talk and chatter characteristic of that gathering. Several of our guys had been served, and others were filling their trays when Pistol Pete decided to say hello. With all the racket, no one heard the shot coming that landed directly in the meat platter. One of Charlie's men was taking a helping from a cook at the time. It was a bloody mess of meat and Marines as the chow hall exploded in chaos. Two cooks, the Marine from Charlie, and a straggler from another battery were killed outright, and a number of others were wounded. No one else from Charlie ate that day. Pistol Pete must have figured out from the commotion that he had found a significant target because for days after that it seemed as if he deliberately fired at meal times, and for some reason our men decided that they liked C rations just fine back in the confines of Charlie Battery's position. If Pistol Pete was going to be ringing the dinner bell at the mess tent, there were not going to be many diners.

Life at Camp Carroll was bearable, but it was during this period that I experienced some of my most emotionally poignant moments. They were occasioned by two separate incidents of incoming that came directly into our area. One day while I was crossing through the battery on some errand, the cry of "Incoming" and the wail of sirens announced that enemy rounds were on the way. I immediately dove for a trench, thinking about yesterday's havoc in the 155mm battery next to us. The NVA had marched their 122mm rockets right across Camp Carroll, and a full volley had landed on Kilo Battery. It was the most devastating artillery attack I had witnessed since arriving in country. The NVA had placed time-delay fuses on some of their rockets, allowing them to penetrate well into the target before exploding. Primarily designed to be effective on bunkers, these rockets had torn up one of the 155mm self-propelled guns on hitting its enclosed breech. The split-second delay caused the rocket to explode from within, and the turret erupted in a mass of tangled metal. Fortunately, no one had been manning the gun, and casualties were light. A few other rockets hit in open spaces, creating craters big enough to put a jeep in. Now lying in the trench, I had racing through my mind thoughts of just how vulnerable we were to that kind of incoming.

In that mind-set, I heard a round impact behind me outside of the perimeter. An earlier one had already landed on the other side of Camp Carroll and just inside the lines. I realized we had been bracketed and that the NVA were adjusting their range on a target that seemed to be one of the batteries in our cluster. As I was lying on the bottom of the deep trench with my face pressed against the bare dirt, it occurred to me that this was not much different from being in an open grave. Another shell landed, and this time it was much closer. In that moment, a feeling came over me that I was surely about to die in one of the next volleys. Their adjustments were just too precise, and our battery seemed to be the center of a classic artillery bracket. The perceived awareness of approaching death did not panic me, but a cold, matter-of-fact realization came over me that my life was about to end.

My thoughts left the stillness of the trench as everyone waited in silence for the next rounds to fall. In the eerie quietness, my mind focused on how much I was going to miss Jody, and profound sadness filled me at the thought. Five rounds came screaming right over our heads and landed about a hundred meters beyond our position. Another adjustment would surely put the rounds right on top of us. I just lay there expecting the end. Moments passed, and I numbly waited, knowing nothing could be done but accept the inevitable. Another minute passed and no rounds. More seconds and nothing. Could it be that it was over? Finally, I realized that they were finished, and I came back from a place I had never been. My life had been given back. There was no elation, only a dull relief mingled with numbness.

I spent the rest of the day in a mentally detached state. Not only had I looked death in the face but also I had had time to sense the loss that comes with it. Unlike combat action, where activity kept you pumped, I could only wait and contemplate the end of existence on this earth. On one other occasion about a week later, I was caught in the trenches in almost the same situation. My thought process functioned in exactly the same way in that I believed I was about to die. I had previously had closer brushes with death and would have several more really dangerous close calls, but on those two occasions I had had the time to focus on the end of my life. Genuine helplessness is a humbling experience, and the reality of how little we control continues to influence my attitude.

The months of January and February blended into a stream of endless days with Charlie Battery firing thousands of rounds in support missions. We took systematic incoming during this period, but that became a rather routine event in itself. Casualties were not heavy, probably because of the series of trenches and bunkers that had been prepared throughout Camp Carroll. During this time, one of the few diversions from the absorption in our around-the-clock firing was my notion of a little garden. I had asked my parents to send me a little tray of radish seeds that had been preplanted in some type of prepared soil. All that needed to be done was add water, and the radishes would grow. When they arrived, I carefully did everything just as the directions instructed and placed the tray on sandbags just outside the entrance to the Exec Pit. I anxiously awaited the new growth like an expectant father and was elated when the first shoots finally came up. The whole Exec Pit crew caught the spirit, probably a result of seeing life nurtured as opposed to our daily missions of destruction. Carefully checking the "garden" several times a day, we noted each new leaf and marked off on a stick the height of the plants as they grew. There was a mystique in tending the would-be garden. In this dreary period of overcast drudgery, the renewal of life represented by the growing plants had created an uplifting effect.

Throughout this time of continuous work, one diversion definitely was not welcome. Convoys had to be run periodically to Dong Ha for resupply, and different batteries rotated security for the trips. Because the NVA periodically mined the road from Camp Carroll to Dong Ha, it was common for vehicles to be disabled on these runs. On those occasions when I drew the duty, I always felt extreme apprehension, an old emotion originating from the convoy runs we had made from the Rockpile to Ca Lu. Convoys exposed us and were dangerous; I hated them. On more than one occasion, vehicles in front of me hit mines, causing delays and much anxiety. Those moments of being stopped dead in your tracks while wondering what was happening up front were not enjoyable. Fortunately for me, the convoys I accompanied were never ambushed on those occasions.

Life at Camp Carroll continued with the pressure of around-the-clock firing, resulting in fatigue and strained nerves. That stress particularly affected the guys who had only recently arrived in country because they were experiencing a radical transition from a stateside environment into a society of men who tended toward the callous. The conditions at Camp Carroll were more like the trench warfare of World War I and totally different from anything the newcomers had ever seen. There is an inclination to miss home under even normal circumstances, but for some the initial shock of the DMZ was too much. At Camp Carroll there had been several cases of new guys deliberately injuring themselves so that they could be medevaced. Only recently, men from other batteries had on two occasions shot themselves in the foot. We talked of those incidents with scorn and with the smugness of never having had such a thing happen in Charlie Battery. Then it happened to us. A Marine who had been with us for only two days went into the privy and shot himself in the foot. Charlie Battery, with its immense sense of pride and tradition, was incensed. From the lowest ammo humper to the officers, we were indignant. To top it all off, the guy tried to claim it was an accident, but we noted that, unless he happened to be a contortionist, he could hardly turn around in the privy, much less shoot himself in the foot. Our feelings of disgust gradually changed, however, and were replaced by a greater sensitivity to the new guys. Although no one in Charlie Battery wanted to be associated with anything resembling cowardice, I think most of the men came to realize that there were some things we could do, or not do, to lessen the chance of pushing a new guy over the edge.

The trench warfare environment ground on at Camp Carroll and came complete with very cold weather, something I had never imagined back stateside. Monsoon season arrived in the mountains in full force, and although we did not have freezing temperatures, it was a wet and bitter cold. We wore field jackets during the day and slept in snug, warm, mummy-style sleeping bags at night, never shaking the chill. Almost needless to say, the open-air showers rarely saw use, and we learned to live with extremely smelly people. During this period, circumstances took a decidedly different course for Charlie Battery.

One cold, gray morning, all the COs and XOs of the various units were told to report to battalion headquarters at eight in the morning. On walking into the bunker, I immediately sensed that something was up. Captain Schwerer and I found chairs near the rear while noting that the regimental colonel from Dong Ha was in attendance. We rarely saw full colonels out this way, and when they showed up it usually meant something big in the works. After passing around real coffee, not the C ration kind, Colonel Opfar had a few words and turned the meeting over to the regimental CO, Colonel Edwin S. Schick Jr. He briefed us on the Tet Offensive and then got to the heart of the matter. It seemed that General Raymond G. Davis (who had recently taken over as commander of our 3d Marine Division) had decided to make some changes. General Davis was a no-nonsense, hard-charging veteran of World War II whose credentials included the Medal of Honor. He maintained a reputation for efficiency, and many regarded him as one of the best generals in the Corps. After a study of recent operations on the DMZ, he had concluded that our forces needed to be more mobile and less tied to the base camps, believing that a better strategy would entail moving infantry and artillery units around more. That would make it more difficult for the NVA to know where we were and give us more flexibility in our own fire support as well. In theory, the enemy would be kept guessing and, through that process, would be limited in their freedom of movement.

Khe Sanh, on the western end of the DMZ, had been effectively under siege since January 20, and we were told that when the monsoon season dissipated that there would be a campaign to relieve those forces. The closest Marine-held strongpoint was Ca Lu on Route 9, and any relief effort would have to originate from there. I had been on many convoy runs to Ca Lu in my early days at the Rockpile and knew it well. The colonel indicated that it would be beefed up and artillery moved in to support the upcoming operation. As the meeting broke up, Major

Capenas called Captain Schwerer and me over to his office where he informed us that Charlie Battery would be the first artillery unit sent to Ca Lu. Division obviously was taking a major interest in this operation because we were even being provided with a small bulldozer and given two weeks to prepare the position before the guns actually arrived. Captain Schwerer and Major Capenas, after some discussion, decided that I would be sent along with eight men and Gunny Mac to oversee preparations. An infantry battalion already manned the perimeter there, and we would be free to set things up as we saw fit. When our guns arrived later, the parapets and bunkers would already be in place.

Leaving the major's office, I thought to myself how filled with irony life was. After spending seven months in the field with the infantry, much longer than typical for an artillery officer, I was headed back into the thick of it. Ca Lu, being the nearest outpost to Khe Sanh on Route 9, would certainly draw the attention of the North Vietnamese. Its strategic position as the only relief approach by land made it important to anyone concerned with the siege of Khe Sanh. I had been in country about nine months, and the realization that we were about to be sitting adjacent to several NVA divisions surrounding Khe Sanh sobered me considerably. Having seen the tenacity of the North Vietnamese regulars at Con Thien, I was greatly concerned about their proximity to Ca Lu.

Even more ironic than being thrust back into a really dangerous area was the fact that most men in Vietnam would never really see combat at such an intense level. They were in such places as Da Nang or Saigon and lived in a totally different world. It just did not seem right for some people to get all the breaks. We "tough Marines," however, were not supposed to be concerned with such trivialities as safety, so I sucked it up and focused on the job at hand. After all, I was the brilliant guy who had been afraid the war was going to end before I could participate and the one who had volunteered for FO duty with an outfit likely to see action.

13

Ca Lu

As the morning convoy left Camp Carroll for Ca Lu, the countryside looked considerably more springlike than the bleak monsoon winter we had been experiencing. Back up the road at Camp Carroll, perched on its bald hill, my surroundings had principally consisted of trenches, bunkers, and sandbags, with little vegetation. Everything inside the perimeter was so congested that hardly anything grew in what was either the mud or dust, depending on the season. Outside of the perimeter, everything had been cut back for several hundred feet to allow clear fields of fire, and that barren expanse removed us from the natural foliage and wildlife of the area. Even birds were rarely heard because of the ongoing artillery missions being fired. Riding down the road from Camp Carroll that morning, I was pleased to see trees and birds again. Life does go on, and being reminded of that helped a great deal. An uplifting mood buoyed us until we began approaching the Rockpile. Here again, that otherworldly foreboding of overhanging mountains with their mysterious jungles began to loom around us. I again had the ominous sense that unfriendly eyes watched, and the scalp at the back of my head tingled as we crept westward along narrow Route 9. Jungle reached out from the left, and for a way the river ran on our right. The scenery was beautiful, but there remained what seemed to be an almost physical presence, sinister in nature. Finally, rounding a bend in the valley road, we saw, imposing as ever, the fortresslike Rockpile looming upward in the middle of the valley surrounded by mountains. Even though I had been away for months, the incredibly stirring spirit of the place remained as strong as ever. Those of us who had served here with 3/3 last summer were on full mental alert. Too much had happened for us to feel comfortable in these surroundings loaded with such traumatic memories.

We paused briefly at the Rockpile base camp to confer with the infantry battalion because they would be the closest help available if we were ambushed. Soon moving again down Route 9 between overhanging mountains, we passed by the sites of the big ambushes from last summer, with each curve and rock seeming to hold a memory for me. Here was the place where the CP group was ambushed. There was the rock that Corporal Olivari and I had jumped behind when the ambush began. It had been the only thing separating us from the NVA soldiers in the ditch on the other side. I reached down and felt the piece of shrapnel still remaining in my left hand from that encounter and remembered Major Harrington lying in the road. The memory made me wonder how he had fared after being medevaced.

So many of the early players were gone now. That was the thing about Vietnam. The cast changed constantly because of KIAs, medevacs, or the unique feature in this war of people constantly rotating after thirteen months in country. We rarely heard the outcome of those who were seriously wounded and corresponded infrequently with those who had returned to the States. The outfit that a Marine finished with in 'Nam bore little resemblance, personnelwise, to the unit he began with. This was even more so with field artillery because those men often began their tours attached to the infantry and then rotated to the battery several months later. So for me this return to a familiar place, while holding many memories, had a whole new set of faces to go with it.

Not only were those things different but also there was a sense of change in the air. The past was real, but the coming activities promised a new measure of assertiveness, something that had not been apparent before. Khe Sanh needed relief, and the powers that be seemed intent on doing something positive. I, of course, had no idea how this venture would unfold, but clearly we were taking a new, more aggressive posture on the DMZ. My experience had been that we mostly waited for the NVA to come to us, the notable exception having been the three-battalion sweep around Con Thien back in the fall. Now plans were afoot to reopen Route 9 all the way to Laos.

General Davis continued to make it clear that Marines were going to become much more mobile than they had been and that the 105mm batteries would be placed much closer to field operations. This meant batteries would be flown in by helicopter and positioned to give the roving infantry quick and direct assistance. There would be less emphasis on base camps such as those at Camp Carroll and the Rockpile. Until those operations began, however, we would make preparations at Ca Lu. With the large numbers of the NVA between us and Khe Sanh, I could only wonder how we would be affected. Ca Lu was only twelve miles from Khe Sanh, a distance no farther than most people drive to work in America each morning, and because it was the obvious point of any relief effort, I did not envision the NVA sitting idly around while we beefed up the position.

When the convoy rolled into Ca Lu, it was apparent that things were happening with significantly more activity than I had ever seen in my trips there last summer. Pulling off the road to the left onto a flat knoll, we took in the panorama. Ca Lu was about twenty miles below the DMZ proper at the intersection of two valleys, one valley running back north to the Rockpile from where we had just come and the other, the Ba Long valley, running east-west from the Quang Tri coastal area all the way to Khe Sanh. Mountains formed a giant amphitheater at this intersection, and a large hill in the center was crowned by the French fort from the French Indochina war. The fort was imposing and prominent with stark concrete parapets overlooking the three approaches to the intersection. The diameter of the amphitheater formed by the mountain crests varied from two to three miles across. Eventually Ca Lu's perimeter would have a diameter of about a quarter of a mile by the time Khe Sanh was actually relieved. Later, Ca Lu became part of a major base called Vandegrift Combat Base and encompassed a huge area.

We unloaded the truck, and I asked directions to the command post. On learning that it was on the hill in the old fort, I hiked up a steep path through tall elephant grass to find the CO. With its austere concrete construction, the fort reminded me of a screen set from a French foreign legion film. In my meeting with the CO, he pointed out where he wanted the battery placed, which happened to be where we were already parked. That pleased me because it would be easy to set up the guns there in a classic circular formation. Another positive was that to the right of this area sat a hut that had been built by South Vietnamese workers for some previous Marine unit. It rested on stilts, had a thatched grass roof, and would make a great headquarters. Barbed wire encompassed Ca Lu's perimeter, and the terrain sloped off gently to a stream. I did not like the nearness of the stream, however, because its high banks could provide cover for an NVA attack. Finally, the CO pointed out that a small bull-dozer had been left by the thatched hooch for our use, and he further suggested that we make haste getting our work done because he expected the activity to draw NVA attention.

As I walked down the hill, it dawned on me that although we had been given the use of the bulldozer, no driver had been provided. Fortu-nately, I had grown up operating heavy equipment on our farm and could personally handle that part of the project. Besides, that would al-low me to tailor the position exactly as I liked.

When Gunny Mac heard we would be at the position with the thatched roof hooch, he was elated. Nicer than anything we had lived in for months, it had been built by the Montagnards for an infantry unit before the recent buildup began. The floor was about three and one-half feet off the ground and made of woven bamboo. The walls were made of C ration boxes, and with a roof of thatched grass, the hut never leaked even in the most severe of downpours. The first thing I had the men do was dig deep foxholes right next to it. The hut could be a death trap if there was not a quick way to take cover during incoming. In retrospect, setting up in the hooch probably was not the smartest thing to do, but the appeal of having a houselike shelter was too tempting to those of us who had been bunkered down at Camp Carroll for the last several months.

The working conditions in the days that followed were great because the weather was passing from the cold monsoon season to springlike conditions. Nights were another matter, and we continued to snuggle in mummy-style sleeping bags. The mood of our activity was consistently upbeat because the break from the drudgery of Camp Carroll was so complete. There we had fired twenty-four hours a day and never seemed to get a full night's sleep. Here, our ten-man contingent worked really hard during the day but relaxed at night just like real people back in the States. That was possible because the infantry had full responsibility for securing the perimeter, and we were strictly here for construction purposes. So for a few glorious days we lived in our grass hooch and slept like babies at night. The interlude was made even better by the lack of incoming. In fact, this was one of the two times in my tour when I experienced peaceful relaxed moments, the other time having been my posting on top of the Rockpile. Why we did not get hit here was a mystery, but we were not asking any questions.

All things come to an end, both good and bad, and our two-week period of nirvana vanished with the arrival of Charlie Battery. Our mission had been accomplished by construction of a really fine gun line, and the earthworks surrounding each gun location had bunker holes for the crews. All that remained for the battery to do was put sandbag roofs on their living quarters, the heavy work having already been done. Charlie Battery would be as protected as could be expected in the vicinity of the DMZ. When the guns arrived, organized chaos returned, and two hours later we were firing missions.

Not only did our firing routine resume, but incoming began as well. That first night we received the first mortar attack since we had been here, and it was obviously intended for Charlie Battery because the rounds fell only on our side of the Ca Lu perimeter. Fortunately, most of them landed near the creek that ran along our exterior lines, but the thump, thump of heavy mortars brought those of us who had been living the good life out here for the last two weeks back to reality. It was also a wake-up call to those who had been with the guns back at Camp Carroll. There, most incoming had consisted of rockets or artillery, but these mortar attacks were far more intimidating. Their shrapnel dispersed in an extremely effective 360-degree pattern, and their short range reminded everyone that the people firing them were very near. Between mortars and rockets, our stay at Ca Lu would be an adventure. The NVA knew why we were there and wanted to discourage us in every way they could.

Two nights later, the NVA probed the entire base and were accompanied by rockets and mortars. Small arms crackled all about while enemy units tested several points around the perimeter. This particular night was different, however, in that we were exposed to one of our new weapon systems we had heard of but never seen. "Puff the Magic Dragon" arrived in all his power and splendor. This converted cargo plane flew around dropping big parachute flares and, more important, fired Gatling guns capable of discharging six thousand rounds per minute. The effect of giant parachute flares lighting up the countryside as they floated gently in the night sky was quite otherworldly, but the accompanying stream of tracers from high-speed machine guns could be mesmerizing. The guns fired so fast that they sounded like a hum in the sky, and the tracers looked like a thin wand being waved across the landscape in an undulating thread of red, unbroken light. The visual impact of this scene was awesome. It also reminded us that if we rated this kind of backup, then the high command was definitely giving this operation high priority. From our point of view, that meant we were at high risk, and that was never comforting. "Spooky," another nickname for Puff, was nevertheless impressive and extremely welcome. His presence psychologically devastated enemy forces and was one of the more effective weapons we employed in night battles. Many a man's prayer was answered in the heart of a dark night with unseen enemy attacking when high overhead the drone of Puff's engines underscored the string of giant parachute flares strung out across the sky. Then the threadlike wand would wave across the battlefield, reassuring us that Puff the Magic Dragon was dispensing death to those spirits out there trying to extinguish our souls. These occasions were always surreal experiences.

The action lasted about an hour and a half and terminated much quicker than usual because of Puff's arrival. The next day I heard more than one refrain from the popular song "Puff the Magic Dragon" being sung or hummed by the troops. In fact, even today when I hear that song, the sound of Gatling guns reaches out from the recesses of my subconciousness, and a red wand waves in the eye of my mind.

About a week later we received the unwelcome news that we were being moved from the battery position we had spent so much time in building. This move would only be to the other side of Ca Lu's perimeter, but all the effort of creating the "perfect" position was going to benefit somebody else. The powers that be had decided that a 175mm Army battery was needed to support the coming relief effort, and, unfortunately for us, the position we had prepared was really the only practical location for the giant guns. Charlie Battery would be squeezed in on a narrow ridge on the western side of the perimeter nearest Khe Sanh. Although we would have a spectacular view of the valley in that direction, we also knew that every enemy eye would be on us as well.

Only one feature about the position seemed helpful. McNamara, with his scheme for building a series of defensive strongpoints, had caused the Army to construct some well-built bunkers. One of those was on the ridge we were to occupy, and it seemed that "McNamara's Folly" might at least be of some use. That engineered marvel seemed perfect for our command post. Our Exec Pit as well as the FDC could be operated from there, divided as the bunker was into two sections. We had never had anything quite so fancy at the battery level, and the gun line could even be seen from the two entrances.

A major problem with the new position, however, was that we would not have a dozer to build adequate parapets or gun crew bunkers. That equipment had long ago been moved to some other sector, prohibiting us from doing anything more than scratching out foxholes in the rocky ground and putting up the most rudimentary of parapets. The rocky hardness of the ridge hardly allowed even that. To top it all off, we stood out in silhouette to all of the NVA up and down the valley to Khe Sanh. Every enemy mortar and rocket unit had line-of-sight adjustments on us whenever they fired. What the hell, at least the view was great, and the troops, for some weird notion, seemed to relish the perceived danger.

The fact of the matter was that Charlie Battery continued in an upbeat macho manner. Feelings of tradition among this bunch of guys were something special and not artificially contrived by the staff to keep up morale. This key part of the collective personality and mentality of Charlie Battery had evolved over time and was exemplified by the continuing problem of our gunners trying to outdo each other in showing their lack of concern for incoming. With practically no parapets up here, the crews walked around as if it were merely raining when the shrapnel started to fly. As at Camp Carroll, I had to raise absolute hell to keep these guys from catching spent shrapnel with their helmets. Something about being high on the exposed ridge with little protection seemed to give the men an even more devil-may-care attitude than usual. Also, about this time, we received the latest issue of *Stars and Stripes*, the in-country newspaper. Unbeknownst to me, some of the troops had sent in pictures of our gun crews with the caption "Best Damn Battery in Vietnam." We were given a full-page layout in the paper, and the troop's cockiness soared even higher than its already lofty altitude.

The following week saw an increase in enemy mortar and rocket attacks, and we, in turn, kept on pumping rounds up the valley toward Khe Sanh. To those of us with field experience, it seemed like we needed a lot more troops than we had at Ca Lu. In particular, we noticed an imbalance of enemy positions on the high ridges to either side of the road going to Khe Sanh. Troops would physically have to root out a way through that gauntlet when the relief effort began; artillery and air would not likely be adequate by itself. Our situation was evolving into an active combat environment, and we now traded fire with the NVA's rockets and mortars on a regular basis. The sense that something was getting ready to happen energized us, and Charlie was mentally ready for whatever that was. A jovial mood pervaded the outlook of the men even though we occasionally took casualties.

During this time, an incident occurred that I could compare only to scenes from movies I had seen. This event occurred during a major rocket attack on a cloudy afternoon. I was outside the big fortresslike bunker that McNamara had provided us and was doing paperwork in the better light. A rocket came screaming overhead, sending everyone for cover and me for safety in the big bunker. Charlie Battery always returned fire as soon as we determined the direction of the incoming, and because someone had detected the point of origin early on, we began scrambling to crank off some rounds. After consulting with the FDC on where best to return fire, I started toward the doorway to give data to the guns. I had barely taken two steps when a 122mm rocket hit our bunker dead center, and just like in the movies, beams shattered, and the roof came tumbling down in a cloud of dust and smoke. Missing from the movies was the heat of the blast and the intense smell of the explosive from the warhead. Talk about doing a fast, low crawl over timbers and sandbags. I think I set a record lunging toward the hazy light where the door was supposed to be. To hell with incoming on the outside; the fear of being buried alive in a bunker intimidated me much more. Outside, after gathering my wits, I went back in to see who had survived. Incredibly, no one was seriously hurt. Only a few knots on the head mixed with scrapes and bruises were there to show for our troubles. Almost needless to say, we never again used the center of the big bunker for our command post. From that time on, we set up at the two entrances, where we could easily evacuate if hit again. This makeshift arrangement was much preferred to the possibility of being trapped in a collapsing tomb of beams and sandbags.

As the intensity of combat increased, I began to notice that the quirks and superstitions normally present in most outfits were reaching extremes in Charlie Battery. Some guys constantly wore a particular article of clothing, and others carried lucky charms. Often these good-luck pieces were worn around the neck but could be carried anywhere. Even I had a few quirks. With me always was the little New Testament that had been provided by the Gideons, and it now stayed in the left cargo pocket of my trousers. I had also acquired a special fondness for the camouflaged helmet cover I had worn over my steel helmet throughout the Rockpile and Con Thien campaigns, and I took extremely good care of it. One day I saw one of the radiomen using my helmet to drive a nail, and I responded with a knee-jerk reaction. To his surprise, I blew up at him. I grabbed the helmet and found that he had ripped the cloth slightly. A sick feeling came over me, as if I had been made vulnerable by a tear in my protective shield. Childishly, I made him sew it up as neatly as he could.

Spring really began to break out now, and we cast anxious eyes down the valley toward Khe Sanh. We knew the NVA were watching us as well and realized that there were a whole lot more of them than there were of us. We did, however, take some comfort in the gradual buildup taking place; almost every day new units were arriving.

During this time we picked up several new members for Charlie Battery. Among them was a second lieutenant who, from the beginning, was obviously a special person. From Amarillo, Texas, this former Baylor football player was full of the enthusiasm so characteristic of new lieutenants. Young Marine officers fresh out of Basic School were typically charged up and ready to take on the world, but this new guy had not only that but something extra as well. His dedication to excellence went beyond the norm, and he maintained a superb work ethic. It did not take me long to realize that he had a knack for quickly adapting to whatever circumstances in which he found himself. What a welcome addition he was to the team. His name was Mike Dewlen.

Charlie grew even closer as a unit during that period, and we experienced an incredible feeling of pride and loyalty to the battery. Operating away from Camp Carroll, without Battalion administration and oversight, gave us a new sense of independence that we were not accustomed to. At Ca Lu we were a little world unto our own, with only radio contact keeping us tied to Battalion. Of course, we had to comply with the orders of the CO in charge of the compound here, but he had plenty of other things on his mind. We communicated with Camp Carroll but lived an independent existence perched high on our ridge.

We even developed an arrogance, probably needed, when the Army's Air Cavalry arrived. This group was, in effect, a mechanized infantry outfit, but their mode of transportation was helicopters. They were insufferable and, in spite of being a top-notch Army unit, rubbed us the wrong way. With their helicopter resources, they received cold beer and hot, kitchen-prepared meals every night. The only thing we got hot was beer on occasion and had eaten only C rations for the last month. They wore nice new uniforms that were clean and fresh, like they had just come back from the cleaners. Our clothes were what some might call rags, and many of us still carried the phased-out M-14 rifle. The crowning blow affecting our attitude was their daily supply of ice cream, which arrived every afternoon by chopper. Obviously, it was hard to feel kindly toward these pampered pogues from the south of Vietnam. Naturally, we assumed a surface indifference and aloofness around these guys, all of which contributed to Charlie Battery's "attitude." Feeling that our outfit was getting the short end of the stick bonded us even tighter.

Ca Lu continued to grow as a base. The perimeter expanded, and another artillery battery moved in. Obviously, something would happen soon. Personally, although I did not discuss it with anybody, I would have preferred to rotate before we began the big push to relieve Khe Sanh. This attitude was even stronger now that I had become a relative short-timer with less than three months left in country. I had already seen more action than I had ever imagined, and with my feelings about the way politicians were running the war, I just wanted out in one piece and alive. On the other hand, I felt pride in being executive officer of Charlie Battery, an outfit recognized as one of the best artillery units on the DMZ. In addition, a real sense of "family" affected us all. People who grow to depend on each other as much as we had over the last months develop attitudes transcending self. The conflicting emotions of the will to survive and the loyalty to comrades with whom I had shared the angst of battle made for a frustrating experience. Only those who have been so totally engrossed in a common endeavor can understand the deepness of such relationships. It does not have to be a war that brings men into such closeness; any situation that requires sacrifice for the common good will achieve the same effect. The bond is real and heartfelt.

In this environment I waited out my days and became quite jealous of Joe Schwerer, who would be rotating sooner than originally scheduled. I wondered how the luck of the draw would treat us when we got a new commander. I had seen some real jerks among the many sharp officers. I rationalized that it did not matter, that I could handle any situation with less than three months left to go. About this time, Battalion radioed for Captain Schwerer to return to Camp Carroll for a conference, and I assumed it would be a meeting to deal with his replacement.

Captain Schwerer was gone overnight, generating the usual speculation among the staff. A change in leadership always created uncertainty. The talk swung wildly from the concern about having a new and untested CO to the possibility that we might be pulled back to Camp Carroll because the Air Cavalry was at Ca Lu in full force. When Captain Schwerer returned to the position the next day, he created a stir because everybody was anxious to find out how the change of command would affect Charlie Battery. A staff meeting was called for three o'clock that afternoon, and we knew from his manner that something was up.

I did not get to visit with him privately because he went directly over to the Ca Lu base commander's headquarters for a conference involving all the COs at Ca Lu. That prompted speculation that something bigger than a change of command was in the making. At the appointed time for our meeting, he still was at the big powwow, so we waited around and wondered some more. Finally, he returned in a serious mood, and we figured we were about to get an earful.

He opened the meeting by saying intelligence had determined that some of the NVA troops had pulled away from Khe Sanh and that we would take advantage of the reduced enemy strength to break through to the encircled base. He said it had been decided that the Air Cavalry would spearhead this operation and that the Marine hierarchy was upset about the Army being given that task. He reminded us, however, that Westmoreland was calling the shots and probably wanted to give the Army the prestige of leading the relief effort. The official reason given was that the Army Air Cavalry existed specifically for helicopter assaults and therefore was best equipped to facilitate a leapfrog effort into the base. Although the Marines had helicopters for transporting troops, they did not have a large contingent of supporting gunships and in reality were not trained as extensively in pure helicopter tactics as the Air Cavalry was. Captain Schwerer then laid out the Marine Corps' role in the relief effort, which mainly consisted of moving in behind the Air Cavalry and repairing the road into Khe Sanh. Following that effort, the Marines would begin a series of sweeps around the base to drive the NVA away. As General Davis had earlier indicated, the artillery's role would be expanded to the extent that 105mm batteries would be airlifted to strategic points for closer support of the infantry units. That reminded me that things could get very hot for the artillery when they were sitting out there in no-man's-land without fortifications. Surely that would be like putting bait out for the NVA. Three 105mm batteries, including Charlie, would have this close support role.

We then found out the reason for Captain Schwerer's somberness. Because his departure date had been accelerated for some type of personal hardship going on back in the States, he would not be accompanying the battery to Khe Sanh. He would now be leaving Vietnam in ten days, and Battalion believed that someone was needed who could provide continuity of command throughout the entire upcoming operation. He paused and looked around the room, and then his eyes stopped on me, and he said, "Lieutenant Brown, you are the new CO of Charlie Battery." Talk about being inwardly rattled. I could not forget that I was a short-timer, too, in spite of the hearty congratulations being offered by the staff. This could not be happening. Sure, I was flattered, but I really just wanted out of Vietnam alive and in good health. The honor of commanding a Marine battery was great, but the responsibility being thrown at me in my final days seemed ill timed. If this had come sooner, I might have savored the situation. Nevertheless, I acted pleased and dealt with the butterflies fluttering in my stomach.

Later digesting the moment, I realized just how unusual this situation really was. The commanding officer of a 105mm battery was normally a captain, and to have a lieutenant in charge was highly irregular. A factor at work here was that they had run out of experienced artillery captains because of some mix-up with new arrivals and the inflexibility of rigid rotation dates. That, coupled with a need in the coming relief effort for experienced leadership and someone accustomed to the character of the participating units, resulted in my being thrust into the role of battery commander.

Obviously, all routine functions in my life were over. I would be so busy preparing for the move to Khe Sanh that little time would remain for me to dwell on my personal plight. Everything had to be carefully organized and all contingency preparations thought out. Because I had been XO since December, the move to commanding officer would be relatively easy, but preparing for the new concept of a roving and mobile artillery battery was extremely different from past artillery operations. Heretofore, we had not particularly had to worry about logistics on the battery level. Supplies and ammunition had been handled by Battalion headquarters, and the battery's main responsibility was to shoot fire missions while keeping the personnel organized and disciplined. Even fire direction had been run from Battalion's central FDC until we had moved to Ca Lu. Now each battery carried its own fire direction staff, anticipating that communications with Battalion would either be frequently interrupted or too far distant for adequate transmissions. All in all, the responsibilities were going to be significantly different from what they had been.

I spent the first several days going over with Captain Schwerer how he viewed the state of the battery and his take on the coming operation. The biggest changes for me would be paperwork and logistical planning. I had essentially been directing day-to-day operations of the battery since December, but the new administrative duties would require some adjustments. Compounding my lack of experience in that area was that what had worked well at Camp Carroll and Ca Lu would not be at all practical for the Khe Sanh expedition. With the anticipated mobility of the battery in a crude combat environment, it would be very difficult to handle the necessary paperwork. After much discussion, it was agreed that day-to-day administration should be left to 1st Sergeant Zipkas, who would continue to remain at Camp Carroll with an office staff. If he had to have an officer's signature he could see Major Capenas, the operations officer, and have him sign whatever was needed. Major Capenas could handle these matters until we returned. He was in full agreement that the unusual circumstances made that the best solution for the time being. This suited me fine and allowed me to concentrate primarily on the pressing needs of the looming operation.

My first difficult task concerned organizing the battery's officer staff. Charlie Battery's fire direction officer was Lieutenant Dave Duchow, an extremely qualified man in that capacity. He had been supervising officer at the centralized battalion FDC but, as the senior officer behind me, should have replaced me as executive officer. On the other hand, no other officer had the experience I thought was necessary for the critical FDC job, especially when we would be left entirely to our own resources. We did have one well-qualified staff sergeant and three corporals with adequate know-how, but obviously I needed a highly experienced officer. Dave had plotted thousands of missions and would be able to set up and operate in the primitive conditions we anticipated. He was going to have to be put in charge, and that is where the difficulty came in.

There was a shortage of artillery officers as a result of the rotation system, and Charlie Battery had only one other officer available unless I pulled an FO in from the field. None of the FOs had operated in a battery environment, and, again, experience was vital in the coming operation. That left only Lieutenant Mike Dewlen, who had been with us about a month. Circumstances and fate left me no choice but to make him executive officer. New second lieutenants were hardly ever given that responsibility until they had months of experience. Fortunately, he had impressed me with his abilities, and I felt no reluctance in assigning him the job. My only reservation was that it was not fair to Lieutenant

Duchow not to be made XO. Thus it was that a very unusual situation decreed roles for these men that would soon affect them in the grand scheme of life.

Captain Schwerer saw things coming together in an efficient manner and, with the wisdom and unselfishness of a true leader, backed off from running the show. This allowed me to slide into my new role quickly. I already owed him a great deal for having helped me develop organizational and executive skills, and what I learned from him then is a part of my makeup today. He was a professional of the first order whom I admired and respected. In fact Charlie Battery had been commanded by two top-notch COs before me, and I was taking over a finely tuned team. Both Captain Pate and Captain Schwerer had trained the battery well, and even though these two men would not be physically with us when we went to Khe Sanh, their efforts and influence made us stronger for the test ahead.

A brief change-of-command meeting took place at Ca Lu, and Joe Schwerer left for that dreamed-of journey home. He was truly upset at having to leave what he expected would be one of Charlie Battery's biggest adventures, and uncharacteristic tears appeared in his eyes as he climbed in the jeep for the trip to Camp Carroll. His last words to me were, "She's yours now, Jim. Take good care of her!" My own concerns did not seem as big on seeing his deep devotion to the battery and hearing his final charge. I could only think that it was a privilege to be a part of such a unit.

The last days before our departure were filled with hundreds of details, foremost being the selection of which troopers we should take. Some would remain to handle administration, and others would be used to handle the equipment and supplies left behind. I made sure that only the most capable were going with us to Khe Sanh. There were always a few people in any unit who did not belong, and they were definitely going back to Carroll. Incompetence or troublemaking could not be tolerated where we were headed. As usual, the best and the brightest would be the ones facing danger, the more competent being asked to carry the load. America's best men are ground up on the battlefields of our wars, regardless of whether it is a popular conflict or not. The rewards of valor and competence carry severe consequences, and thus the true tragedy of all war is in proportion to the degree of necessity for the conflict in the first place.

About ninety men made the final cut for the operation. We would carry our normal six guns, eight trucks, and as many supplies as we could load. We had been told there would be plenty of ammunition, but as a precaution for logistical foul-ups, I ordered each gun crew to carry two plastic antitank rounds and three rounds of beehive. The antitank rounds were being carried because Lang Vei, an Army Special Forces position outside of Khe Sanh, had been recently overrun by enemy tanks, and I wanted something that would give us a fighting chance if we found ourselves in a similar situation. The beehive was for enemy ground troops. Canister had been used effectively to repel attacks since the Civil War; beehive was merely a sophisticated upgrade of that already wicked tool.

The operation began with the Air Cavalry moving out in their helicopters along Route 9. By April 8 they had hooked up with the Marines at Khe Sanh. Resistance was minimal, and within another week the roads and bridges had been repaired by Marine engineers. During this time we fired continuous missions down the valley toward Khe Sanh in support of the operation, which was code-named Pegasus. How they came up with these names sometimes baffled me, but this one was fairly obvious. The winged horse symbolized the air tactics of the Air Cavalry, who had been given the lead role. We poured out artillery rounds at whatever targets they called in and hoped nothing would be left when we ourselves followed.

At last we received the word to stand down and prepare to move out the next day. That night was another long and sleepless event of war. What would the next day bring? A lot of letters were written. In my own correspondence I made a real effort not to convey the anxiety I felt. Besides, the siege had been lifted, and intelligence said many of the NVA were gone. Surely it could not be that bad and would, we hoped, be a nonevent. In any case I would not have somebody from Battalion or Regiment looking over my shoulder if I made mistakes as battery commander. Sleep, however, came only fitfully that last night in Ca Lu.

14

Khe Sanh

Dawn broke with everyone in Charlie Battery hustling into activity. We really did not know what to expect, and cautious excitement filled the air. Charlie Battery's macho Marine spirit was at a peak this morning, but I wondered just how many of the guys were actually experiencing queasy feelings beneath the confident bravado that abounded. On the other hand, seeing people acting with such confidence bolstered everyone's resolve. This bold attitude had evolved over a period of months and resulted from knowing we had handled everything thrown at us so far. Combat either made men and units stronger or drained their very souls. Fortunately, this battery had developed an iron-minded spirit for which men were willing to die. Certainly, no one wants to die, but some concepts are stronger than death; when that mentality exists, the dynamics of a group can vastly increase. Such was the Charlie Battery that set out that day on the road to Khe Sanh.

Our convoy, accompanied by a platoon of infantry, left Ca Lu on a misty, foggy morning. The jungled ridges on either side of the valley were rugged with jagged rock formations piercing upward through the trees. A stream ran along one side of the road, and recent work by the Engineer Battalion was in evidence where bridges had been rebuilt. On our departure, helicopter gunships appeared as if from nowhere and began searching the ridges for NVA. For about five miles down the road, the terrain looked much like that around the Rockpile and Ca Lu, but after that the surroundings took on a different feel, with big bomb craters and shattered trees appearing more frequently as the valley widened and vegetation decreased. Eventually, we moved onto a gently rolling plain, well away from the ridges, and nothing was the same. I could not relate the panorama to anything I had ever seen and could only imagine that the surface of the moon must look like this. Our little track of a road wandered through massive bomb craters void of anything green. Occasionally, blackened tree limbs protruded grotesquely from piles of raw earth, and an awesome feeling of insignificance overwhelmed me as I viewed the total destruction. This hardly imaginable wasteland resulted from one of the most massive conventional bombing assaults in history. We had watched B-52s at close range in previous actions and been duly impressed, but seeing the results of their power in the middle of the impact zone was humbling. This devastation extended in a two-mile-wide band encircling the entire base of Khe Sanh. As I thought on this, it occurred to me that the entire DMZ region was really nothing more than a big impact zone. This was just the concentrated manifestation of it. The destruction around us made me wonder how the enemy could have even considered attempting a siege, much less actually accomplishing one for two and one-half months. Charlie Battery, even with its cool bravado, had always respected the NVA, but seeing how much they had endured in this incredible air assault added to that respect.

Nearing the perimeter, we were in for another eye-opener as we gazed on a maze of barbed wire surrounding what seemed to be the most colossal garbage dump of all time. Everything behind the wire was jumbled and smashed, indicating that the NVA had put their licks in on us as well. In addition to rockets and mortars, powerful artillery had zeroed in on the base, creating its own zone of destruction. Their firepower was massed on an imposing mountain named Co Roc, across the Laotian border. Its sheer cliffs faced us broadside, and the NVA had placed their artillery in caves throughout the face of this mountain. When they were ready to fire, they simply rolled their guns out and pounded the base until they were finished or an air strike forced them back in. No amount of bombing had diminished their ability to wreak havoc at Khe Sanh, and all normal structures had been demolished; everyone lived underground. Driving into the base, we saw nothing but wrecked guns, vehicles, military equipment, and, finally at the airstrip, smashed airplanes and choppers. Everything was strewn about in complete chaos, and a musty smell of decay attacked our senses. Standing out like some giant monument to the siege, a tail section of what seemed to be a large cargo plane pointed straight up at the sky. In the intensity of incoming fire, it would have been insanity to try to keep things orderly.

The NVA took due note of our entry and welcomed us with artillery, prompting a mad dash to the position where we had been assigned. We had picked up a guide at the main gate, and he led us on a wild ride. Whoever selected the position must have had a sardonic sense of humor because it was the old ammo dump. It had been hit long ago, and hundreds of artillery rounds were scattered everywhere. The base engineers, using bulldozers, had pushed up parapets for our six guns in the midst of all this, and unexploded shells poked out at every angle from the low walls. Because we were already taking incoming when we arrived, we did not worry too much about the condition of the site but hastily guided the guns into the parapets. The barrage of incoming was more than enough to occupy our thoughts, and all we wanted to do was place the guns so we could prepare for whatever came next. At that moment we did not know whether this was a major attack or, as it turned out, just routine incoming. Men and equipment were extremely exposed, and my priority was simply to throw the guns into their parapets quickly so we could find protection for the men. There were no trenches and few depressions to take cover in, so things ran helter-skelter for a few moments. If bunkers were available, they were not obvious in this huge junkyard.

At this point, no one had briefed us on anything, and with the incoming, they were not likely to do so. The only sign of life we had seen had been Marines on the perimeter by the gate and the guide who had joined us there. Even he had quickly disappeared when we reached the battery's new position. With the welcome wagon out from Co Roc, everyone at Khe Sanh had gone underground, and we were on our own. After randomly scattering the trucks away from the guns, we yelled to the troops to find whatever shelter they could, and following a mad scramble, we all just kind of froze in place and became very still. Immediately, the guns of Co Roc fell silent, and it hit me hard that Khe Sanh was going to be a miserable affair even though the siege was supposed to be over. We had hoped that with the road reopened to Ca Lu we might find an environment similar to other bases on the DMZ. It was not to be.

After a respectable time had elapsed following the welcoming barrage, the battery staff hooked up to determine what we were going to do for cover. We did find a small, low bunker near one of the gun parapets, and though filthy and putrid, it had a sandbagged roof. Nothing else near us had overhead protection, so we set up both the command post and fire direction center in there. Normally we separated the two, but for the time being, there was no alternative. After further survey, we found out we were on the eastern end of the landing strip and right next to the wire. Two infantry troopers in a foxhole by the wire filled us in on the peculiarities of the position but were none too excited about our arrival because we made a highly visible target for the NVA. After quizzing them at length, Gunny Mac developed a sense of the area and found out where some of the key points were. Taking me over to the perimeter, he showed me trenches outside the wire coming toward us in a zigzag pattern to a point fifty yards away from our lines. This NVA design prevented us from firing directly into their trenches and, by weaving back and forth as it did, allowed them to advance incredibly close to Khe Sanh. The northern forces in the Civil War had used much the same type of trench approach at the battle of Vicksburg, the outline still being visible to this day. The infantry troopers also warned the Gunny that snipers would occasionally pop up from those trenches and crank off a round, making me decide that we needed additional foxholes of our own near the wire. I also decided that they should be manned by Charlie Battery. I wanted to insure that we knew for ourselves what was going on out there in no-man's-land. The Gunny also found out that the base command post was located near the middle of the landing strip and next to the aid station, which was Company C, 3d Medical Battalion, or "Charlie Med." With the lack of orientation we had received so far, I thought it would be a good idea to check in right away and find out both what our role was supposed to be and anything else useful to survival.

After giving directions to Lieutenants Duchow and Dewlen on where to set everything up, Gunny Mac and I headed out on foot to find the CP. By keeping close to the airstrip, we found it easily in spite of having to weave through mazes of junk and wrecks. Demolished aircraft and equipment were scattered all up and down the runway. Obviously, when planes and choppers had been hit, the expedient thing to do had been merely to push them off with dozers. The airstrip was Khe Sanh's lifeline, and keeping it open had been the priority. Neatness and order were forgotten in the struggle for survival. Moving along the airstrip we began noticing scruffy Marines, most of whom could be seen sitting near the entrances of bunkers. Clearly, they wanted a quick escape hatch in the event of incoming.

We noticed Charlie Med first and distinguished it because of the activity generated by the recent incoming. It was conveniently located next to the airstrip for evacuations, and a few wounded Marines were now being helped down into a deep bunker. Adjacent to Charlie Med, and for the same ease of access to the runway, was the morgue. It, however, was above ground because its occupants, although no longer needing protection, did need fresh air. Near both of these, but a little further away from the strip, was the headquarters bunker. Low and massive, it prickled with radio antennas, and the sandbagged roof was only about two feet above the ground. Going down a set of stairs, we found operations and also the other two 105mm battery commanders, who had been there a short time. They were somewhat agitated because they did not know anything more than I did, which was nothing. The CO of Alpha Battery was a "Mustang," or ex-enlisted man, who had come up through the ranks and been made a lieutenant. The other was Lieutenant Koestler, the CO of Bravo Battery. It puzzled me that the Marine Corps did not have enough captains to fill these billets. Either there had been poor administrative planning, or we were really stretched thin in the officer corps. Waiting with them to be briefed, I found out that both of their batteries had taken over existing artillery locations and that only Charlie Battery had needed to scratch out a new position. I never found out why we were so lucky.

Finally we met with the CO of Khe Sanh and were informed that for now we would fill in for the batteries that had been there during the siege but that later we would be used to assist in the mop-up operation around the hills of Khe Sanh. He did not seem to know a whole lot about our future roles and was primarily interested in making sure we handled counter-battery fire as the previous batteries had done. He did make clear that all artillery missions would be controlled from Khe Sanh's main FDC until we went out on the sweep-up operation. That suited me just fine because we did not have adequate bunker facilities for an FDC of our own. Our personnel would take shifts and supplement the staff at the base operation. Lieutenant Duchow and his staff would be delighted with that news because they could now get some rest, being in a rotation sequence with other batteries. Besides, the main FDC bunker was one of the safest locations in Khe Sanh. It was evident to all by now that being above ground at Khe Sanh was not a healthy place to be.

Our job would be to shoot fire missions and return counter-battery fire whenever we took incoming. This we were expert at, and it sounded like we would simply be doing the same things we had done for months. The CO further cautioned us that the less activity generated, the better. He pointed out that any time a lot of movement took place, the NVA usually cranked in a few rounds to discourage whatever was going on. This was discomfiting because I wondered how we were going to fire our guns without creating activity. Our stay at Khe Sanh promised to be very interesting.

The following days tested our ingenuity, but we created some order out of the disarray around us. It was C rations and heat tabs for the whole time and the worst of living conditions in the surrounding squalor. Here the rats thought they ruled the place and scampered about at will as if we were not even there. The troops slept with buddies watching to be sure rats did not crawl over them because the rodents had lost all fear of man. Of course Charlie Battery, with its salty attitude, managed to make the most of the situation, and soon the men were devising contests for ingenious ways to kill rats.

From time to time we fired artillery missions, and Khe Sanh routinely took incoming. During this period and by some incredible stroke of luck, we had no one wounded or killed. The base was very big, and most of the incoming landed elsewhere. Only two rounds landed in the battery area itself, and everyone happened to be in foxholes at the time. Our routine was similar to Camp Carroll, but living conditions were deplorable.

Late one afternoon an unusual incident occurred that was noteworthy in an abstract sort of way. I had taken my jeep and driver and gone on some errand near the western side of the base. A total calm filled the air as the sky yellowed to a hazy half-light. On several other occasions I had seen similar atmospheric conditions, probably resulting from late afternoon sun filtering through clouds in a prismatic sort of way. The base was extremely quiet, and the yellow glow gave an unreal feeling to the moment. The only sign of life was our jeep as it began meandering back to the battery. We had not gone far when we heard an artillery shell pass over our heads followed by the sharp crack of its impact a moment later. In that split second of awareness, I nonchalantly wondered whether they were shooting at our jeep driving through the acres of devastation or just cranking off rounds at random into the base. More shells came in, but for some reason we did not stop or take cover. We rode on in this otherworldly scene with no panic, no tension, only a calm compulsion pressing us back to the battery. We could hear the shells whistling overhead and see the flash of their impact, but we just drove through the junk heap of Khe Sanh like we were out for a Sunday drive. What possessed us not to take cover I will never understand. When we reached the battery in the yellow haze of the weird twilight, the incoming stopped.

Since arriving at Khe Sanh, the battery had maintained a good-natured attitude in spite of the conditions, and morale was no problem. The fact that we had not taken casualties in the midst of this insanity uplifted us enough. Of course, in Charlie Battery someone was always cooking up some mischief, and that kept our minds off the seriousness of our situation. If it was not something such as a new angle on the war with the rats, then someone was playing a practical joke on another member of the battery.

During this period I had time to think about my personal situation and found it hard to believe that I had less than two months left in country and yet here I was in the midst of one of the most dangerous times of my tour. I fully expected things to get even hotter when the mop-up operation started around Khe Sanh. Proud though I was of Charlie Battery, the gravity of the circumstances and the irony of being so close to the end of my tour left me introspective and sober. Life takes twists and turns that are hard to comprehend. In any event, it pleased me to be CO and to know that Charlie Battery was performing well.

Finally, the long-anticipated word came that the mop-up operation was about to begin. At a briefing in the base command bunker, I learned that Marine infantry had been deployed south of Khe Sanh and that we would provide close support. General Davis, the commander of the 3d Marine Division, remained determined to change the role of the Marines from guarding bases or strongpoints to that of a more mobile, self-contained strike force. Certainly, that approach was more in keeping with the aggressive posture Marines traditionally assumed.

The artillery's role would be radically different from what it had been since my arrival in Vietnam. Batteries typically are placed behind the lines in protected positions or, as was the case in Vietnam, well-protected base camps. The new plan involved airlifting us out to provide close-to-the-action fire support because the operation was taking place in a remote area. General Davis wanted artillery to be quickly available and effectively positioned if the sweep units encountered NVA artillery or mortar fire. We would be operating along the Laotian border near the Ho Chi Minh Trail, giving the NVA ready access to their own artillery and supplies. There were even supposed to be enemy tanks operating in the area. General Davis hoped to level the playing field by reinforcing the troops with 105mm howitzers at close range.

Charlie and Bravo Batteries would be going to a hilltop very near the Laotian border, and I found out that a small bulldozer would be dropped in ahead of us to prepare parapets. We would follow the next day, a company of Marine infantry being already there for security. Furthermore, we were instructed to take only seventy men per battery. This was supposed to be a lightning quick operation, and we would carry minimal supplies. Adequate artillery rounds would be dropped in for plenty of firepower, but fewer men meant fewer supplies and, of course, fewer resupply trips.

We learned that the infantry had found large caches of NVA supplies and arms; even more interesting, however, a road had been found that was frequently used by enemy vehicles. Apparently, we were heading into serious "Indian Country," and the question on everyone's mind was, "Are the NVA still there in force?" This possibility was viewed as a threat to the future security of Khe Sanh and was the reason given to us for the necessity of sending us into such a remote and dangerous area near the Laotian border. They had definitely been there earlier in strength, but it was not now clear whether they still had heavy concentrations of troops.

Well, this was it. I had at least one more gauntlet to run before my rotation back to the States, and I knew I would have to concentrate fully on this operation if Charlie Battery was going to run smoothly. Going home must be purged from my thoughts and my whole being thrown into this endeavor. Adrenaline began to pump, and my focus became clear. The mission was set. It was time.

My first tasks were to select the seventy who would go and to be sure everyone was mentally prepared for whatever lay ahead. Even though I believed we had already weeded out the marginal men before leaving Ca Lu, I thought I ought to give anyone with serious hang-ups a way out. It would be best to have only the truly dedicated with us in the coming tense days. I went ahead and made my decisions on whom to take but was prepared to adjust this if some of the men did not want to go. A meeting of the full battery seemed like the way to handle the situation, so I scheduled one for immediately after dark when we would not draw the attention of NVA gunners.

In the meantime, the staff and I began making decisions on what equipment we would take and started loading excess gear on the trucks to be left behind. Those vehicles would return to Camp Carroll carrying the equipment and men who were not going. Daily convoys were being run now, and it would be relatively easy to send everything back.

My decisions on what to take were influenced by the news of active NVA roads. After hearing that report, I thought a confrontation with tanks seemed a real possibility. Fortunately, I still had the plastic antitank rounds that we had brought from Ca Lu as well as our beehive rounds. Each gun crew was directed to carry in one plastic and three beehive rounds for their gun. That was about as much as they could carry along with their other basic equipment because they would physically have to carry these rounds in their arms. I was not about to take a chance on logistical foul-ups and for some reason not receive them with the regular ammo airlift. Each gun crew would have four or five men, so they could handle this with relative ease. Personal gear consisted of no more than could fit in a backpack; everything else would go back to Camp Carroll with the trucks.

Another item of note concerned the artillery and had been brought up in our briefing. A new, highly classified artillery round called COFRAM (controlled fragmentation munitions) was being made available for our use. This shell was so restricted that it had to have clearance from the president before it could be used. It was first authorized for use at Khe Sanh. Code-named Firecracker, it was allegedly a wicked weapon, but we had never seen it in use. The shell was fired like an ordinary round but functioned by exploding over the target and casting golf ball–sized bomblets across the area beneath. After landing on the ground, they would explode and have the effect of hand grenades going off all over the place; it sounded deadly. These rounds would be supplied with the regular ammo in the helicopter insertion.

Darkness finally fell amid much speculation by the troops over what was coming down. At the appointed time, we gathered at Gun One. In the partial darkness it could have been a gathering of ghosts because only the silhouettes of the men were visible. What had fate decreed this time? You could hear the rustling and whispering of ninety men waiting for me to begin.

I opened by telling them that Charlie Battery had been selected to be dropped into an area that had essentially been NVA territory since the French defeat at Dien Bien Phu years ago. We would be the first U.S. military group in years, other than recon units, to go into the area, and we would provide independent fire support for the infantry units sweeping through. Contact with Battalion would be difficult, and most fire support decisions would be made on our own to accommodate the needs of the infantry. I explained that we had been given this latitude in order to increase our ability to respond quickly to changing circumstances. The infantry did not know what to expect and would make rapid adjustments in the field as the situation dictated; so would we. I pointed out that it was an honor to have been selected for this unusual task and that obviously a great deal of confidence was being placed in Charlie Battery and the other 105 batteries if we were being allowed to operate in such an independent manner. All that I told them was the truth as I understood it at the time, and I spoke with an emotional pride.

The troops took it all in silence, and I concluded the briefing by letting them know we could take only seventy men. I explained to them that there might be short-timers or others who might not want to go for any number of reasons and that we were giving them an opportunity to request to remain behind. Because time was short, I instructed them to turn in their names if they did not want to go or had a problem, and I would take it under consideration. At the meeting's conclusion, the position began to buzz with conversation like church had just let out. I could not see their faces, but you could feel excitement in the night. I hoped I had pumped them up but would have to wait a while to find out their reaction.

An hour later I got my answer; no one had volunteered to stay behind. I then gave the Gunny the names of the people who would be left so everyone could immediately begin the appropriate packing and preparations. Was I in for a surprise! Half of the guys who had been designated to return to Camp Carroll were requesting meetings with me. This was highly irregular, and normally I would not have taken the time to listen to bellyaching over assignments. After some persuasion from the staff, however, I agreed to meet with these men individually. They came to me in the lighted command bunker, and I was able to read each man's face as he pleaded his case. Some came in teary eyed, and almost all made highly emotional appeals as to why he should be included on the mission. I was quite moved on hearing these guys pour their hearts out, and the genuine brotherhood of the battery affected my own attitude. After hearing them out I told them I would get back to them later that night.

The Gunny and I went over each of their requests and decided that there would be three changes, mainly because he pointed out that we had overlooked several men who were really short, each having less than a week left in country. We made those changes, and then I had requests for meetings from the three new additions to the list. I left it to the Gunny to explain that we were sending them out because their time was so short and that we were not meeting with them or anybody else on the matter.

The next morning there were long faces among those not going, but the rest of the battery was pumped, and adrenaline began to flow. We also received word that we were to be airlifted out at ten o'clock the next morning. Thinking that it might be helpful to talk to the CO of the other battery, I met with Lieutenant Koestler and discussed the coming operation at length. He and I concluded that before we were dropped in on the LZ, we really needed to see the position firsthand in order to know how to set up the guns. We put in a request for a chopper and, after receiving permission for the recon, were told to be over at Charlie Med by three that afternoon so they could have us back by dark.

Lieutenant Koestler and I arrived early and thus began an interesting but brief relationship. He was not one to talk a lot, but he was intelligent and certainly fit the image of a Marine officer. I learned he was a Harvard graduate who had grown up in Boston and, having been around him on several occasions in the past, judged him to be solid. His tenure as CO had been about the same length of time as mine, so we both could identify with the other's problems, particularly the responsibilities of command. Before this day was over we would know each other much better.

The chopper picked us up right on schedule, and on a beautiful day we were soon passing over green hills outside the ring of destruction that the B-52 bombs had made. We had not been gone long when the crew chief came back and handed me a headset to put on. The pilot then informed me that he had been diverted to an emergency evacuation and would have to drop off Lieutenant Koestler and me at a nearby infantry position. This suited the heck out of me because I sure did not want to fly into a firefight to remove medevacs. All we could have done was watch as passengers. I passed the phones to Lieutenant Koestler, and he mirrored my own feelings when I saw him roll his eyes. Moments later we clambered off the chopper and onto a hill covered with elephant grass. The Marine who had directed in our landing then took us over to the CO of the infantry company holding the hill; it turned out they had just arrived themselves. They were going to be there only for the night because they were participating in a search-and-destroy sweep and would be moving out early the next morning. I had thought that my days of being in the hills with infantry were behind me, but fate was up to its usual tricks.

The most startling information, however, was the nature of the emergency that had stranded us in the boondocks. It seemed that the guns of Co Roc had swung and were firing on the hill where we were supposed to be dropped the next morning. Not only was that happening but the position was taking heavy mortar fire as well. Evidently, the bulldozer's activity had attracted considerable NVA attention. Nothing about this development sounded good to Lieutenant Koestler and me as we contemplated our scheduled arrival the next day.

The next concern was trying to get a helicopter to take us back so we could supervise preparations for liftoff. Normally, it would have been high priority to return two COs to their commands, but as we monitored radio traffic, it became apparent that every available chopper was being used to medevac casualties. The hill was, in fact, taking a deadly pounding from the guns of Co Roc. When darkness finally fell without a chopper having picked us up, we knew we were there for the night. The anxiety of not being with our batteries as they prepared for the next day's liftoff was intense. In fact, this sequence of events was almost unbelievable.

Lieutenant Koestler and I found a bomb crater on top of the hill we were on and settled in for the evening. It was away from the infantry command post but had a view, giving us good surveillance in all directions. We sure hoped this infantry company had a solid perimeter because all we had were our .45 pistols. The CO did loan us a backpack radio with a greater range than a handheld unit so we could talk back to Khe Sanh. It would prove to be a sleepless night as we monitored radio traffic.

After taking turns talking to our battery officers, we finally had a chance to tune in the frequency of the unit that had been taking heat that afternoon. It was important to know as much as possible about the situation out there. In only a few minutes, we found out those guys were facing a major ground attack, and the awareness that our batteries were about to be airlifted into this meat grinder sank in with a sick feeling. You could hear and feel the strain of desperation in their voices. It was a big-time, serious affair, and now we could see Puff on the night horizon dropping its flares and waving his red thread of machine-gun fire. The flares cast eerie shadows as far away as our own position, and we had enough light to read the expressions on each of our faces. They were somber ones. Occasionally the flares would stop, and in the ensuing darkness, stars could be seen brightly twinkling overhead. It made us feel very insignificant in the vastness of the universe, sitting as we did on a bleak hilltop halfway around the world and crouched in a hole with someone we hardly knew. It was a lonely feeling, and we talked about our families and backgrounds to make it less so.

From time to time the action at the distant hill would pick up, and in would come Puff dropping flares and saturating the area with miniguns. It did not look good for tomorrow, and I prayed someone would have the good sense to cancel the airlift. Evidently, no one had anticipated that the artillery fire from Co Roc and Laos would be so intense. In my opinion the position was much too close to the Laotian border. As the time crept by, the night seemed to be lasting longer than any I had ever experienced, and all we could do was sit there with nothing to do but let our minds ponder the meaning of it all while listening to anguished calls for assistance. My silent prayers grew more intense, and I unabashedly asked God not to let them send us in tomorrow.

The following morning found us still awake and alert, and we spent the hour before dawn lobbying Khe Sanh for a chopper. Finally, some of the artillery units relayed to Camp Carroll the dilemma of two COs being separated from their batteries, and we promptly received a first priority on the next helicopter out of Khe Sanh. I heard later that the CO of 1/12 had personally taken a hand in seeing to it that we were returned when he learned of the situation.

Early after first light, a chopper came in, and we were whisked back to Khe Sanh. The battery was in good shape, and everything was primed to go. After checking preparations, I went over to the Khe Sanh command post and, on reporting in, received the most welcome words I had ever heard. A decision had been made to relocate the artillery strongpoint to another location. It would be more to the south and about the same distance from the Laotian border but significantly further away from the guns at Co Roc. No one can imagine the relief I felt. It was all

I could do to maintain some semblance of dignity and not give a hearty cheer. On the walk back to the battery, I prayed a continuous prayer of thanksgiving.

The battery stood down from the airlift, and we returned to our previous role of shooting fire missions for targets controlled from Khe Sanh. I never shared my feelings with anyone in the battery about how bad it would have been if we had been dropped on that LZ. As it turned out, the position was overrun, with the loss of much life and the abandonment of the dozer. It had been a real wipeout. Charlie's troops, however, continued to be enthusiastic about the prospects of getting in the thick of it, and I did not say anything to dampen that spirit. I strongly suspected we were going to need every positive mental vibration that we could muster in the days ahead.

The next morning, word came down that we would move out to a new location the following day. This time it would be Charlie and Alpha batteries that would go to the new position, code-named LZ Torch. There we would be dropped on hills about a mile apart, and each would have a company of Marines for security. Battalion threw me another surprise as well. Because we would be operating so far away from Camp Carroll and because the communication by relays had not been up to par on the previous airlift attempt, it was decided to give one officer the authority to make tactical decisions for all the artillery support of the infantry. Both batteries would be operating fire direction centers, and there could be confusion if there was not a central point for clearing missions. I got the job, which meant the other battery had to clear everything through Charlie Battery. My fire direction center would monitor all firing from both locations. Fortunately, Lieutenant Duchow had worked in the battalion FDC at Camp Carroll and could easily handle the routine part of clearing these missions. I would insure that we provided the proper fire support and maintained harmonious relations between both batteries and the infantry.

The complexity of my position was not lost on me. Here I was, a lieutenant filling a captain's billet as battery CO, going into what promised to be a really critical operation, and having the responsibility for coordinating two batteries. It was like having an independent command in a remote theater of operation with no one to turn to for advice. Was this really happening? Never, back in the States, would I have imagined such a scenario involving so many responsibilities while still just a lieutenant. Fate has a way of creating the most improbable sets of circumstances, and the expected can never be taken for granted.

Later that afternoon the Khe Sanh command gave us more details for the following day. First, they told us that they were not going to send a dozer to prepare positions and that each battery would have to construct for itself whatever protection it needed. They did point out, though, that there would be adequate infantry for security. Furthermore, there would not be a helicopter recon to check out the position. I guess they had decided that the early work of the previous dozer had been too much of an alert to the NVA, and they also did not want to take a chance on having two COs separated from their batteries again. After really raising a ruckus, I did get the concession to have the Gunny, three FDC personnel, and me dropped in an hour before the battery arrived. That way I could designate where to put the six guns and could have the FDC operational by the time the guns got there. I explained to the Khe Sanh command that by doing this, we could have aiming stakes in place and be ready to fire missions within ten minutes of the guns' arrival. That argument, in combination with previous positive comments from infantry units about our speed and accuracy, was appealing to them; I also think they realized we could deliver better support if accommodated just a little bit.

Returning to the battery, I found everyone already in full swing with preparations, the troops already checking gear and busying themselves with details. The place buzzed like a beehive and looked like an anthill. Charlie Battery was ready and impatient. The previous false start had been hard to take, but the men were not having any trouble getting pumped up again.

15

LZ Torch

The battery was scheduled to lift off at ten o'clock the following morning. Hoping there might be an early bird I could get my advance crew on, I took Gunny Mac and the three FDC personnel over to Charlie Med at seven in the morning. There we settled down next to a sandbagged bunker and found ourselves in the old hurry-up-and-wait mode to which we were so accustomed. Unfortunately, over here away from the battery, we did not have anything to do but think. I was soon dealing with butterflies in the stomach, again being reminded of the pregame jitters that used to come in my football days. Also contributing to our discomfort was the proximity of the makeshift morgue, hardly more than a few pieces of canvas hung over a wood frame to screen bodies from general view. When the wind puffed, the canvas would flap, and plastic body bags containing dead Marines could be seen laid out in a row. The tattered state of that final way station with all its starkness sobered us, to say the least. No one made small talk as each man dealt with his own inner feelings, and the waiting dragged on.

Another thirty minutes, seemingly forever, passed before we finally heard choppers coming in from the south. Hoping one was for us, we automatically began gathering our gear. About that time a corpsman from Charlie Med came running over, quickly explained that they were shorthanded, and asked us to help them unload some medevacs. We, of course, dropped our gear and ran over to the landing pad as a big double-rotored helicopter settled down. Following the corpsmen, we ap-

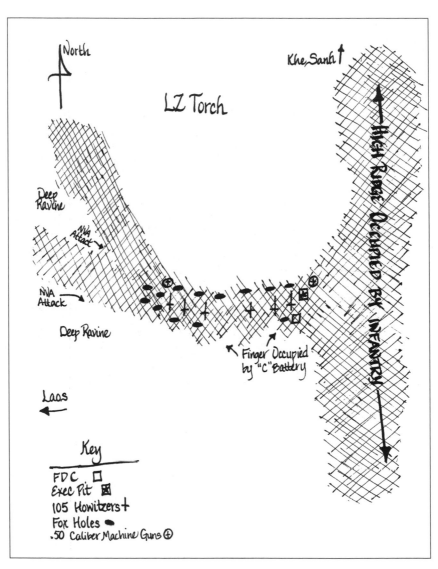

LZ Torch

proached the rear of the big chopper in order to run up the rear ramp as soon as it dropped. It opened slowly, and there before us was a bloody pile of men either sitting up or sprawled out all the way to the front of the aircraft. In mild shock at the sight, I focused on one of the crewmen dragging a Marine down the ramp. His head bounced up and down on the deck, and my first reaction was to knock the crewman away. I do not know what I had been thinking, but when I reached down to pick up the Marine, I saw that the top of his head was gone and that only a cavity remained where his brain had been. It finally hit me that he was dead. I still did not want him dragged like a sack of meat, however, so I picked up his body in my arms as if it were a child. Every bone in his body must have been broken, and his limbs flapped and sloshed like I was carrying jelly. Carrying him as gently as possible, I took him over to the morgue and laid him on the ground inside. Then, with tears running down my face, I returned to the chopper and helped unload the rest of the dead and wounded.

Returning to our gear by the bunker, I found the butterflies in my stomach were now merely a sick, numb sensation. Looking at the silent faces of my guys, I knew this was affecting them, too. We needed to get out of here in a hurry, so I went over to the command bunker to try to find out what was taking so long. As it turned out, the casualties were coming in from the operation we were about to join, and the choppers we had just unloaded had returned for more wounded. Fortunately, however, the infantry now decided they wanted our batteries out there in a hurry and promised us a ride on the next bird out.

Rejoining my men, I calmly told them what was going on, but my inner self struggled with the trauma of the moment. Never had I felt such stress. Beyond a doubt we were going into a hot zone. I imagined we must be experiencing something similar to what Marines in World War II must have felt while waiting for the landing crafts that would storm the beaches in the Pacific. Maybe our situation was even worse because we had just unloaded the carnage from the zone we were going into. It was just wait and pray; I genuinely tried to make my peace with God. During all this and for the sake of the men with me, I acted as if it was not any big deal. They were all giving the "thousand-mile stare," that stare of shock when one seems to be looking at things in the distance and not focusing at all on what is near; no one seemed to want to look anyone else in the eye. One of the troopers got sick, and the staff sergeant of the FDC gave me a letter to mail in case he did not make it. I took it with a nod. This was pure stress, and nothing would give relief but the first lick of the ball game.

Finally, a chopper came in, and we were on it in no time. I think we had genuinely been in shock since unloading the casualties, but the moving about seemed to help. Never mind that we might be dropping into a firefight or whatever; the relief of finally doing something made us all feel better. I was glad to be on the way, come what may. We soon arrived at LZ Torch, and as we began to circle, I edged over to the open gunner's door to check out the terrain. We were in steep hill country with a lot of elephant grass, and we could see nearby mountains on the Laotian border. Occasional patches of trees marked draws and creek beds, but the hills were mostly distinguished by a covering of grass. LZ Torch itself was obvious because a colored smoke grenade had been popped to guide us in. It was a big ridge running north-south with fingers coming off on either side.

On landing, I immediately located the CO of the infantry company to find out where the guns were supposed to go, and he quickly pointed toward a finger that ran off the main ridge to the west. Then he dropped a bomb on me. After telling me that he had only enough men to man the main ridge, he said we would have to provide for our own perimeter defense on the designated finger. "Some security!" I thought, recalling the briefing back at Khe Sanh. By now I had no idea of how long it would take for the battery to arrive, and that prompted us into high gear to at least be able to show the choppers where to drop each gun. There was certainly no time to take issue or attempt to find a better location. My only option was to take the situation as the infantry captain presented it.

I ran down through the elephant grass to the battery's new position and designated a place to set up the FDC. The spot was located near the top of the finger where it met the main ridge. That crew began setting up immediately, having been placed where they would be least likely to be affected if we were overrun by ground troops. The FDC had to be given as much security as possible because they were the nerve center for all firing data. We could lose all guns but one and still be functional if we had the FDC, but if we did not have them, we were inoperative for supporting fire, period. I instructed them to set up their charts in the open and to have them ready for fire missions when the guns arrived. They could start digging in after they were operational.

Gunny Mac and I then quickly headed down the finger to get a sense of the position. Not only did we have to figure out where to place the guns, but we now had to set up our own lines as well. Proceeding farther, I went out a much greater distance than I intended to place the battery because I wanted to find likely enemy approach points. The positioning of the guns and arrangement of our perimeter defense would depend on the terrain in front of us. Running at a half trot on this recon with only a shotgun and my .45 pistol, I was sure glad we did not run into any NVA because there was no infantry at all on this finger. At this point I really began to appreciate the Marine Corps' method of training that prepared every Marine first as an infantryman before going on to some other specialty such as artillery. Consequently, in Basic School I had set up numerous positions and spent hours learning the concepts of infantry tactics. I thanked the Corps for what they had given me back then because now I needed every skill I could muster.

We soon determined that the most likely NVA approach route would be from the end of the finger and particularly to the right or northern side. The ground was not very steep there, and a jungle-filled ravine came up at that point. I figured the NVA would use that approach for cover if they came. Having a somewhat better feel for our surroundings, we returned to the top of the finger to select gun locations. Unfortunately, the crest was so narrow that, without a dozer to cut gun pads, we were left with only one option. The guns would have to be stretched out on line along the ridge in order to keep them somewhat level. Gun One was to be near the FDC, and the other guns would be dropped sequentially down the gradually sloping finger. The last gun in the line would be Gun Six, and consequently it would be the most vulnerable. I also positioned the guns much closer than normal for two reasons. First, there was a steep drop-off not too far down the ridge. Second, because we had to provide for our own security, I did not have enough personnel to man a very large perimeter.

My plan was simple and dictated by the terrain. The north or right side of the finger already provided good fields of fire. The south side was an extremely steep ravine and would likely discourage serious attacks from that direction. That left the extended ridge beyond Gun Six as the most likely point for an attack. I would place two fighting holes on the north side of each gun and one on the less vulnerable south side. To protect the more dangerous north side, I would also place one of our two .50-caliber machine guns high on the ridge near the FDC. It would provide excellent coverage of the open ground to the north of our gun line. At the lower end of the gun line, around Gun Six, I planned to beef up the defenses considerably with three holes facing down the extended finger. In addition to those, three more would be added below where the finger dropped off sharply. The fighting holes closest to Gun Six could fire freely over that additional row without hitting the occupants. I then planned to knock down all the elephant grass for about thirty yards to the likely NVA approach from the ravine. To cover that danger point, I would put our other .50-caliber machine gun in the far right hole of the forward line.

With that arrangement in mind, I began helping Gunny Mac lay out big markers showing gun numbers that would designate where each gun was to be dropped. After finishing that, we began setting out aiming stakes with our instruments as if the guns were already in place. We would, of course, have to make adjustments when the guns actually arrived and fine-tune everything, but with these preliminary preparations, we should be able to have the guns ready to fire in minutes.

While attending to this tedious task, I noticed three light helicopters coming into the area. They were too small to be transporting our battery, so I did not pay a lot of attention when they landed on the main ridge with the infantry. Gunny Mac and I went on with our business, methodically sighting in and setting up the aiming stakes. Then, out here in the middle of nowhere, I experienced one of the biggest surprises I would ever have. Striding down our fresh trail through high grass came a Marine general. I could not believe my eyes. I had been in country for a year now and had seen only one general. He happened to be visiting the top of the Rockpile, and he had been an Army one at that. I had seen no Marine generals at all and only a few Marine full colonels since my arrival in Vietnam, so this was an exceptional moment. It startled me so much that I came to attention and popped off a crisp salute, not the thing to do out in the field like this. He returned the salute as an aide introduced us to General Davis, commander of the 3d Marine Division. He calmly quizzed me about the position and put me at ease, and I answered questions about what we were doing to protect ourselves and the overall plan of support for the infantry. Gunny Mac just stood wide-eyed, holding an aiming stake and looking on with incredulity. General Davis had the reputation in the Corps of being one of our sharpest generals, and I was duly impressed that he would even be out here in such an exposed forward position. After hearing what I had to say, he looked me in the eyes and said, "Lieutenant, you had better dig your men in good because they're going to be coming after your guns." With that he stuck his hand out, shook mine, and was gone.

Gunny Mac and I just stood there with our mouths open. Had this scene really happened? Everything had been so unreal earlier this morning back at Khe Sanh, and now this had happened. One thing for sure, Charlie Battery was going to do some digging when it got here. If anybody should have an accurate idea of what was coming, it ought to be the division commander.

After all the aiming stakes were in place, I began marking locations for fighting holes. The more that could be done before the battery arrived, the smoother things would be when it finally got here. It would be chaotic enough with seventy men and six guns arriving all at once.

I now had time to review our defensive plan and became even more concerned about the jungled draw so near our position down the finger. The NVA could get dangerously close before we even knew they were there. Realizing this to be a critical factor in our defensive strategy, I decided to put a listening post down the finger in front of our lines to provide, I hoped, some warning if NVA came from that direction. As was typical, the LP would consist of two men who would alternate four-hour shifts during the night. The Gunny and I reconnoitered the area until we found a spot that would accommodate an LP yet minimize the chances of those men being trapped in front of the lines if we were attacked. It was to the right of the finger, much farther down on the edge of the ravine itself. At that point a clump of trees about seventy yards from our lines spilled out of the draw. The trees would give our men the ability to sit up so they could hear well and still not be seen when flares floated overhead. I instructed the Gunny to be sure they did not dig there and to leave the area looking as natural as possible; NVA observers would be less likely to notice it during the daytime. He would take the LP out only after dark, and they would return before day, decreasing the chances of their being detected.

As the Gunny and I made our way back to the position, we finally heard what must be our battery coming in from the north. The *thump, thump* of the many choppers pumped up our adrenaline, and soon we saw them headed toward us with guns slung below. Already hot and sweaty from intense tropical heat, we nevertheless double-timed it back through head-high elephant grass. We made it there just in time to supervise the off loading, and a whirlwind of cool relief greeted us as helicopter blades turned the ridge into a dust cloud of swirling debris.

The first two choppers rapidly unloaded personnel to help detach the guns, and the fieldpieces swinging beneath the bellies of the other big choppers were easily released as the choppers settled down. More choppers unloaded the rest of the men up the ridge by the FDC, and in short order all of Charlie Battery had been deposited on our finger. Within ten minutes we had the guns sighted in and ready to fire, and I immediately had the FDC notify all infantry units in the area that we were ready to provide operational support. Forty-five minutes later, Alpha Battery reported in that they were operational also.

Now the priority of the moment was digging in and clearing fields of fire. It was hot, humid, and itchy, but the work progressed at a rapid pace. Adrenaline continued to flow when the troops found out that we would not have infantry around us, and under the circumstances it did not take much prompting to get them to dig their holes. They fully understood that these foxholes would be more than just protection from incoming mortars and artillery. Another concern was water. The three canteens that each man had been instructed to bring would not last long with the kind of exertion we were putting out, and for some reason our big water bladder had not arrived with the ammunition like it was supposed to. After much radio communication and a lot of ranting and raving, we would finally receive it late in the afternoon.

The Exec Pit was set up near the FDC and, at that high point of the ridge, provided an excellent overview of the surrounding terrain. I told Lieutenant Dewlen to have one of his men constantly scan the hills for any indication of enemy activity. To accomplish this, he set up the BC scope, a type of binocular mounted on a tripod, and established a watch to do nothing but observe the hills and draws. Ironically, I noticed that one of the men assigned to the scope, Corporal Gary Conner, had only recently been brought back to the battery because he had spent an inordinate amount of time in the field as a radio operator. Now, here he was where it was not supposed to be so dangerous.

The work preparations went well, and we began shooting fire missions soon after notifying the infantry that we were ready. This made it tough on some of the men who were preparing foxholes because the guns had to shoot directly over them. Digging had to go on whether the guns fired or not, and the concussion from the muzzle blasts was a real aggravation. Fortunately, the targets were close, so we did not have to use full powder charges. The smell of cordite or gunpowder, always a staple in an active battery, was extreme today because of the congested position, and that contributed to the excitement of the moment as it merged with the noise and fervid activity. Moreover, the battery soon began receiving compliments from the infantry for accurate and quick fire support, which added to that high. Charlie Battery was living what usually was only read about in books or seen in movies.

Around four in the afternoon, while down at Gun Six overseeing the final touches of setting up defenses, I received an urgent call from Mike Dewlen to come up to the Exec Pit. On arriving there, I could not help but notice that everyone was excited. Mike was glued to the BC scope and looking southwest at the first hill across the valley where people could be seen stirring around. The man on watch had noticed movement earlier, and now Lieutenant Dewlen had confirmed seeing it, too. In an excited voice he told me, "There are a lot of people in uniform running around on a hill over there, but they don't have helmets on." I took a look, and, sure enough, people could be seen scurrying around a clump of trees on the top of a hill. I sent Mike up to the infantry CO to be sure those people were not one of his patrols or another Marine unit we did not know about, and he returned with the report that there definitely were no friendlies in that area. I decided to do something at once, suspecting that the activity might well be an indication of NVA intentions to mortar us.

This situation was exceptional in that it was extremely unusual for an artillery battery to be able to call in missions from its own gun position. Targets were usually much farther away and called in by forward observers. It occurred to me also that this was an excellent opportunity to try out the new Firecracker rounds we had heard so much about. Now we could see firsthand just how effective they were. By this time everybody on the ridge knew we had the NVA in sight less than a mile away, and all work stopped when we called for the Firecracker. Lieutenant Dewlen, as XO, gave commands to the guns over the headset, and I, with far more experience than anyone else as a forward observer, took over that function. Standing near the FDC, I gave the fire commands directly to that group without even using a radio. I wondered how many times that had happened in the history of the Marine Corps. It could not have been often, I was willing to bet.

Using regular rounds, I adjusted the fire to target with three shots from Gun Three. The whole battery was now watching the enemy hill. After the third round hit the target, I gave the command to "fire for effect," and all six guns fired off a round of Firecracker. About sixty feet over the enemy position, shells popped in puffs of smoke, and a few seconds later, small explosions covered the target area. The sound from this distance could be compared with strings of Chinese firecrackers crackling in unison.

I sent another volley of six rounds, and soon the area looked like an anthill as enemy troops scurried away from this new agent of destruction. There must have been close to a platoon out there from the number of NVA we saw clearing out amid the crumpled body heaps scattered around the hill. For good measure I pumped in another volley but this time used our regular rounds to conserve the limited supply of Firecracker. If a mortar attack had been intended, it was not likely going to happen from that location. The NVA now knew that we literally had them zeroed in on that hill.

After the mission's conclusion, we got the troops back to work on our own defenses. Night would be here before we knew it, and everybody needed to be dug in. There was no doubt now that we were in a hot zone of enemy activity and that plenty of incoming and probably a ground attack were likely. Six 105mm howitzers sitting right in the middle of enemy territory had to be a tempting prize for the NVA. We continued firing support missions for the infantry and occasionally sent a six-gun volley back to the hill where the Firecracker had been used.

About an hour before dark, we took our first mortar attack. Interestingly, the rounds fell well outside of our perimeter, an occurrence significantly different from what we had experienced in the base camps. There, the NVA practically had surveyed coordinates of our locations, and the rounds usually fell in our position on the first volley. Here, it took them a number of adjusting rounds before they even came close. To me, this indicated that General Davis's strategy of moving the batteries to new and unexpected locations had merit. He must have been a student of General Nathan Bedford Forrest because Davis was using artillery in much the same way as that Civil War genius had more than one hundred years before. By the time the first rounds struck, we had determined from the pop of their tube that they must be behind a high ridge to the northwest. After we pumped rounds to the rear of the hill we thought was shielding them, the incoming stopped. Only two of their rounds had impacted in our area, and those had been up on the big ridge with the infantry. We were hardly affected by that and continued preparing our position.

When darkness fell, Gunny Mac took the first pair of LPs out to the designated post. They had been given careful instructions on how to communicate back to us silently by using a series of clicks on the radio mike. If they heard nothing, then they could whisper back at regular check-in times. If they thought they were hearing something or felt the need to operate silently, then they could operate by a clicking code we had devised. Contact back to the battery was to be every fifteen minutes. On the battery perimeter, one man would stand watch in each foxhole and rotate watches with another man sharing the hole.

During that first night we fired a number of support missions for the infantry and occasionally fired rounds at suspected approach routes. On three occasions we fired volleys at the hill where all the enemy activity had been seen earlier. That night there were no NVA mortar attacks and no probes of our lines, but we did not do a lot of sleeping.

When day finally broke, the finger we were on looked a whole lot different from how it had when we first arrived. Spent brass from fired artillery rounds lay all over the place, and empty ammo boxes cluttered the area. Things were anything but neat and orderly. The elephant grass, which had been head high when we landed, was now trampled down completely on the gun line and was substantially down to the north and west from where we believed enemy attacks would likely come.

About an hour after dawn, we received our first resupply of artillery rounds, having fired a large number already. I had asked for double the initial supply, and the request was promptly granted. Evidently, the infantry liked the generous support they were receiving. When the choppers brought in the first of two loads, it was again mass chaos in the backwash of the helicopter blades. This time, however, every poncho and tee shirt that was not on somebody seemed to go up in the dust storm. With their eyes shut, the troopers just tried to lie on as much as they could, holding down anything in reach, while the choppers dropped ammunition pallets at random along the gun line. Neatness was out of the question as yesterday's trash littered the entire ridge amid a hodgepodge of used pallets.

An hour later our second lift came in, but this time NVA mortars arrived just as the last loads were dropped. Fortunately, none of the rounds landed in our position, but the pallets were scattered out even more because the pilots were having a fit to get unhitched. One pallet was dropped so close to Gun Four that the gun could not be turned, and another ended up twenty yards outside of our perimeter. We had to break those two pallets up immediately in order to put Gun Four back in operation and retrieve the other rounds to the security of our lines.

We fired all day in support of the infantry who were moving about on sweeps and on at least one occasion backed up a unit in a firefight for an intense hour and a half. By mid-afternoon, I decided that, at this rate, we were going to need still another supply of artillery rounds. This time the airdrop came right before dark, and again the NVA started throwing in mortars. We took two rounds up near the FDC but still received no casualties.

I, of course, was relieved that no one had been hurt, but we did incur one serious problem in this last attack. Our water bladder, the only source of water, had been hit by mortar shrapnel and was gushing like a fountain. The Gunny had the men come up and catch the spewing streams in canteens and anything else that would hold water. With the heavy physical demands resulting from around-the-clock ammo humping, water was now a big item with us.

Night finally fell, and the guns stood silent for the first time that day. The infantry had put in their night protective coordinates before dark, and no one was having contact at the moment. We had now been here for two days and one night, and I hoped they would wind down the operation or send us someplace new. General Davis's new strategy of frequently moving the guns had impressed me; the NVA seemed to be taking an inordinate amount of time adjusting to our battery's presence.

Going into the evening, I assessed our defenses and felt good about the progress. The fighting holes were now adequate for repelling a ground attack, and fields of fire were well defined, with the elephant grass having been knocked down considerably. My major concern still was the approach below Gun Six, and I was counting heavily on the LP for an early warning there if the NVA approached. If a ground attack did come from the ravine to our front, the .50-caliber machine gun in the forward tier of fighting holes should really help out. Again, after dark, the same two LPs headed out to their position with instructions to do everything just like they had the night before. Their system for signaling had worked well, and no one had dozed off. I think the stimulus of sitting out in front of the lines all alone and separated from the battery was enough to keep anyone awake; I counted on the same alertness for tonight.

It was an unusually calm evening as far as infantry requests for fire support, and by midnight only two fire missions had been called in from the field. Some of the troops were getting much-needed sleep, and Gunny Mac was making regular visits around the perimeter to be sure at least one man was awake on each post. I went up to the Exec Pit to get a little sleep myself, planning to relieve the Gunny later. It seemed like I had barely dozed off when Lieutenant Dewlen shook me awake shortly after midnight. He said that Gunny Mac had called in and needed me down on Gun Six right away. I quickly headed down there, and the gun crew told me that the Gunny was out on the second row of foxholes to their front. The night was not very dark, and I soon came across him in one of the holes. With enough light to distinguish facial features of the men, it was apparent that they were intent on something to the front. Gunny Mac's first words to me were, "Skipper, the LP says there are lots of gooks moving through the ravine, and I have called them back in." They had been signaling by clicking the radio mike for about twenty minutes, but when asked whether they thought they ought to come in, they had whispered back in the affirmative. The men in the LP had been selected because of their reliability, and the Gunny did not think they were letting their imaginations get the best of them, as is often the case. We had both agreed earlier that if there seemed to be movement, then we must get them back quickly for their own protection. When they reached our lines, I quizzed them at length and decided they really believed that people were moving in the ravine. Returning to Gun Six, I got on the gun loop and put the battery on 100 percent alert. Then I had Lieutenant Dewlen put together a reaction team made up of the Exec Pit crew and anybody else nearby; they would be used for reinforcements at the point of an NVA attack wherever that happened to come. The word was also passed to the infantry on the big ridge above us.

Going back to the foxhole where the Gunny remained, I settled in to listen myself. We had no mortars available to shoot into the ravine and to have opened fire with rifles would have achieved little because any NVA out there would have been in defilade. In absolute silence, we strained to hear any sound. It reminded me of nights as a young boy back in the Mississippi Delta. Many times in those days before air conditioning I had lain awake in a sweat, letting my mind play tricks on me while listening to night sounds and imagining some unknown threat in the outside darkness. Then, none of my fears had come to pass although they had seemed real at the time; now I felt those old anxieties coming over me again. Soon, I thought I could hear the slightest of movements out front and to the left of the ridge on the steep side of the finger away from the ravine. For some reason the insects had stopped chirping, and even the smallest sounds seemed clear. Was my imagination playing tricks on me as it had long ago? On hearing what sounded like a piece of gravel rolling down a bank followed by crawling sounds in the grass with the distinct clink of metal on stone, I knew an attack was coming.

Hustling back to Gun Six, I got on the headset to the rest of the battery and told everyone that the NVA were about to attack. Lieutenant Dewlen was ordered to bring his reaction force quietly down to the left of Gun Six where I was hearing the noise. I wanted reinforcements for that part of the perimeter before the enemy realized we knew they were there. We could then start chunking grenades and open fire with rifles and machine guns. All of this happened in the span of only several minutes from the time I had personally heard the enemy movement out to the front. About that time a tremendous flash of light and explosion occurred, and I saw the .50-caliber machine gun to the front right of Gun Six being blown twenty feet straight up in the air. Everyone in the battery who had a hand flare must have popped it simultaneously because the position lit up at once. I headed back to the Exec Pit to coordinate our defense from there and passed Lieutenant Dewlen and six or seven Marines on the fly as they ran down the hill. It was the last time I would see Mike alive.

A furious firefight was in full swing below Gun Six by the time I reached the Exec Pit. Our other .50-caliber machine gun, high up on the ridge, was cranking away, and the M-60 machine guns, which were scattered around the perimeter, were ripping it up as well. Eerie shadows from the flares filled the night while tracer rounds interspersed through a scene that was clearly visible as action increased around Gun Six. Things were happening so quickly. I was on the headsets talking to the guns and getting reports but receiving no response from Guns Five or Six. I would just have to rely on Lieutenant Dewlen to take charge down there. Incoming small-arms fire was everywhere and sounded like the flight of bees buzzing by. The NVA had automatic weapons and were using them freely; their distinctive sound added to the chaos. This went on for a number of minutes, and I could easily see the action down the ridge. The fury of the fight had drawn dangerously close to Gun Six, and it seemed they might be overrun. Gun Four confirmed this with a report that NVA were almost at Gun Six, convincing me that the enemy would soon be in our position. An overwhelming feeling of indignation welled up inside me, and I resolved that I was not going to lose any guns on my watch. I was the new CO of one of the finest Marine units in the Corps, and I would die before allowing that to happen.

I gathered all the men from the FDC except Lieutenant Duchow, who was left to coordinate things, and grabbed everyone else nearby. We started down the hill, our group totaling eight, and, scattering out on line, began a fast walk down the ridge. Screaming above the din, I told them to stay abreast of me all the way to Gun Six. As we fanned out across the ridge I started giving rebel yells, and soon the troopers were doing the same. Bullets ripped around us like hornets, and I noticed one of the Marines to my right go down as we swept forward. We would not actually fire our own weapons until we reached Gun Six, but the troopers were in the spirit of things, and everyone yelled at the top of their lungs. Some men from the gun crews we were passing could not resist the excitement of the moment and joined us on our fast march to the front. Another man fell beside me. I could not believe I had not been hit. A strange but distinct feeling came over me that God must surely be saving me for something.

Reaching Gun Six, we opened fire and pushed through to the fighting holes on the other side. A maelstrom of explosions and automatic-weapons fire rang out everywhere, and light flashed all around from exploding satchel charges and concussion grenades. On passing Gun Six, I ran over to an unopened pallet of artillery shells that I hoped might give some protection while I tried to get a handle on things. These rounds were in wooden boxes stacked about four feet high, and, kneeling behind them, I held my shotgun high with my right hand and peered toward the heaviest enemy firing. Evidently, an NVA soldier was very near because a satchel charge landed on top of the boxes protecting me and exploded. The blast blew my shotgun in half while still in my hand, but fortunately for me, my head was lower than the top of the ammo pile, thus shielding my body. In fact, everyone around Gun Six was very lucky because if the stack of artillery rounds on which the satchel charge

landed had detonated, there would not have been much left on this end
of the gun line.

Everyone fought furiously, and I saw Marines in hand-to-hand combat about ten yards away near one of the foxholes. Pulling my .45 pistol
from my shoulder holster, I started running toward them. I took no more
than three steps in a low crouch when a concussion grenade or satchel
charge exploded on the ground in front of me. The blast, in a blinding
flash of light, blew my helmet backward off of my head, and I could only
crawl around on the ground trying to open my eyes just to find out
whether I could still see. My face and eyes burned, and I could not force
my eyes open to find out how bad off I really was. About that time a
trooper crawled over to see whether I was all right, and I had him pour
canteen water in my eyes. This flushed out enough trash and debris for
me to know that I still had vision, and I realized I was all right for the
moment. With one eye open, I ran around making sure we kept up the
firing.

It occurred to me in the melee that we had to get more firepower
going into the heart of the attack, and I remembered the beehive on each
gun. Seeing Gunny Mac nearby, I shouted at him to turn Gun Six and
to point it down the slope. Because of its position at the very end of the
gun line, it was the only one we could turn directly toward the main
enemy thrust. Getting Gun Six moved was no easy task, however, because both of its big rubber tires were flat from rifle fire. The guns could
normally be swung around with four men, but with flat tires and with-
ering enemy fire, it took closer to eight. At least two of the men went
down with bullet wounds while helping swing the gun.

When the gun finally pointed down the slope, we started pumping
beehive down the ridge. The tide of the fight changed immediately, and
enemy small-arms fire dropped off sharply. Thirty minutes later, another
factor came into play, giving us even more firepower as well as a morale
boost. When the attack had begun, the infantry had called for Puff, and
that gunship, equipped with miniguns and giant flares, finally arrived.
What a thrilling sight it was to see the red stream of machine-gun bullets waving a long thread over the draws and crevasses that we could not
reach with our own fire. Their flares turned our area into day, and the

light comforted us after the previous semidarkness that had been filled with flashes from explosions and rifle muzzles. Just knowing others were attempting to aid us made us feel better.

Prior to Puff's arrival, I had gotten all the beehive to Gun Six and had fired those rounds until only five remained. By then the attack was over, and these last shells were being held in reserve. The beehive quite possibly had saved us, and I was so thankful that we had brought them in. Using regular shells now, we continued firing direct fire down the ridge and to either side of the ravine. There was no calling in of missions here. It was just aim and shoot. The noise of the gun firing reassured us psychologically, regardless of whether we hit anything, so I kept up the firing for some time.

We continued to take distant rifle fire for a while, but even that eventually tapered off. The concern now became the condition of Charlie Battery. The NVA had made a concentrated effort to knock out our guns, and wounded were scattered everywhere. We started gathering casualties and taking them up by Gun One. The boys who had been killed were left where they fell for the time being; nothing could be done for them now, and we had our hands full with the wounded. I ordered a casualty report, and I soon had the news. Seven had been killed, and twenty-two were seriously wounded. A number of these were critical and would have to be medevaced if they were to have any chance of survival. At least two of these, including one of our corpsmen, had lost a leg, and others were in equally traumatic circumstances. A medevac chopper was requested, and we spent a lot of effort stabilizing those guys until we could get them out. Many other casualties were not critical, and those men would stay with us until morning to help hold off another attack if it came.

Puff continued dropping flares and occasionally waved its wand of fire into draws or creek beds. Our appreciation for that guardian angel had never been greater. Gun Six fired periodically down the ridge and into the valley. We had plenty of artillery rounds, but I learned we were getting extremely low on rifle and machine-gun ammunition. Our water supply was also getting low, the exertion and stress having created a terrific thirst. We would be down to nothing by daybreak at this rate.

Now the priority, other than casualties, had become replenishing the low supply of rifle ammunition. Water could wait, but if the NVA attacked again, we could easily run out of ammo. It was about two thirty in the morning now, and enough time remained for them to make another assault before day. By using radio relays, I got word back to Battalion at Camp Carroll that we desperately needed rifle and machine-gun ammunition, and they passed the word back that they would get right on it.

Around three o'clock the medevac chopper radioed that they were coming in and had us light a hand flare to show them where to land. It had occurred to me earlier that we would have a wild time loading the wounded if we started taking mortars during the extraction. To reduce that chance I had directed Gun Six to pick up the firing pace and instructed Lieutenant Duchow to start firing missions with Guns Two, Three, and Four at preplotted suspected enemy positions. Puff also continued to work the area over.

After we popped the hand flare, the big double-rotored CH-46 chopper came in quickly, dropping its rear loading ramp right by Gun One. The inside of the long chopper was lit up with red lights, supposedly to make it hard for the enemy to see from a distance, but for us it created a surreal scene as we loaded wounded into the big cargo cabin. They had to be stacked helter-skelter to get them all in, and looking into the red-hued cavern with its writhing cargo of torn and tattered men was like viewing a scene from hell. The ramp slowly closed back up, and the chopper roared away. The hill then faded into silence, disturbed only by an occasional round fired from Gun Six.

Thirty minutes later, one of the infantry units started getting a probe, and we traversed back into the battery's normal routine of fire missions. We could use only Guns One through Four, however, because the tires on Five and Six had been shot out and could not shift easily. Besides, the men were exhausted, and I did not want to use up their energy moving crippled guns around.

My efforts now turned to trying to speed up the resupply of rifle ammo. The thought of what could happen if we were hit again really concerned me. After much begging, pleading, and raising Cain, we were finally told that a resupply chopper would be in shortly. The only catch was that it would have to land up on the big ridge with the infantry because our position was a wreck by now. It was one thing for the pilots to take risks getting the wounded out at Gun One, but it was another if we were not under attack. They did not want to bring their choppers into the clutter of the battery area, so we would just have to hump up to the infantry's ridge and carry the ammo back down the hill. No one seemed to mind, though, because we all realized how crucial it was to be ready for another ground assault.

As daylight approached, Puff finally left, leaving us in inky darkness, and when the infantry stopped calling in fire missions, our position became extremely quiet. Everyone breathed easier, and individuals started checking themselves over. In my own case, my throat rasped with a raw hoarseness from all the yelling, and my eyes burned painfully, the right one being worse than the left.

Gunny Mac and I walked the gun line and circled the perimeter, talking to the men. The old familiar exhilaration I had experienced after previous combat experiences returned and felt good. I suppose this high comes from looking death in the eye and realizing that you are still here to tell about it. There are often subtle questions that reside in a man's heart as to whether he has what it takes to deal with great personal danger, and when those tests do take place, where your very life is at stake, there is a joy in their successful conclusion that is hard to describe. Feelings of grief and sadness would come later, but in the immediate period after intense combat, an elevated state of being was for me always the dominant emotion.

Walking the lines and interacting with the men, I sensed similar feelings of elation. The men were talkative, and their comments showed great pride that the NVA had not taken our guns. Charlie Battery had added yet another chapter to its epic journey, and already stories were taking shape that would grow in the retelling. These vignettes would be embellished and eventually become legend in the lore of Charlie Battery, just as they had before at places such as Gio Linh. Those previous events had occurred before my arrival in country, yet I had heard the accounts so many times that I felt as if I had participated myself. On this night already, I had listened to several variations of how Corporal Fake had killed an NVA with his folding pocket knife. Lieutenant Dewlen's charge into the teeth of the attack with the Exec Pit crew was being viewed as the courageous act that had given us just enough time to re-group. And then there was Gunny Mac who, fed up with being pinned down in a foxhole, had become a wild man in repulsing the attack. Fi-nally running out of ammo, he was seen to throw his pistol at an NVA soldier. And it would go on. This was one of Charlie's finest hours, and the battery knew it.

Day finally dawned, and I could only wish that we had an American flag. It would have been so appropriate to have it hoisted on our battle-strewn hill to let the NVA know we were still there. For now, though, it was more important to think about trying to get some water flown in. After a few radio requests, we finally got the word that a chopper would be in around seven o'clock with water and to pick up our seven KIAs.

The mood became quite somber in the freshness of the morning as we gently carried our fallen men up to a clear spot just above the FDC. For some reason, no one attempted to cover them up. It was like every-one wanted to be with them just as they were for a little time longer. To have covered them would have been too final. They were carried to the LZ with their faces up and on the shoulders of their buddies. I helped carry Mike Dewlen, who had taken a bullet in the neck right below his ear; he had died instantly. It was like a ceremonial procession in which fallen warriors were being carried to their funeral bier, and we laid them all out side by side to await the chopper. More than a few silent prayers were said over these men, and the Catholics, making the sign of the cross, symbolically expressed what was not being said in words. The heli-copter arrived on schedule and, after dropping its big water bladder, settled in to pick up our boys. We loaded them aboard respectfully, and they were gone.

In the quiet that followed I thought back over the night. Of the seven guys we had just put on the chopper, three had been from Lieutenant Dewlen's Exec Pit crew that had gone into the breach at Gun Six. Two others from his group had been wounded and were medevaced earlier in the night. That charge had probably made the difference in holding the position or losing it. Victory or defeat sometimes hinges on the slightest of moments. The tide can shift either way, with seemingly minor events affecting the outcome, and then the new direction takes on a momentum of its own. I thanked God for our good fortune.

Now in the full light of day, I checked the ridge out in detail. It really looked the part of a battlefield. Shattered weapons, helmets, and personal gear were scattered everywhere in the midst of the expended shell casings surrounding the guns. Down at Gun Six, a number of NVA bodies still lay where they had fallen. They had actually been in our position and, for a while, had engaged in hand-to-hand combat with our troops. These enemy soldiers were fully uniformed, lacking only helmets, and appeared quite professional. Some carried folding stock machine guns, leading me to believe that they were no ordinary troops. A number of unexploded satchel charges were scattered about, having been brought in to blow the guns, and concussion grenades littered the entire area. The latter were nothing more than bags of powder that if thrown in a fighting hole could kill a man but would not throw shrapnel. This feature allowed the NVA attackers to do their damage and not be hit by their own weapon. It was later confirmed that these troops were part of a sapper battalion whose role was to do just what they had tried to do to us.

It was at Gun Six, with hand-to-hand fighting so heavy, where so many had distinguished themselves. Here, Sergeant Rutledge, a Marine who had already received the Silver Star in a previous engagement, again fought with special bravery. He was, in fact, the man who crawled over to me and helped wash out my eyes when the concussion grenade got me. Nearby was the hole in which Corporal Fake had fought the enemy soldier with his pocket knife. And then there was Corporal Gary Conner, who had just returned to the battery from 3/3. He would receive the Bronze Star for his actions at Gun Six. A number of other men would be decorated for individual acts of bravery, but for every man receiving personal recognition, many others did as much or more than those formally cited. Frequently, acts of bravery are not seen by others in the heat of combat, and, of course, many observers are killed or traumatized by wounds received in the height of the action. Still, every one of the men on LZ Torch that night can take pride in just having been a member of Charlie Battery. The common bond of being an intimate part of a band of warriors who stood and fought will be accolade enough for most.

As morning wore on, the adrenaline that had sustained us dissipated, and with everyone exhausted by now, we arranged a shift system to let people get some sleep. It was also time to check out the injuries of those who had not been wounded badly enough to rate medevac last night. One of our two corpsmen had been evacuated, so we borrowed another one from the infantry up on the ridge. They checked everyone out and reported in to me that several men had serious conditions. One corpsman came over to me and asked to take a closer look at my face and eyes. He called the other corpsman to confer, and then both said that I really should be medevaced myself. They pointed out that my face, particularly around the eyes, had significant powder burns and that a kind of filmy glaze covered my cornea. They concurred that there was a real chance of vision loss if my eyes were not treated in a sterile environment.

At that moment I was not comfortable leaving until the battery had been reorganized and preparations made for the coming night, so I declined the medevac. About an hour later, Lieutenant Duchow suggested that I get some rest. I turned things over to him and fell asleep instantly, only to awake two hours later with a burning thirst. I tried to open my eyes, but they were stuck together, and I had a very panicky moment as the possibilities of what that might mean ran through my mind. Finally, pouring canteen water on them, I got them unstuck and could see again. The right eye was extremely painful, and both were quite puffy. I put a bandage over the right one and by using my left was able to see well enough to get around.

After a quick tour of the position, I found everybody to be snapping back into the routine of the battery quite well. While checking things out, I passed our corpsman, who again insisted on looking at my eyes. This time he said it was critical that I have them checked by specialists. By now, suspecting he was right, I got on the radio relay to Camp Carroll to let them know, and Major Capenas directed me to get on the next chopper.

With this development it was clear enough what had to be done. Lieutenant Duchow was to take charge of the battery because no other officers were left. He knew every aspect of the battery and was quite capable of command. He would have to run the FDC as well as be CO until someone else could be sent out. Battalion assured me they would be getting replacements to us quickly but emphasized that I should not wait.

About two o'clock in the afternoon we received word that a medevac chopper was on the way to pick up casualties, and I began to say my good-byes. It was an emotional moment for me because I could only wonder whether I would ever see any of these guys again. Because I was so close to rotation and because I did not know just how bad off my eyes really were, it was possible that I would not even return to the battery at all. When the chopper finally landed, it was with conflicting emotions that I went up the ramp. On the one hand there was a feeling of sadness at leaving people with whom I had shared so much. On the other hand, I felt relief at leaving so much danger. It kind of melded into a feeling of guilt and made me question whether I was doing the right thing.

There were no seats in the helicopter, so I sat down on the metal deck. Several other Marines had already been loaded on board, but I was not paying attention because I had adjusted the bandages down over my eyes to keep out debris. Then, moments later, the chopper roared off the hill, and the air from the helicopter rotor blades blew back my bandages to a point where I could see the men around me. Looking over at a Marine from the infantry company, I felt even guiltier for being medevaced. He was lying there in pain and with fear in his eyes. A bullet had passed through both of his thighs and his scrotum. Fortunately, the bullet had not expanded or torn him up, but he had received one of the most dreaded of wounds; his manhood was at risk. Because the wound was so clean, I hoped he had a chance to heal to a point where he could function again normally, and I prayed fervently that the Lord would see him through his ordeal. The maiming and death of the last several days was being brought sharply into focus by this young man at my side, and the dark side of war was all I could see as we raced back to Dong Ha. Combat has been glorified in countless books and movies through the years, but witnessing such agony on this trip out left me with a hollow emptiness. The elation I had earlier experienced now faded as the carnage around me overwhelmed my emotions. War reflects the degradation of man in the sense that no matter how necessary or just the cause for which one is fighting, the destruction of another human being is still the basic goal. We wrap the sacrifices of our comrades in a cloak of honor and attempt to live with the baseness of it all. Yes, war is essential in many cases, but we should never forget the price that is paid in death, pain, and degradation of the soul. Realizing that, you just move on and do your duty as you hope God would have you do.

The chopper took us to D Med, the field hospital at Dong Ha and the main medical facility on the DMZ. Typically, this was the first place the seriously wounded were treated other than the first-aid measures applied in the field. Here, real doctors performed extensive medical procedures that could not be handled in combat zones, and the facility was geared up to receive masses of wounded at one time. On arrival, corpsmen quickly took me to a frame building, one of the few wooden structures that even existed on the DMZ. One wall had wooden patient tables built into it, and those could be folded up when not in use. On this same wall, garden hoses were rolled up at intervals for easy availability when needed to wash away the blood from the concrete floor. The other sides of the building were open, and I supposed that was for ventilation. They pulled one of the tables down and had me lie down on my back, and I waited there for some time with my eyes covered. Listening to them work on some of the men near me, I realized there were others in critical shape who were being attended to. The doctors sounded professional and efficient.

As I lay there, my thoughts returned to my own problems after having been emotionally consumed with the plight of the young Marine on the chopper. As I waited, with the sounds of trauma all around, my mind began imagining all kinds of things, and I wondered whether I might be worse off than I had thought earlier. My eyes and face burned painfully, and I now wanted to be checked out in a hurry.

With those disturbing thoughts racing through my mind, I felt a big hand squeeze my shoulder and heard a voice with an Alabama drawl gently say, "Lieutenant Brown, I heard they had brought you in, and I just wanted to come over and check on you." It was Lance Corporal Elvin Murray from Charlie Battery, affectionately dubbed "Big Un." He had been medevaced the night before with significant neck wounds. A giant of a man who had grown up in the coal mine area around Birmingham, Alabama, he had heard the call to arms and, like many of us, volunteered. He was one of the most-liked men in the battery, and it was like hearing family as I lay on that operating table. "Big Un" stayed there talking and held my shoulder until the doctors arrived. It was truly comforting to have one of my own with me at a time like that. He filled me in on the casualties from the night before. One of the first he told about was the radioman who some weeks ago had torn my helmet cover while using my headgear as a hammer. On finding out that he had now been killed, a spooky feeling came over me as I recalled my superstitious concerns. Two other men had lost legs, and several others were in critical shape. It was touch and go as to whether they would even make it. Four or five were going to be fine and would return to the battery in a few weeks. The rest were headed to various hospitals. Of particular interest to me was hearing that the brass from Regiment had come down on the arrival of the wounded and congratulated the men on the job Charlie Battery had done, specifically citing their defense of the guns. It was good to know that the efforts had been appreciated and that the senior officers had cared enough to tell the men.

Finally, a Navy doctor showed up and checked me out. After flushing out my eyes and studying them for a while, he said I needed to be sent out to the *Repose* for examination by an eye specialist. The *Repose* was one of two hospital ships stationed in the China Sea off the coast of Vietnam, and the thought of going there made me uncomfortable because I wondered whether this eye situation might be more serious than I had previously thought.

"Big Un" waited with me until a chopper flew in to take me to the ship, and I will be forever grateful for his concern and support at the time. When the medevac arrived, I was put on a stretcher, although I could have walked, and strapped into place along with several other Marines. Fifteen minutes later, we began our landing approach to the ship.

16

The *Repose*

On touchdown, medical personnel came scurrying up from all over the place and would not let me get off of the stretcher. Whisking me into the ship, they put me in a receiving room. From time to time I peeked out from my bandages to see what was happening and to keep my eyelids from sticking together. What I saw contrasted sharply to the medical facilities I had passed through back in Dong Ha. The interior of the ship was as up-to-date as any hospital I had ever seen back stateside. Shiny instruments and equipment sparkled in a pristine and sterile environment while Navy corpsmen and doctors in neat scrubs hustled busily about. By comparison, D Med at Dong Ha had been a crude and dusty barn.

Now, in what seemed to be an emergency operating room filled with lights and equipment, they x-rayed me from head to toe and flushed my eyes out again. A corpsman rubbed something on my facial burns, and the doctor bandaged up my eyes after putting some type of salve in them. I was instructed not to remove the bandages on my own and to avoid getting them wet, all of which made me nervous and caused me to start quizzing the doctor. He explained that he expected me to be fine, but to avoid complications he was keeping me on the ship for a while.

I was then wheeled to the officer's section, where I heard a real American female voice for the first time since Hawaii. What a pleasant sound it was! It was a Navy nurse, and this voice from the "real" world was just wonderful. A corpsman wheeled me to a private room, and the nurse told me I needed a shower. Being exhausted, however, I convinced her that I needed rest more than a shower. Sleep came instantly. The realization that I did not have to concern myself with mortars and such had relaxed me to a point where I was almost comatose.

The next thing I knew, someone was gently shaking me awake. I had no idea how long I had been out because I had slept the sleep of the dead. They gave me a shot and took my temperature, and the nurse now insisted on getting me out of my filthy clothes to take a shower. I must have smelled to high heaven. A corpsman led me down a hall and put me in a shower stall, cautioning me not to get my bandages wet. The luxury of that stream of warm, clean water was incredible, and I washed away more than four weeks of grime accumulated since leaving Ca Lu. Much sooner than I wanted, the corpsman returned with clean hospital garb and led me back to bed, where the nurse cleaned my head and neck. I fell asleep before she was through and again slept for what must have been a very long time.

When I next awoke, a different nurse was there, and she made some conversation while I ate. My mind was beginning to function again, and I began to get a sense of my surroundings. The events of the preceding days now came creeping back into my consciousness, but remembering LZ Torch and Charlie Battery was like trying to recall a dream. Asking questions, I found out that I had been on the ship since yesterday and that it would soon be the second night of my stay. Later after supper, the nurse turned on a radio or some type of music, and I again faded off to sleep.

The following morning a doctor removed my bandages and put some kind of solution on my eyes to unstick them. Then, after shining a light into my pupils, he told me I was coming along fine. A full bandage was placed on one eye so I could not see anything from it, and he loosely wrapped both eyes. This left me where I could peek beneath the bandage by raising it slightly. Now I would be able to start moving around some. The doc concluded by saying that, if things went as expected, he would remove all the bandages in two days.

After he left, a nurse came by and announced that I could eat the noon meal at the dining table. I had been eating in bed for two days, so I welcomed this diversion. At noon she brought in a wheelchair and pushed me down to a table where others were already seated. I lifted my bandage a little to get the lay of the land and wished I had not. The guys around me were missing hands, arms, legs, and an eye or two. What was I doing here with these guys who were so seriously wounded? Guilt overwhelmed me, and I felt like crying for these men. Ironically, they were in the best of spirits. A few nurses assisted them, and everyone was joking around. I felt completely out of place and had the uneasy feeling that I did not deserve to be in the company of people who had given so much. One man, a captain, really stood out. He had lost both legs, an arm, and an eye and had been hit in the groin. All this was the result of having stepped on a land mine. There must have been a hundred stitched-up cuts where they had taken shrapnel out of his body. War definitely stunk from this perspective. Death and this kind of carnage can barely be accepted if what you are fighting for is worth it to begin with, but by now I questioned what our leaders were really up to. The campaign in Vietnam was not being conducted in a traditional manner; instead, we fought one day over a piece of terrain, only to give it back the next. Lines were drawn that we could not cross, yet the enemy roved wherever he willed. Most frustrating of all, body counts seemed to be what mattered most to the politicians. Now, seeing the results of a suspect war up close and personal like this, I could only search my soul as to the legitimacy of this war.

Every meal was uncomfortable from that time on. I just did not believe I was injured enough to be with men so mangled. Keeping my composure around them was difficult, and I did everything I could to not let them know how much their conditions depressed me. They were upbeat and acted as if it was just another day at the office, but I am sure they were making their own special effort to cover their real feelings. At any rate I ate my meals quickly and retreated to my room, where I did not have to face them. I felt like a phony in their presence.

Progressing well with no complications, I ended up spending seven days on the *Repose*. After that first meal at the dining table, I could not wait to get off the ship, and when the staff finally told me I could leave, I quickly got my new clothes together and hastened up to the helicopter landing pad to catch the first chopper available.

The flight I finally caught happened to go to Hue. During Tet, that city had been one of the major targets of the NVA, and fighting around the Citadel had been as rough as it gets. It was interesting seeing the aftermath of that battle, but the destruction hardly compared with the devastation at Khe Sanh. On arrival, I found out that it would be another day before I could catch a flight to Dong Ha. That was good because one of my childhood friends from Leland, Tommy Rousseau, happened to be stationed here, and I could look him up. Besides being a friendly face from home, he had been one of those who had helped shape my notions concerning the military. We had played war in his aunt Geraldine's backyard in the summers and thrown numerous magnolia cones at each other, pretending they were hand grenades. Now, here we were at war for real, and it seemed only appropriate that I visit him in this setting.

An Army major by now, Tommy was not difficult to find in the Army complex, and I spent an interesting and enjoyable evening with him. It was so good to be with someone who had been a part of my growing up. In a way I felt closer to home just being with him, and we had plenty of catching up to do because I had not seen him since he had gone off to West Point. Another interesting aspect of the visit was seeing the luxury in which the Army lived. These guys lived in wood frame quarters with air conditioning and had so much more of the things that make life comfortable than I had ever seen at a Marine compound. I just took it all in and enjoyed the luxuries. The next morning I felt rejuvenated, having spent a great evening with an old friend, and was now in the process of mentally adjusting to the notion that my old world still did exist.

17

The Final Days

The following day I hitched a ride on a C-130 to Dong Ha and after reporting in to Regiment was told that Charlie Battery was now back at Ca Lu. It turned out that the battery had stayed at LZ Torch until June 18, seven days after the NVA attack, and had then been airlifted directly back to Ca Lu rather than Khe Sanh. The reason for that was simple enough, but it would be years later before I found out why. The facts are that the decision had already been made to abandon Khe Sanh and level it to the ground before we even flew to LZ Torch. When the time came to take Charlie Battery off the LZ, equipment and personnel were already being removed from Khe Sanh. By July 6, the base did not even exist anymore.

According to his memoir, *A Soldier Reports*, Westmoreland realized that the NVA had taken the pressure off of Khe Sanh by mid-March, or as he said, "It was apparent that the enemy was giving up at Khe Sanh" (page 456). General Cushman, the senior Marine in Vietnam and commander of the III Marine Amphibious Force, had been pressing since at least as early as April 14 to close Khe Sanh. Westmoreland had finally concurred, according to Edward F. Murphy in *Semper Fi: Vietnam* (page 167). In some ways, that could be construed as an admission that Khe Sanh had not really been that important from a tactical or strategic view in spite of Westmoreland's defense of his actions after the war.

Also in *A Soldier Reports*, Westmoreland states that the "critical importance for the plateau" was that "Khe Sanh could serve as a patrol base for blocking enemy infiltration from Laos along Route 9; a base for SOG [Study and Operations Group] operations [unconventional or commando-type operations] to harass the enemy in Laos; an airstrip for reconnaissance planes surveying the Ho Chi Minh Trail; a western anchor for defenses south of the DMZ; and an eventual jump-off for ground operations to cut the Ho Chi Minh Trail" (page 442). It is hard to understand the practicality of such a conclusion when it is recognized that Khe Sanh was isolated and away from the main supply lines, exposed to the artillery imbedded in the caves of Co Roc Mountain, subject to bad winter weather that limited air resupply, and surrounded by high ground, giving it a tactical disadvantage militarily. If those negatives are taken into consideration, only one of the reasons that Westmoreland gave makes sense, and that was the possibility of using Khe Sanh as a launch site into Laos to disrupt the Ho Chi Minh Trail. Even then, if Westmoreland, knowing the difficulty of supplying it during the typically horrible winter months, intended it as a jump-off point, the timing of building it up as a base was seasonally off track in that a much more massive buildup should have begun in April and the attack launched before the winter. It seems more likely that Westmoreland either was drawn into reinforcing the position with enough troops to show the NVA that they could not bully us around in that area or was deliberately dangling Khe Sanh out there as bait. If it was for the former reason, it may possibly have been the result of a planned attempt by the NVA to distract us from their real goal of launching the Tet Offensive. If the latter reason was the case, it gave Westmoreland the perfect opportunity to use the U.S.'s massive munitions capability, which he certainly did and which would have been nothing more than another effort to enhance the body count ratios. This last possibility is raised by Westmoreland himself and indicates that at least it was on his mind when he says in *A Soldier Reports*, "The base no longer served to lure North Vietnamese soldiers to their deaths" (page 457). He also confirms that he recognized some of the impracticality of using Khe Sanh when he explains why it was replaced by the new Vandegrift base at Ca Lu. As he puts it, "That base [Vandegrift] was beyond the range of North Vietnamese artillery positioned inside Laos" (page 457). The significance of that artillery threat has been highlighted in John Prados and Ray

Stubbe's comprehensive book on the siege, *Valley of Decision: The Siege of Khe Sanh*. These authors point out not only that the NVA were estimated to have ninety-six tubes (mortars or guns) at Co Roc (page 269) but also that they had long-distance 152mm guns with a range of 17,260 meters and 130mm guns with an even greater range of 31,000 meters that could pound Khe Sanh. By comparison, the longest range of any gun at Khe Sanh was 14,955 meters (page 280).

Whatever had been Westmoreland's motivation for allowing Khe Sanh to be built up in the way that he did, it evidently no longer mattered because he had finally given in to pressure to shut the base down. At that point, even though Westmoreland had agreed that Khe Sanh must be closed, he would not issue the order himself. He wanted General Abrams, who would relieve him on June 11, to handle that. It would have been extremely awkward for Westmoreland to give the orders to dismantle what he had so fervently pursued. In my opinion he in no way wanted to give an order that might have been construed as a personal admission that he had possibly sacrificed lives unnecessarily and in the process expended an unbelievable amount of ordnance protecting the troops.

In later years, on learning that as early as April 14 the Marines had recommended closing Khe Sanh, I have questioned whether Charlie Battery and the other Marine forces operating near LZ Torch were needlessly put at risk. After all, the action at that remote outpost occurred almost two months after the recommendation had been made to close down the base. The time element is one thing, but the necessity of sending troops out into areas controlled by the NVA and so close to the protective sanctuary of Laos is another matter. Some might say that the operation was merely another search-and-destroy mission that really did not relate to the protection of Khe Sanh. Given the remoteness of the area, the ability of the NVA troops to retreat at will into Laos where we could not follow, and our vulnerability to the artillery and rockets residing in Laos, it is hard for me to believe that the high command would put our troops at such high risk without a deeper motivation than just mopping up and engaging the enemy. It is more likely, in my opinion, that the actions in the vicinity of LZ Torch were viewed as necessary to facilitate a safe withdrawal from Khe Sanh. If either reason was the basis for the operation, then I indeed believe that lives were needlessly put in harm's way. A concentrated bombing effort by B-52s would likely have been just as effective in holding the NVA at bay as it was to deploy troops physically into such dangerous territory.

Once the "siege" was over and the road to Ca Lu reopened, a safer and more practical plan would have been to move the troops out along Route 9 while carpet bombing the surrounding area with B-52s and employing tactical strikes by other aircraft as needed. It certainly was not necessary that the base be plowed under and smoothed out like a landfill, as was actually the case. The NVA would not have benefited from controlling the abandoned trenches, nor did they have a use for the airstrip. It is indeed difficult to find a reason for keeping the base operational after Route 9 was reopened. That conclusion is supported by the Marine high command's strong desire to abandon it at the time. Not only did the Air Cavalry and Marines already control the ridges to either side of Route 9, but the evacuating troops would be putting distance between themselves and the concentrated NVA artillery of Co Roc in Laos. This "retreat," or abandonment, could hardly have been more vulnerable to casualties than were the troops deployed in "Indian country," where the enemy had the decided advantage of operating from the protection of Laos with short supply lines. As it was, those people out at LZ Torch and other spots near the Laotian border took more casualties than were received in the entire "siege" of Khe Sanh, or Operation Scotland, as it was referred to. Prados and Stubbe in *The Valley of Decision* put the matter in perspective when they state that the mobile operations around Khe Sanh, known as Scotland II and lasting from April 16 to July 11, recorded our casualties as a total killed of 326 dead and 1,612 seriously wounded (page 447). Against those numbers the official casualty figures of the "siege" at Khe Sanh were 205 dead and 825 seriously wounded (page 453). In other words, the almost three-month period from the time Khe Sanh was relieved until the base was deserted produced almost double the casualties of the "siege" itself.

The whole affair after April 8, when the road was reopened, seems to me to have been nothing more than a matter of saving face for Westmoreland and Johnson. For whatever reasons, they had decided that Khe Sanh was the place where we would show our ability to stand up to

North Vietnam and that to have abandoned the base immediately after the NVA had pulled back would have only increased the speculation that Khe Sanh had not been that important in the first place. I, of course, knew none of this at the time and returned to the DMZ area proudly believing that Charlie Battery had been an integral part of insuring that Khe Sanh would continue as a vital segment of the total strategic plan for northern I Corps.

When I arrived back at Dong Ha, I learned that I had been replaced by another officer as battery commander and that many new men had already come on board to replace the casualties who would not be coming back. The rumor was that Charlie was getting fitted out for another operation. It was also apparent that we were getting a lot of publicity for the job we had done in support of the infantry and for the stand we had made when we were overrun. All of this was news to me because I had had no contact with anyone from Charlie Battery or 1/12 since my medevac, and it pleased me immensely to know that the battery was being recognized for its actions at LZ Torch.

The next day I caught a convoy to Camp Carroll and again experienced the negative memories associated with that method of transportation. I soon saw, however, that they had bulldozed the sides of the roads back considerably and that the jungle and grass had been defoliated back even further. Gunships accompanied the convoy as well, and the new precautions made me feel much better.

After arriving without incident at Camp Carroll, I checked in with the administrative personnel who had been stationed there since we had left for Ca Lu. It felt like a homecoming to me, and I enjoyed immensely getting to see 1st Sergeant Zipkas along with other members of the battery. In fact, I felt as if I was with family again. Everyone enthusiastically told me of the accolades that we had been receiving since LZ Torch, and it seemed that we had made an impression throughout the division. Of particular significance were two official documents that Sergeant Zipkas showed me. They read as follows.

A. CG TASK FORCE HOTEL 210825Z JUNE 68 NOTAL PASEP

1. The congratulatory remarks contained in ref a pertaining to the Robin South Action are a source of great pride to this command.

2. The final results of the operation were: 635 enemy KIA; 33 POW's; 38 Detainees; 186 individual weapons captured and 37 crew served weapons captured. These statistics attest, in part to the outstanding performance of not only the infantry battalions but also the tremendously effective support provided by Det Co. A 3rd Engr BN and 1st BN 12th Marines. In addition to artillery support, members of the 12th Marines also performed aggressively and courageously in defense of artillery positions threatened by a determined enemy ground attack on Fire Base Torch.

3. All hands can take justifiable pride in a job well done. Col Miller sends. BT

HEADQUARTERS
12th Marines
3rd Marine Division (Rein), FMF
Fpo San Francisco 96602
6/WAK/geb
1611
15 Jun 1968
From: Commanding Officer
To: Commanding Officer, 1st Battalion, 12th Marines
Subj: Performance of Duty

1. The accomplishments of Battery "C", 1st Battalion, 12th Marines at Landing Zone Torch have been a source of pride for all of us in the Regiment. Naturally, the loss of our comrades who fell and the injury and pain of the wounded, brings home to all the price that was paid to achieve the gallant reputation and high respect that is reflected on we who are less exposed. I am sure this feeling of pride will act as bulwark if our turn to stand the test arises.

2. While talking to one of the WIA's, I was not told how rough it was, only—"Colonel they didn't get the guns." With this spirit, I am sure they never will.

W. A. Kluckman

Well, there it was in writing. We had done our job in a way that we could only take pride in. On reading those documents, I believed that whatever I might have personally needed to prove to myself had been accomplished. Charlie Battery had stood the test, and I had been a part of it. It was particularly gratifying to have been commanding officer at the time.

By now, there were only about ten days remaining before I would leave Vietnam. I spent the first two of them helping 1st Sergeant Zipkas take care of administrative matters and then received permission from Battalion to go to Ca Lu to say good-bye to Charlie Battery. The only way to get there was by convoy, which of course I hated, but it was only appropriate that I make a proper departure from the men with whom I had been through so much. The ride brought back many memories as we passed the turnoff to Con Thien, the Rockpile, and other familiar locations. The ride along Route 9 through the valley, surrounded by the ominous and ever-mysterious mountains, was always a sobering experience, but this time it was as if the ghosts of past battles and encounters were watching me pass. This road had been the highway to everywhere along the DMZ, and so much had happened on or near it.

Arriving at Ca Lu, I found the battery located in the original position we had built on moving there several months ago. The area now looked like a major base, and the perimeter extended well back toward the Rockpile, the entire complex having been designated with the formal name of Vandegrift Combat Base. Learning that the infantry now stayed in force up on the mountain ridges to prevent surprise attacks, I was overjoyed because any kind of attack was the last thing I wanted to experience now. A true short-timer, I did not want to add any more war stories to my repertoire.

My reunion with the battery was filled with smiles and handshakes, and it was a special day for me as I visited with as many of the men as I could. They filled me in on their perceptions of the fight at LZ Torch and brought me up to date on the guys who had been wounded. Lieutenant Duchow accompanied me while I wandered through the battery.

About four o'clock a battery formation was held, and there, in a formal ceremony, I was presented with the remnants of my shotgun that had been blown apart in my hand. They gave it to me in a sandbag sack, and on removing it I wondered how I still had a hand. Then going through the formation, I visited with each man individually for the purpose of saying good-bye and gave each a salute as I moved on. Most of the guys had something to say, so it took awhile to get through the formality of it all. It was quite touching speaking with them, and I consider it one of the high points of my life. When the formation was over, I spent the evening visiting with Gunny Mac and Lieutenant Duchow.

Early the next morning, it was my good fortune to catch a ride on a helicopter going to Camp Carroll, and I was back in no time. It sure beat the heck out of riding in a convoy. By the end of the day, all of the paperwork that I had to sign had been completed, and nothing was left for me to do. My responsibilities were over. I went over to visit Major Capenas and to seek permission for an early return to Da Nang. An old friend from Sewanee, Don Griffis, was stationed there, and I wanted to visit him before leaving the country. Major Capenas worked it out with Regiment, and I was cleared to leave the next day.

The final morning at Camp Carroll was an anxious one. It was still a very active combat zone out here, and I did not want anything going wrong. Those numerous stories of men who had served for a full tour, only to be killed on their last day, continued with a life of their own. Regardless of whether those odds were great or small, there was no question that one successful convoy ride to Dong Ha followed by a flight to Da Nang would significantly increase my chances of survival. Butter-flies fluttered in my stomach as I climbed on a truck for the last run of the gauntlet, but thankfully the trip was uneventful.

After a two-hour wait at the landing strip, I caught a transport plane headed to Da Nang, and when we were high in the sky, I finally breathed a sigh of relief. It was like a load had been lifted from my shoulders, and all of a sudden I felt exhausted. Being on the DMZ had been like being in North Vietnam's "V-ring," or gunsights, and in that vast impact zone, incoming had always been possible. Now that feeling was slipping away. Da Nang should be much better.

On arrival, I immediately checked into the R&R Center and quickly luxuriated in a real shower with hot and cold running water. I was emo-tionally drained, and the warmth of the shower left me weak and hungering for sleep. It was now mid-afternoon, and I crawled into a bed with white sheets. I fell asleep before my head hit the pillow. The next morning, when I finally did awake, it took me several minutes to realize that I was almost home and nearly out of danger.

At noon, I went over to the restaurant at the R&R Center and had three cheeseburgers with fries and two chocolate malts. It was wonderful. That all-American dish had never been so appreciated, and that day it took me closer to home. The last meal like that had been months ago in Hawaii with Jody. How sweet the transition to the real world was becoming. Little things were what mattered most to me now.

In the afternoon I found a real stateside-type telephone and started trying to locate my buddy Don. He had been one of my closest friends since college and was even the godfather of my daughter, Cathy. Recently graduated from the University of Texas School of Law, he was now a captain and assigned to the Judge Advocate General, or JAG, arm of the Marine Corps in Da Nang. He had been such a hard charger in the past, and I wondered how he would handle sitting behind a desk with a war going on around him. Finally, after umpteen phone attempts, I found him and made arrangements to visit. Don's outfit was on the outskirts of the city near the perimeter, which I did not like, but I really wanted to see him. Leaving the middle of town, with its relative safety, was not appealing to me at all.

Later that afternoon, after a real hassle of a search, I finally found him at his hooch. What a great reunion it was to see such a close friend after all of my recent experiences and in the unique setting of Vietnam. After a lot of backslapping and joking, we caught up on what had been going on with each of us. I quickly related to him how things had gone on the DMZ, and then he flabbergasted me with an account of his new job. In addition to his daytime work in JAG, he had volunteered to lead a perimeter security company that ran night patrols and set up ambushes outside the lines. I thought he had gone crazy and told him so. After seeing how things were being done over here, I did not think it was worth getting killed over if you did not have to. Volunteering to go in harm's way was, in my opinion, just plain dumb in a war that to me was a product of political posturing. It was one thing to go out and do your job in a manner so as not to discredit yourself or the Marine Corps, but it was an entirely different thing to risk your life needlessly. I firmly believed that politicians such as Johnson and McNamara had made irresponsible decisions by making our troops fight this war with one hand tied behind their backs. Don just laughed at my ideas and, like most new guys in country, did not really want to believe me. Oh well, knowing Don to be the eternal optimist, I suspected it was a waste of time trying to reason with him.

After visiting for a while, I began noticing his living quarters. It had a real tin roof and wooden floors, and from about four feet up, there were even screens to keep out bugs. I proceeded to give him hell about the luxury he lived in and did my best, in the way good buddies do, to make him feel like a worm. It was all in good fun, but deep down it was hard to accept that Marines back in Da Nang could live like this when on the DMZ we often lived like rats. Don took the ribbing in stride and gave as good as he got. It was great being with him again.

About that time a siren went off, throwing my senses on full alert. Seeing Don sitting calmly on his bunk, I abruptly inquired as to what that was all about. When he replied, "We are taking incoming," I about knocked the door off the hinges in an attempt to reach the bunker I had seen just outside the hooch. Huddling down in the hole, I looked back up at Griffis, who now stood in the door looking down at me like I was some kind of idiot. Spouting off to him, I said, "Griffis, have you lost your mind? We're taking incoming. Get down!" He nonchalantly came down in the hole and said, "Brown, we take incoming every other night or so in Da Nang, and it's not that big of a deal. That incoming might be a mile away." Evidently, whenever they took incoming anywhere in Da Nang, sirens went off all over the city, which included an area of several square miles. Well, it was a big deal to me! I was three days short of going home, and I did not like incoming even if it happened to be two miles away. Where I had come from, the cry "Incoming!" caused instant pandemonium as people hit the deck or dived for holes. Don must have thought I had gone wacky, but everything is relative to what one has experienced. If a person had not lived through what many had on the DMZ, it probably was hard to understand how someone could be so jumpy. I spent an uneasy night at Don's after the incoming scare and was tired when we got up. It did not take much to make me edgy, it seemed.

The next morning at breakfast, Griffis, with his normal enthusiasm, informed me that it was the Fourth of July and what a neat day it was going to be. He gave me a rundown of the activities planned around Da Nang, but only one appealed to me. A big celebration was planned for that night at the Stone Elephant, the officer's club I had visited on my way to meet Jody on R&R. It was the only place I had been in Vietnam that did not seem like Vietnam, and in many ways it was as nice as the better restaurants back home. I reasoned that it would be just the thing to help with a transition back to the real world. Unfortunately, Don had perimeter duty that night because Da Nang was going on full alert for the evening. American holidays often triggered enemy attacks, and Don's security unit would be trying to discourage any such attempts. Because he also had his daily responsibilities to take care of, I hustled on back to the R&R Center to have my khakis pressed. They had been in my bags for months, and tonight's occasion would require them. Getting that attended to took up much of the afternoon.

The evening at the Stone Elephant was surreal. Again, I ran across numerous men whom I had been with at OCS and Basic School. Of special note, I ran into my old buddy Ross Blanchard, who, it turned out, was returning on the same flight with me. When he saw me he reacted as though he had seen a ghost and told me that he had heard I had been killed on the DMZ. I was most happy to inform him of the erroneous report, and we caught up on our activities for the last thirteen long months. The festivities were wild in the bar area, but I took time out early in the evening to have dinner with old friends and enjoyed a full-course meal complete with tablecloths and wine. I had almost forgotten what it was like. How sweet it was coming back into a world so taken for granted.

After that fine repast, I returned to the bar with its dance floor and took in the scene. It was full of Navy and Marine officers, and again women were in the crowd. Seeing them made me intensely homesick, and I could think only of Jody. As the night wore on, the drinks did their job, and before long the whole bar was singing patriotic songs. "God Bless America" seemed as if it was sung every third song, and in the setting of that room filled with uniforms, chills went down my spine each time we sang it. The Fourth of July had never been as meaningful as it was that night, and it never has been since. At that moment in Vietnam, surrounded by people knowing firsthand the sacrifices being made, a spirit of the heart manifested itself in song that transcended the ordinary. It was a special evening, and I returned to the R&R Center feeling proud to be an American. Despite how politicians might be mishandling things, there were still people fighting this war for love of country. The vast majority of personnel in Vietnam believed that it was an honor to serve country, family, and their branch of service by doing their jobs to the best of their abilities.

The next morning I awoke with a first-class hangover, something that had not happened in a long time. Where I had been the past months, few would risk the possibility of diminishing their senses with heavy drinking when so much was at stake. By noon I managed to come back to the land of the living and again headed out to Don's. I am sure I was not the most congenial of conversationalists when I got there, but I could carry on a reasonably decent dialogue by mid-afternoon. It was important to me that I make one last effort to give Don my impressions of the war in Vietnam.

In a nutshell, I reiterated to him that I did not believe it was worth getting killed to satisfy some politician's agenda and told him the method of conducting this war was dead wrong. I argued how foolhardy it was to volunteer for duty that put him at risk when the objective of our leaders was not to win the war but to avoid difficult political situations. If Don went into combat in the normal course of events, that was one thing, but for him to seek it out was, in my opinion, a mistake. He let all of this roll over him, and I could tell he thought I was just a jaded short-timer who had seen too much action. Don was not listening to me and believed that the war had a sound basis. Later, after I returned to the States, he confirmed my evaluation of his attitude by continuing his extra activities; he eventually received the Bronze Star with Combat V for performance in the field.

By late afternoon I had said all I could think of that might persuade him to be more careful, and I began getting ready to head back to the R&R Center. The idea of spending another night with Don reminded me too much of being in a combat zone. With his help I found a truck, and soon we were saying good-bye. As I jumped up into the back of the vehicle, I looked down at Don and said one more time, "It ain't worth dying for, Griffis," and the truck sped away. He stood waving in a cloud of dust, and I said a silent prayer for him.

July 6, 1968, finally arrived. I had been counting the days down for months, and it was hard to believe it was here. The feeling that something could go wrong was still strong even at this late date. Nothing would do but for me to get on over to the airstrip as soon as possible, and I found myself there about two hours early. Of no surprise, a large crowd was already waiting for the same flight. It seemed that I was not the only anxious one wanting to get out of 'Nam.

Not so strangely, I started running into guys I had flown over with thirteen months ago. I had not thought about it until now, but their rotation date was logically the same as mine. There were a lot of strangers, too, reminding the rest of us that the war had taken a toll on the original group that had flown over together. Thirteen months in I Corps was more than enough time for significant attrition.

The mood of the group was decidedly exuberant, and we caught up on what had happened to whom during the last year. Nobody seemed to be down on this special day, and time passed quickly as we waited for boarding procedures to begin. We processed through smoothly because everyone had made sure his necessary paperwork had been checked and double-checked before leaving his unit. About that time, word went through the crowd that our plane was coming in, and everybody started searching the horizon. Then, there it was, a big TWA jet with a golden tail. I sent up a prayer that we would not get mortared or such and that nothing would go wrong at this last minute. Home was too close for us to be shot at again. When the big plane touched the runway, a gigantic cheer went up from the Marines around me, and I cheered, too. No sight had ever looked better.

We all now crowded near the gate, watching the new guys coming off the airliner for their tour of duty. It was not hard to remember the apprehension we had felt when we had been in their place thirteen months ago. Nevertheless, the troops showed them no mercy as they harassed the new men with comments about what they were getting into.

At last, the loading began, and I do not think any airliner ever filled faster. Real female stewardesses greeted us, helping everyone get settled, and I just lay back in my seat and prayed that we would get off the ground before something bad happened. Soon, we were roaring down the runway with everyone strapped in and seats upright. When the plane lifted off, the cabin immediately erupted with cheers and clapping. It was over. We were leaving behind experiences that would be difficult to describe adequately to those who had not been there, but we were carrying away memories that would be with us forever. As the shoreline of Vietnam faded away, a relaxing calm seemed to come over the plane. In no time at all, I was asleep, and the experience of a lifetime was over, except in my dreams.

Afterword

While working on this manuscript, I read many books about Vietnam, and some are cited in this book. Readers who want to check these books further might find the following listing of references helpful.

Karnow, Stanley. *Vietnam: A History.* New York: Penguin, 1984.

Lehrack, Otto J., ed. *No Shining Armor: The Marines at War in Vietnam: An Oral History.* Lawrence: University Press of Kansas, 1992.

McNamara, Robert. *In Retrospect: The Tragedy and Lessons of Vietnam.* New York: Times Books, 1995.

Murphy, Edward F. *Semper Fi: Vietnam: From Da Nang to the DMZ, Marine Corps Campaigns, 1965–1975.* San Marin, Calif.: Presidio Press, 2000.

Pisor, Robert. *The End of the Line: The Siege of Khe Sanh.* New York: Ballantine Books, 1993.

Prados, John, and Ray Stubbe. *Valley of Decision: The Siege of Khe Sanh.* New York: Houghton Mifflin, 1991.

Telfer, Gary, Lane Rogers, and Keith Fleming. *U.S. Marines in Vietnam: Fighting the North Vietnamese, 1967.* Washington, D.C.: Headquarters and Museums Division, U.S. Marine Corps, 1984.

Westmoreland, William C. *A Soldier Reports.* New York: Dell, 1980.

Glossary of Military Terms and Acronyms

airburst Shell that exploded in the air.

Air Cavalry Helicopter-borne Army infantry.

ammo Ammunition.

ammo humper Gun crew member who carried rounds to the gun when firing.

base camp Home base for units operating in the field.

battalion Military unit consisting of four or five companies or batteries.

battery Military unit of artillery pieces or heavy mortars (usually four to six); would typically contain from 100 to 130 men.

beehive Slang for a type of artillery shell that contained hundreds of flechettes or little nails with fins on the back to stabilize them in flight. The beehive was like the canister from the Civil War and created an effect similar to a shotgun when fired from an artillery piece.

bird Slang for aircraft.

bracketed In the adjustment of artillery fire, a target was considered bracketed when there had been adjusting rounds fired over and below the target. In theory, the next adjusting round should be near or on target.

CH-46 chopper Large helicopter.

Chicom Slang for hand grenades of the enemy. Word stemmed from the words "Chinese Communist."

chopper Helicopter.

claymore Type of antipersonnel mine fired by hand from an electrical wire connected to a detonator at some distance. It could be placed at key points for directional firing and had the effect of a shotgun blast.

CO Commanding officer.

company Unit made up of three or four platoons and typically containing between 100 and 180 men.

concussion grenades Grenades made without shrapnel so they would not injure the attackers when overrunning a position.

CP Command post.

C rations Prepackaged meals of boxed canned goods that could be prepared without a field kitchen. A heating tablet, instant coffee, and toilet paper were contained in each package.

defilade A depression in the terrain that direct-fire weapons could not hit because the missile would pass overhead.

DEROS Date eligible to return from overseas.

DMZ Technically, the no-man's-land separating North and South Vietnam. Typically, the entire area bordering that no-man's-land was referred to as the DMZ. Stands for demilitarized zone.

FDC Fire direction center; where firing data were prepared for the guns.

fighting holes Proper term for foxholes. These holes were dug to prevent soldiers from getting hit by direct rifle and machine-gun fire. They were also helpful in protecting the occupant from shrapnel.

Firecracker Code name for COFRAM (controlled fragmentation munitions); artillery shells with bomblets that were expelled from the shell over a target and exploded like grenades when they hit the ground.

firefight Combat skirmish where rifle or machine-gun fire was involved.

flare ship Cargo plane used to drop parachute flares that would light up the night. Often used in night combat.

FO Forward observer.

folding-stock machine gun Compact, handheld machine gun with a stock that could fold down to make it even more compact.

friendlies Troops or civilian personnel who were not the enemy.

friendly fire Weapons fire that came from our own troops, allies, or civilians who were on our side.

gungy An attitude that showed one had experience.

gun loop Communications system linked by wire to all the guns in a battery and the command center ("Exec Pit")

gun pad Area where the gun was placed or positioned, often within parapets.

H&I Harassing and interdiction fire.

heating tablets Tablets a little larger than an Alka-Seltzer that when lit would burn for approximately five minutes; used to heat canned meals in C rations; also called heat tabs.

helicopter insertion The insertion of troops by helicopter into an area.

hooch Living quarters; could be a shack, bunker, tent, house, or similar structure.

humping Hard or heavy marching; used in such phrases as "humping the hills."

in country To be in Vietnam.

Indian country Dangerous area or territory controlled or dominated by the enemy.

JAG Judge Advocate General; the legal branch of the Marines.

KIA Killed in action.

LP Listening post; a man or team of two men set up in front of the lines in the dark for early detection of the enemy.

LZ Landing zone

M-60 machine gun The standard lightweight, belt-fed machine gun of all U.S. military forces in Vietnam.

medevac Medical evacuation.

meters One meter is equal to 39.37 inches, and one kilometer is equal to

0.6214 of a mile. The military tends to use the metric system to describe distances much more than they use the English system.

minigun Type of Gatling gun that fired rounds at an extremely high rate. Often used in cargo planes high over a target to saturate the area. Used in the cargo aircraft called "Puff" and sometimes "Snoopy."

NCO Noncommissioned officer; corporals and various grades of sergeant.

NVA North Vietnamese Army; term used both in the singular (referring to single soldier) and in the plural.

OCS Officer Candidate School.

pogue Derogatory term used to describe people who were not highly regarded.

R&R Rest and relaxation; referred to time off from the fighting or one's duty. In particular referred to the one week of vacation that each member of the military was entitled to during a tour of duty in Vietnam.

recon Reconnaissance.

salty Term used to describe someone who is experienced and somewhat cocky about it.

sapper NVA soldier trained to overrun and destroy positions using explosives.

satchel charges Explosives carried in a large bag and used to blow up large objects such as artillery pieces or reinforced bunkers.

search and destroy Type of military operation where soldiers swept an area in hope of finding the enemy and destroying him.

short-timer Soldier who has only a short time remaining before being rotated back to the States after tour of duty.

spider holes Excavations approximately two feet in diameter and more than four feet deep in which an enemy could conceal himself.

V-ring The rear sight of a rifle. To have something in the V-ring meant you were sighted in directly on the target.

XO Executive officer; the second in command of a company, battery, or battalion, for example.

Index

1st Battalion, 12th Marine Artillery Regiment, 17, 67
2d Battalion, 4th Marines, 90
3d Battalion, 3d Marine Infantry Regiment (3/3), 17, 23, 106
3d Battalion, 4th Marines, 48
3d Marine Amphibious Force, 247
3d Marine Division, 15, 17
12th Marines, 16, 17, 67
40mm antiaircraft gun (twin forties), 55, 62
75mm Pack Howitzer, 178
81mm mortars, 63
105mm towed battery, 20–21
122mm rockets, 66, 123
130mm guns, 69
140mm rockets, 66
175mm battery, 22
175mm Long Toms, 137
804th NVA Regiment, 74

Abrahms, General, 249
adjusting fire, 38, 53
aiming stakes, 222, 223
airburst, 263
Air Cavalry, 195, 196, 200, 263
air strike, 53
Alpha Battery, 205, 215, 224
ambushes, 60–81; August 21, 1967, on the road to Ca Lu, 62–64; between the Rockpile and Ca Lu, 79; Sept. 7, 1967, on the road to Ca Lu, 70–76
ambush patrol, 50–51
American public: growing skepticism about war, 112, 154–55; opinion of Vietnam War, 86–87; support of World War II, 2
American soldier, image of, 9
ammo, 263
ammo humper, 263
Anderson, Lieutenant John, 35, 46; death of, 55–56
antitank rounds, 200, 209
antiwar movement, 86; effect on troops, 57–58; student protests, 1, 152
Arc Light, 114–15
Arizona memorial, 173
Army, luxury of living quarters, 246
Army Air Cavalry, 194
Army Special Forces, 200

artillery, role in Khe Sanh, 208
artillery attacks, at C2 Bridge, 102
artillery liaison officer, 30, 66
artillery spotting plane, 74
attrition, game of, 87, 119, 154

B-52s, 202, 250
B-52 bomb crater, 41
B-52 strike, 114–15
Ba Long valley, 187
bamboo viper, 52
Bangkok, 164
base camps, 16, 263
battalion, 263
battalion operations bunker, 61
battery, 263
BC scope, 225
Bebee, Corporal Rayford R.: at C-2
    Bridge, 100, 102, 105, 118; Con
    Thien offensive, 137; profile of,
    31–32; status among the infan-
    try, 33
beehive, 21, 200, 209, 233, 234, 263
bee marauding incident, 162–63
beer ration, 161, 164
"Best Damn Battery in Vietnam,"
    161, 192
birds, of Vietnam, 40
birds (aircraft), 263
Blanchard, Ross, 9–10, 12, 15, 257
body counts, 154, 155, 245
Bo Ho Su, 17
bonding, in a common cause, 56–57
booby trap, 19
bracketed, 263
Bravo Battery, 205, 208
Brennan, Walter, 9–10
Bronze Star, 238
Bronze Star with Combat V, 258

Brown, Cathy, 172
Brown, Jody, 4, 5, 172, 173, 174,
    257; on the veranda of the Illikia
    Hotel in Hawaii during R&R,
    photo, 131
Brown, Lieutenant Jim: complex po-
    sition going into LZ Torch, 215–
    16; departure from DMZ, 254; as
    executive officer, giving firing di-
    rections to guns during a live fire
    mission, photo, 129; as executive
    officer and second in command at
    Camp Carroll, 156–65; farewell
    to C battery at Ca Lu, 253–54; in
    front of the operations bunker,
    photo, 132; on the gun line at the
    second position in Ca Lu, photo,
    130; introspection, 207–8; as new
    CO of Charlie Battery, 196–200;
    photo taken at arrival at Camp
    Carroll, 127; presented with Sil-
    ver Star at Camp Lejeune, North
    Carolina, photo, 134; unloading
    the dead and wounded, 219; using
    the battery commander's scope
    at Ca Lu, photo, 131; on the
    veranda of the Ilikai Hotel in
    Hawaii during R&R, photo, 131
bunkers: at Ca Lu, 191; at Con
    Thien, 90, 153, 191; at Khe Sanh,
    153; of NVA, 123

C-2 Bridge, 90, 91, 97–126; Arc
    Light, 114–15; bunkers, 104;
    casualties, 103, 110–11, 116;
    continuing strength of NVA,
    114; daytime artillery attacks,
    102, 107; FO teams, 105, 109;
    "friendly fire" casualties, 101, 110–

11; latrines, 108; listening posts, 104; map of, 96; massive NVA offensive on, 94; memorial services, 116–17; perimeter protective fires, 99–100; sniper fire, 107; supply truck unloading, 103; vulnerability to any kind of attack, 152

Ca Lu, 17, 18, 183, 185–200, 187; 122mm rocket hit on bunker, 192–93; active combat environment, 192; bunkers, 191; convoy to, 79, 185–86; key location on the DMZ, 33–34; mortar attacks, 189; strategic position, 184; vulnerability to any kind of attack, 152

Cam Lo, 17, 18, 81; refugee camp, 18, 77, 84

Camp Carroll, 17, 151–65, 152; arrival at, 20–21; bee marauding incident, 161–63; FDC personnel for all plotting, 159; outstanding defensive location, 160; reduced chance of ground attack, 152; return to from Con Thien, 151, 155; and Tet offensive, 177–84; water supply, 33

Camp Hansen, 12

Camp Lejuene, 158

Camp Pendleton, 2, 7

canisters, 200

Capenas, Major, 159–60, 161, 183–84, 198, 239, 254

Carroll, Captain J. J., 48

casualty figures for the "siege" at Khe Sanh, 250

C Battery, 1st Battalion, 10th Marines, Camp Lejuene, 158

C Battery (Charlie Battery), 1st Battalion, 10th Marines, 20; accolades received from LZ Torch, 251–53; artillery, 21–22; "attitude," 194; at Ca Lu, 184, 189, 191; collective personality, 24–25, 191–92; esprit de corps, 26, 135, 158–59; lore of, 236; at LZ Torch, 247; quirks and superstitions, 193; role in relief of Khe Sanh, 196, 201–16; sense of "family," 195

CH-46 chopper, 235, 263

Chicom grenades, 147, 263

China Sea, 17

chopper, 264

Christian faith, as mechanism to deal with the harshness of war, 85

Christmas in Vietnam, 163

CINCPAC, 88

the Citadel, 246

Civil War: artillery use, 227; trench approach at the battle of Vicksburg, 204

classic artillery bracket, 180

classic offensive thrust, 136

claymore mines, 49, 264

clothing, at C-2 Bridge, 117

"Club Charlie," 177

CO, 157, 264

COFRAM (controlled fragmentation munitions), first authorized for use at Khe Sanh, 210

combat: concentration on the job, 75–76; exhilaration after, 75, 236

combat patrol, 50

company, 264

Company C, 3d Medical Battalion (Charlie Med), 204, 205

concussion grenades, 232, 238, 264

Conner, Corporal Gary, 225, 238

Con Thien, 17; ground attacks, 152; intense and deadly action, 80, 81; primary target on North Vietnam's DMZ firing range, 122; well-built bunkers and trench systems, 90, 153

Con Thien offensive, 135–50; air support, 142; casualties, 148–49; directing counterfire, 141; fire support plan, 136–37; hand-to-hand combat, 140; Jolly Green Giant, 143–44; night defensive perimeter, 145–46; night firefight, 147–48; standoff engagement, 143

convoys: to Ca Lu, 79, 185–86; to Dong Ha, 181–82

"coordination from the field," 73

cordite, 225

Co Roc Mountain, 202, 203, 213, 214, 248, 249, 250

corpsmen (Navy medical personnel), 74

CP, 264

C rations, 33, 51, 264

Cushman, General, 247

Da Nang, 168; arrival in, 15; Fourth of July in, 257–58; incoming, 256; rear area support groups, 86; R&R center, 168

Davis, General Raymond G.: meeting with at LZ Torch, 223; new artillery strategy, 227, 229; new role for Marines in DMZ, 183, 187, 208

"dawn's early light," special meaning of in DMZ, 117–18

day patrols, 45

death, realization of, 180–81

defilade, 22, 230, 264

dehydration, 38

demilitarized zone (DMZ). See DMZ

DEROS, 156, 264

desensitization, 106

Dewlen, Lieutenant Mike, 193–94; death of, 237; at Khe Sanh, 204; at LZ Torch, 225, 226, 230, 231, 236–37; as XO of Charlie Battery, 198

DiCaprio, Corporal, 158–59; on the gun line at the second position in Ca Lu, photo, 130

Dien Bien Phu, Battle of, 124, 210

D Med, 241, 243

DMZ, 17, 264; American troops not permitted to enter, 57; difference in warfare versus southern South Vietnam, 18–19; higher ratios of enemy troops than in other parts of Vietnam, 112; new, aggressive posture, 186–87; Northern I Corps, 28; NVA advantages, 152–53; refugee camp concept, 18; skepticism about war, 57; spirit of troops, 56

Dong Ha, 16–17, 81; ammo dump hit, 69; first view of, 18; main base on the DMZ, 82; stateside environment, 85, 89

Dong Ha Mountain, 58, 92, 178

Don Ho, 173

draft dodgers, 57, 86

drug use, 68

dry heat, 29

Duchow, Lieutenant Dave: as CO of Charlie Battery, 239, 253; as

FDC, 198; at Khe Sanh, 204, 206, 215; at LZ Torch, 232, 235, 239
Dudley, Lieutenant Dan, 25
dust, 29

Eager, Lieutenant John, 24, 52, 159, 161
elephant grass, 20, 29, 35, 39
encephalitis, 24
enemy foxholes, 40
Engineer Battalion, 201
esprit de corps, 26, 135, 158–59
Exec Pit at LZ Torch, 225
executive officer. *See* XO

Fake, Corporal, 236, 238
fighting holes, 264
Findlay, Captain Ray, 109, 110
Firecracker, 210, 226, 264
fire direction center (FDC): Camp Carroll, 22; defined, 264; at LZ Torch, 220–22; role of, 157
fire direction officer, 198
firefight, 264
"fire for effect," 110, 226
fire missions, 22, 53, 74; Lt. Brown's first, 37–38
first sergeant, role of, 157
fitness report, 68
flak jackets, 83
flare ship, 148, 264
flechettes, 21
folding-stock machine gun, 265
Forrest, General Nathan Bedford, 227
Fort Sill, Oklahoma, 5
forward observer (FO), 20, 22, 33, 105, 226, 264

Fourth of July in Da Nang, 257–58
foxholes, 37, 143
Foy, Corporal Patrick, 61–62, 63
free fire zone, 19
French fort, 187–88
French-Indochina war, 34, 187
friendlies, 265
friendly fire, 101, 111, 265
friendship, 56
frontline troops, pride in their individual units or the United States, 85–86
fruit cocktail, 38

gardening, 181
Gatling guns, 190
Geneva Convention, 17
"Ghost Mountain," 48
Giap, General, 123–24
Gio Linh, 17, 25–26, 80, 81, 158; ground attacks, 152
good-luck pieces, 193
Goodridge, Sergeant Duane, 44, 53, 54, 60, 62, 70; Bronze Star, 65; helpful information about Rockpile, 46; outstanding job of calling in supporting fire during ambush, 64–65; photos of, 132, 133; profile of, 30–31; rotation, 100; skilled with protocol, 31, 32
Greenville, Mississippi, 3
Griffis, Don, 254, 255–59
gun crews, 22
gungy, 265
gun loop, 265
gunnery data, 157
gun pad, 265

hand flares, 147

hand-to-hand combat, at LZ Torch, 233, 238

Harper, Major, 61, 77, 90, 103, 104, 125

Harrington, Major Mike, 61, 67, 71, 72, 73, 186

Hawaii, 11

Hay, Captain Orville C., 71, 73, 76, 90; photo, 132

Headquarters Company, 139

heat and humidity, 11, 15, 34

heat casualties, 34

heating tablets, 51, 265

heat stroke, 35

helicopter crash, 114

helicopter insertion, 265

helicopter pilots, as heroes of Vietnam, 42, 47

helicopter resupply at the outpost on top of the Rockpile, photo, 127

high-angle fire, 21

high-explosive (HE) shell, 21

H&I (harassing and interdiction mission), 101, 265

Hill 881, vulnerability to any kind of attack, 152

Ho Chi Minh Trail, 153, 208, 248

honor, 56, 135

hooch, 48, 265

Hope, Bob, 10

"House of the Rising Sun," 12

Hue, 86, 245–46

humping, 229, 265

hyperventilation, 44

illuminating flares, 21

immoral leadership, 136

"in country," 265

India Company, 33, 70, 73

"Indian country," 145, 265

infantry liaison officer, 22

infantry tactics, 221

inspections, unannounced, 24

introspection, 207–8

JAG (Judge Advocate General), 255, 265

Johnson, Lyndon: concern over war's increasing unpopularity, 87; immoral leadership, 136; irresponsible decision to make troops fight under restricted conditions, 256; political decision to wage war by standards he believed would project America as a protector of South Vietnam, 153–54; political problems, 112; realization that war could not be won through body counts, 155

Joint Chiefs of Staff, 88

"Jolly Green Giant," 143–44

Jones, Perry, 4

Junction City, 152

"jungle rot," 35

jungle utilities, 23

Kagler, Lieutenant Tom, 31; photo, 132

Karnow, Stanley: *Vietnam: A History*, 86

Key, Francis Scott, 118

Khe Sanh, 17, 18, 23; active NVA roads, 209; all normal structures demolished, 202–3; decision to abandon, 247–51; makeshift morgue, 217; massive conventional bombing assault, 202; NVA interference with convoys to, 33, 34; relief of, 201–16; siege of, 55, 69, 81, 183, 184, 250; traffic closed to, 55; underground camp, 206; well-built bunkers and trench systems, 153; Westmoreland's motivation for building up, 247–51; worst of living conditions, 206–7

KIAs (killed in action), 65, 265; memorial services for, 116–17; numbers, 154

Kilo Battery, 179

Kluckman, W. A., 252

Koestler, Lieutenant, 205, 212, 213

Kosovo, 88

landing zone (LZ), 116, 265

Lang Vei, 152, 200

Laos, 249

Laotian border, 17, 23, 220

Leatherneck Square, 81, 83

Lehrack, Otto J.: *No Shining Armor: The Marines at War in Vietnam: An Oral History*, 80

Leland, Mississippi, 2, 3

liberty, 9

light artillery, 21

Lima Company, 73, 113

listening posts (LPs), 104, 223–24, 227, 229, 230, 265

live fire mission, photo, 130

loyalty, 56, 135

lucky charms, 193

LZ Torch, 215, 217–42; artillery plan, 221–22; casualties, 234, 235; Exec Pit, 225; FDC, 220–21; first fire mission, 226; hand-to-hand combat, 233, 238; listening post, 223–24; Lt. Dewlin, 236–37; map of, 218; needless risk of Charlie Battery and the other Marine Forces operating near, 249–50; NVA ground attack, 231–34; Puff, 233–34, 235

M-14 rifle, 194

M-60 machinegun, 265

"The Magnificent Bastards," 90

Marine Corps, 4; and Air Force, 118; cavalier attitude toward elaborate fortifications, 153; method of training that prepared every Marine as infantryman, 221; new role for in DMZ, 183, 187, 208; not programmed for defensive actions, 153; Officer Candidate School (OCS), 5; respect for its history, 56; role in relief of Khe Sanh, 196

Marine Corps Air Station, El Toro, 10

Marine Corps headquarters, Da Nang, 15

Marine high command, desire to appear in control of their sectors, 112

McDavid, Lieutenant Joe, 23–24

McKnight, Jody. *See* Brown, Jody

McLaughlin, Gunnery Sergeant Bernard (Gunny Mac), 120; at Ca Lu, 188; at Camp Carroll, 160–61; drinking binges, 157–58; humor, 121; at Khe Sanh, 204, 205; at LZ Torch, 221, 222–24, 229–30; and NVA attack at LZ Torch, 233, 236, 237; responsible for pushing the troops and keeping order, 157; Tet celebration, 177

McNamara, Robert: irresponsible decision to make troops fight under restrictions, 136, 256; "McNamara's Folly," 191; micro-management of war, 87; *In Retrospect: The Tragedy and Lessons of Vietnam,* 154; theories of quantitative analysis, 154
"McNamara's Wall," 88–89
McNease, Y. C., 4
medevac, 35–36, 265
meters, 265
Mike Company, 35, 55, 110
military indoctrination, 151–52
military occupational specialty (MOS), 5
military protocol, 31, 32
minigun, 266
Mississippi Delta, 3
monsoon season, 182–83
Montagnards, 18, 59, 128, 188
Montagnard village, evacuation of, 76–78
Morrison, Colonel William R., 20
mortar attacks (mortar incoming): at C2 Bridge, 102; at Ca Lu, 189; first attack experienced by Lt. Brown, 44; mostly at night, 45, 117
mortars, effective killing tool, 37
mosquito netting, 44
Mullen, Lieutenant Biff, 92, 93, 94
Murphy, Edward F.: *Semper Fi: Vietnam,* 154, 247
Murray, Lance Corporal Elvin ("Big Un), 241–42
"Mustang," 205
Mutter's Ridge, 53

napalm, 54
NCO (noncommissioned officer), 31, 266
Needham, Colonel Robert C., 67–69, 71, 76, 79–81; and ambush on road to Ca Lu, 63, 64; at C-2 Bridge, 90, 91, 93, 94, 99–105, 110, 112, 114, 118, 119, 122, 125; at Con Thien, 98, 143, 145–46, 147; profile of, 60–61
news media, coverage of War, 173; abandoning of previous reporting restraints, 155, 164; in the first part of 1967, 152; increasingly frequent descriptions of student protests, 152
New Year's Eve, 164–65
nightmares, 117
noncommissioned officer (NCO), 31, 32, 266
North Koreans, 176
North Vietnam: benefit from American disenchantment, 154; "General Offensive, General Uprising" plan, 80–81; invasion of, 153; major artillery attack at Gio Linh, 25
Nui Cay Tre (Mutter's Ridge), 48
NVA (North Vietnamese Army), 17, 266; 320th Division, 175; 804th NVA Regiment, 74; advantages of in DMZ, 152–53; elaborate bunker system and sophisticated foxholes, 123; engineering ability, 141; extensive artillery arsenal, 123; formidable opponents, 123; intercepting radio transmissions of, 45; jungle highway system, 42–43; massive offensive on C-2

Bridge, 94, 114; tactics of stealth and quick strikes, 66

Office Candidate School (OCS), 36, 266
officer-enlisted relationship, 31, 32
Okinawa, 11–13
Olivari, Corporal, 35, 49, 72, 73, 186
Operation Pegasus, 55, 200
Operation Prairie III, 25
Operations Cedar Falls, 152
Operation Scotland, 250
Opfar, Colonel Charles H., 79–80, 159, 175–76, 177, 183
overnight positions, setting up, 37

parachute flares, 190
parapets, at Ca Lu, 191
Parris Island, 4
Pate, Captain, 22–23, 79, 199
patriotism, 135–36
peaceniks, 86
Pearl Harbor, 173
Pegasus, 55, 200
perimeter protective fires, 37–38, 43, 99
personal survival, 45
Pisor, Robert: *The End of the Line: The Siege of Khe Sanh*, 78
"Pistol Pete," 178–79
plastic anti-tank round, 21
Platoon Leaders Course, 4
pogue, 266
poisonous snakes, 40
political considerations, influenced the way war was fought to a greater degree than pure military strategy, 118, 153

Poncet, Father, 78
Prados, John: *Valley of Decision: The Siege of Khe Sanh* (with Stubbe), 248–49, 250
protocol, 31, 32
Pueblo, 176, 177
"Puff the Magic Dragon," 190, 214, 233–34, 235, 236
punji stakes, 142

Quang Tri, 69, 173, 187

radio operators, 22, 35, 105
rats, 44, 206
Razorback, 52
reaction team, 230, 231
recon (reconnaissance mission), 35–43, 266
The *Repose*, 243–46
rest and relaxation. *See* R&R
resupply chopper, 47
reverse triangulation, 63
Rice, Lieutenant Colonel W. H., 21, 67, 68
ridgelines, 22
Ripley, Captain John W., 32, 73
rock apes, 50
Rockpile outpost, 17, 18; ground attacks, 152; key strategic location, 23; maintaining, 45–46; peak of, 47–49; security, 49; spirit of, 185–86; water supply, 33, 58
Rockpile to Ca Lu, road from, photo, 128
Rousseau, Tommy, 246
Route 9, 17, 20, 23, 34, 45, 69, 253
Route 561, 91
R&R Center, 168, 254–255

R&R (rest and relaxation), 163–64, 166–74, 266
Rutledge, Sergeant, 238

"salty," 25, 266
Sanctuary, 48
Sands of Iwo Jima, 3, 90
sapper battalion, 238, 266
satchel charges, 73, 232, 238, 266
Schick, Colonel Edwin S. Jr., 183
Schwerer, Captain Joe, 79–80, 81, 120, 121, 156, 183, 184, 195–96, 199
Scotland II, 250
Seabees, 89
search-and-destroy sweep, 212, 266
self-injury, 182
Sharp, Admiral, 88
short-timer, 266
showers, 32–33
shrapnel, danger from, 103
Silver Star, 238
skepticism about war, 57
sniper fire, 107
SOG [Study and Operations Group] operations [unconventional or commando-type operations], 248
Song Ben Hai River, 17
South China Sea, 48
South Vietnam, map, 14
South Vietnamese 1st Division, 17
spider holes, 70, 266
"spooky," 190
spotter plane, 74
Stars and Stripes, 192
Stockman, Colonel James R., 67
Stone, Pfc. James, 94
Stone Elephant, 169–70, 257

strafing, 142
Stubbe, Ray: *Valley of Decision: The Siege of Khe Sanh* (with Prados). *See* Prados
student antiwar demonstrations, 1, 152
surface-to-air missile, 58

tank, photo of, 129
Tet: at Camp Carroll, 177; significance to both North and South Vietnam, 176
Tet Offensive, 81, 86, 173, 175–84
thatched roof hooch, at Ca Lu, 188
"thousand-mile stare," 219–20
tigers, 50–51
time-delay fuses, 180
trench warfare, 178, 182–83
trip flares, 49
tropical vegetation, 40
tubes (mortars), 63
twin forties (40mm antiaircraft gun), 55, 62

unannounced inspections, 24
unit camaraderie, 10
unit pride, 85–86, 135
University of the South, Sewanee, Tennessee, 4
U.S. Marines in Vietnam: Fighting the North Vietnamese, 1967 (Gary Telfer, Lane Rogers, and Keith Fleming), 88

Valley of Decision: The Siege of Khe Sanh (Prados and Stubbe), 249, 250
Van An Rocket Artillery Regiment, 123

Vandegrift Combat Base, Ca Lu, 187, 248, 253

Vieques, 158

Viet Cong, 74, 81, 123, 136

Vietnam: evenings, 38–39; spectacular beauty, 18, 47

Vietnamese army interpreter, 19

Vietnam veterans, difficulty readjusting to civilian life partially due to shock of indifference and contempt faced at home, 86

Vietnam War: American troop strength in October 1967, 86; as body count affair, 154; constant rotation of troops, 186; fixed return date for each soldier, 156; heightened period of existence, 65; loss of public support for, 112; most responsible soldiers rewarded with added risk, 119, 199; politically mismanaged, 67, 153–54; pride of frontline troops in their individual units or the United States, 85–86, 135; psychological victories, 155; public disinterest in 1967, 1–2; reflections on death, pain, and degradation of the soul, 240–41; troops restricted by rules to which North Vietnam did not adhere, 136, 152, 245; as a war of attrition, 87, 119, 154

Vinh Linh Rocket Battalion, 123

V-ring, 266

water bladder, 229

water purification tablets, 39

Wayne, John, 3, 90

Westmoreland, General, 88, 154, 175, 196; *A Soldier Reports,* 81, 247–48

Wheeler, Major General E. B., 133

white phosphorus, 21

Wilder, Lieutenant Colonel Gary, 32, 33

World War II: public support of, 2; veterans, 3

XO, 121, 157, 266

Zensen, Captain Roger, 113

Zipkas, First Sergeant, 198, 251, 253